# THE EIGHTEENTH DAY

# THE EIGHTEENTH DAY

## The Tragedy
## of King Leopold III
## of Belgium

by REMY

translated by STANLEY R. RADER

Everest House
Publishers          New York

# CONTENTS

6

# FOREWORD

After taking command of his army on May 10, King Leopold III spoke to the nation:

"People of Belgium! Despite the solemn pledges made to the world, the German Empire, for the second time in a quarter of a century, has attacked Belgium, which has always remained loyal and neutral. By nature a nation of peace, we have done everything possible to avoid war, but if made to choose between sacrifice and dishonor, the Belgian will no more hesitate today than he did in 1914.

"We have fulfilled our duties as a neutral country to the utmost, for we have not called upon our two guarantors, who have remained true to their word, until the actual invasion of our country.

"Today the fatherland pays tribute to our valiant army, our brave soldiers. We have full confidence in them. Like the heroes of 1914, they are fighting step by step to halt the enemy's advance through our territory and to limit the extent of the violation of Belgian soil.

"Thanks to the efforts made by the nation, the strength of our resistance is considerably greater than it was in 1914.

"France and England have pledged us their support. Already, the first contingents from them have set off to join our troops. It will be a hard battle. There will be much sacrifice and hardship, but we have no doubt that we will succeed. I shall remain faithful to my constitutional oath of maintaining the independence and integrity of this territory. I have put myself at the head of the Belgian army as my father did in 1914, with the same trust, the same faith. Our motives are pure, and by the grace of God, we shall triumph."

"We have no doubt that we will succeed," said the king. He was right, but he would have to wait five years almost to the day for victory—a costly victory bought at the expense of untold misery and suffering in Belgium as in the rest of the world. On May 28, 1940, after an uneven struggle which came to be known in history as "The Eighteen-Day Campaign," Leopold sorrowfully signed the following order of the day:

"Officers and soldiers of the army: Despite your being thrown into a war of untold violence, you have fought courageously in the defense of our national territory. Now, exhausted by this continuous struggle against an enemy superior both in numbers and resources, we are forced to surrender. History shall testify that our army did its duty. Our honor has been upheld. All the hard fighting and sleepless nights have not been in vain. I appeal to you not to be discouraged, but to bear this with dignity. Let your attitude and discipline continue to command the respect of our Allies.

"I shall not desert you in this hour of great misfortune, and I shall attend to all your needs and those of your families.

"Tomorrow we shall set to work firmly resolved to rebuild our fatherland from these ruins."

—

"Our honor has been upheld," said the king, but someone in France did not share that opinion. Even before that order of the day could reach all the troops concerned, Paul Reynaud—who had succeeded Edouard Daladier as head of the French government the previous March 21—made a radio broadcast at 8:30 A.M. Speaking in a manner that was very different from his usual blustering style so familiar to the French, he said:

"I have an announcement of great importance to make to the French people concerning an event that took place last night.

"France can no longer rely on assistance from the Belgian army. Since four o'clock this morning, the French and British armies have been fighting alone in the north against the enemy.

"I hardly need to explain the situation to you. Following a breach in our front line on May 14, the German army drove a wedge between our troops, forcing them into two groups, one in the north and the other in the south. The French divisions in the south have established a new front line along the Somme and Aisne rivers, thus keeping the Maginot Line intact. In the north are three Allied forces: the Belgian army, the British Expeditionary Force and some French divisions in which many of our loved ones are serving. These Allied forces were under the command of General Blanchard, who depended on reinforcements from Dunkirk, defended by the British and French soldiers in the south and west and the Belgian army in the north.

"By order of the king, the Belgian troops have just surrendered unconditionally, in mid-battle, without so much as a word to their French and British brothers-in-arms, leaving the road to Dunkirk wide open to German divisions. Eighteen days ago, the Belgian king, who up till then had seemed to believe Germany's word as much as the Allies', sent us an appeal for help. And in accordance with agreements made last December by the major Allied countries, we responded to that appeal.

"But now, in the midst of battle, without warning General Blanchard and without a thought or word for the French and British soldiers who answered his anguished appeal for help, King Leopold has laid down his arms. In all history, such a thing is unheard of.

"I understand from members of the Belgian government that the king's decision was made against their unanimous wishes. They have furthermore stated their intent of placing all the forces they can spare at our disposal, and particularly. to raise a new army and help in the task of arming France.

"We must think of our soldiers. *They* can say their honor has been upheld. Their efforts in the front line have been commendable. On each of these eighteen days of battle they have performed countless deeds of bravery. Two young French generals who have just taken over have already become heroes. Our officers and soldiers have formed a barrier, in which we have every confidence and which will earn the admiration of the whole world.

"We knew that darker days would come, and they have. Though France has been invaded hundreds of times in the past, she has never succumbed. Let those brave people in the north remember that. The new spirit of France, which will make her greater than ever, will be forged in the trials that await us. Our faith in victory has not been shaken. The strength of each soldier, of every man and woman of France is ten times greater than it was.

"France has always triumphed in adversity. Today she is more united than ever. We shall hold fast at the new front line established by General Weygand and Marshal Pétain along the Somme and Aisne rivers. And because we shall hold fast, we shall be victorious."

Only one of Reynaud's famous "catchphrases" was missing from this collection of grandiose nonsense and deliberate lies about King Leopold. Shortly before, Reynaud had claimed that France was "the strongest of all," a phrase from his repertoire rather like his famous "the iron road has been cut," which was still pasted on walls long after the expedition to Norway had ended in a fiasco.

The recording of his nasal voice was broadcast again at 12:30 P.M. In the interim there was an announcement that by governmental decree King Leopold III had been struck off the order of the Legion of Honor. The French premier was in a tight corner and had already shown signs of panic when he telephoned Winston Churchill on May 15 to declare that the battle in France was lost. His shameful accusations had an immediate impact on the

French people. In Brittany I had to intervene to protect a dozen or so Belgians, exhausted from their exodus to the Atlantic coast in appalling conditions, from the abuse and threats of people who had heard the Radio-Paris broadcast. At Roanne, five Belgian pilots on a flying mission were handcuffed and thrown into jail. At the Hôtel des Bains in Royan, my friend Dr. Voisin had to deal with some fanatics who were trying to burn the flag of the Belgian consulate there. The consulate had been hastily installed in the hotel to help the distressed and heartbroken soldiers withdrawing from battle.

———

By his web of lies Paul Reynaud was trying to cast a slur on the king's honor, and through it on that of the Belgian army. "We must think of our soldiers. *They* can say their honor has been upheld." I need hardly point out that this indirect insult to the Belgian soldiers was as slanderous as the open insults to the head of their army. His claim, "In all history, such a thing is unheard of," is completely unjustified. When this pretentious man found the carpet pulled from under his feet, he directed the anger of the French people against a king whose integrity toward France and England had never faltered. Belgium's appeal to France and England was not the anguished plea that Reynaud would have us believe. It was a calm and dignified call for help based on a treaty of mutual assistance signed just over three years previously:

"The king's government regrets to announce to the Republic of France and the United Kingdom that Germany's troops have just invaded Belgian territory, despite the declaration signed by the Reich on December 13, 1937, and renewed just prior to this conflict.

"The Belgian government is resolved to take a firm stand against this violation of its territory. We appeal to the governments of France and England for immediate assistance as agreed in the treaty and confirmed by joint declaration on April 24, 1937. Moreover, our government trusts that France and England will also renew the agreements signed at Sainte-Adresse on February 14, 1916. These undertakings, which also apply to the Congo, are stated in letters from the British ambassador, dated September 19, 1914 and April 29, 1916, and in a declaration by the French government of April 19, 1916.

"The king's government has every confidence that, as in the past, through the concerted efforts of France, Britain and Belgium, justice will triumph.

"The Belgian government hopes to receive a reply from the French and British governments as soon as possible."

It is no secret that the arrival of French and British troops in Belgium was part of a plan discussed a long time before by the French high command. Paul Reynaud, who would have liked to make it seem that the Belgian people was responsible, knew this plan better than anyone.

———

Paul-Henri Spaak, the Belgian minister of foreign affairs, said on July 17, 1940, that his countrymen had heard Reynaud's broadcast "with stunned indignation." He added:

"Belgians in France and the government at home listened to the broadcast with feelings of anger and helplessness. But it was soon apparent, after this violent diatribe, that the statement prepared by the Belgian ministers expressing an opposite point of view would only make matters worse.

"During that day and the following afternoon the text was revised. Honorable Belgians who lived through that terrible day of May 28, 1940, will admit that the government's statement avoided a disaster. As soon as people heard Paul Reynaud's speech, all hell broke loose. Many Belgians were insulted, others molested. Some saw the friendliness they had encountered before turn to hostility."

It is worth lingering over this curious explanation which sounds more than anything like a confession. Spaak says that the statement prepared by the Belgian ministers expressed "an opposite point of view." This can only mean they wanted to preserve the honor and dignity of the king, the real target of Paul Reynaud's venomous attack. What disaster could Spaak and his associates possibly fear, except the prospect of falling out with Reynaud, who needed the assurance that his accusations against the king would be supported by them? It was because of this that they wrote a second version of that unsatisfactory first text.

On Tuesday, May 28, at six o'clock in the evening, Pierlot read the revised version of the text over Radio-Paris to the Belgian people:

"Ignoring the advice of the government, the king has just begun negotiations with the enemy. Belgium is shocked, but one man's mistake should not be ascribed to the whole nation. Our army does not deserve such a fate. This action is illegal and does not commit our country in any way. For according to the Constitution, which the king has sworn to abide by, the power rests with the people, and the execution of that power is laid down in the Constitution. No action by the king can take effect unless it is countersigned by a minister. This is a fundamental principle, and one that is basic to the functioning of our institutions. By breaking the ties that bind him to his people, the king has placed himself at the mercy of the enemy. From now on, he is no longer head of this country, for those duties cannot be carried out while he is under alien control. The officers and civil servants of this country are absolved from the obedience incorporated in the oath of allegiance.

"Furthermore, the Belgian Constitution provides for the continuity of power. In a case such as this, where the king is no longer in a position to rule the country, the two Chambers must join together. The constitutional powers of the king then become the responsibility of the ministers, who act on behalf of the Belgian people. This government, which is constitutionally elected and invested by Parliament, approves the right to defend, together with its Allies, Belgian independence and Belgian integrity against all aggression. The government now accepts these powers. In agreement with the two national legislative Assemblies in Paris and the ministers of state with whom we have consulted, this government, in its wish to serve the nation, is determined to continue the struggle to liberate this country. We shall raise a new army from those brave young men who responded to the government's appeal and from the Belgian military who are now in France and Great Britain. They shall fight alongside our Allies. Those who are not eligible for conscription will be assigned to the civilian workforce or to our arms factories, according to their abilities. And so all the help available to us shall be put to serve the cause, the cause which has become ours with Germany's invasion. As from today, measures will be taken to put these plans into effect as quickly as possible. We must give tangible demonstrations of our continuing solidarity with the nations that have supported us in accordance with their pledges.

"We are living through the most painful ordeal of our entire history. The time has come to remember the lessons of bravery and honor taught us by those who served in the 1914–18 war. Come what may, we shall remain worthy of them."

—

In his haste to revise the first text and get it approved by his ministers, Pierlot did not seem to notice that his phrase "the time has come to remember the lessons of bravery and honor taught us by those who served in the 1914–18 war" might be taken as a slight on the Belgian army, like Paul Reynaud's "*They* can say their honor has been upheld," referring to the French soldiers.

There is no need to go over the events that followed, which ended in a railway carriage at Rethondes on June 22, 1940, with the signing of the Franco-German armistice. It was nevertheless alarming to hear the Belgian prime minister say on May 28, "We shall raise a new army.... They shall fight alongside our

Allies," when the British troops had been hastily evacuated the day before, and large sections of the front line held by the French in piecemeal fashion were collapsing under enemy fire. Pierlot was well aware of King Leopold's views about levying a new army. Without wishing to detract from the courage displayed by the Belgian volunteer army which fought on after that country's collapse, it was only effective in a limited way. This was due to the simple reason that the strict surveillance of Belgium's coastline made it impossible for them to head for England. The only road open to the volunteers was the long, perilous journey across the borders of France and Spain to Gibraltar. As it happened, the greatest battle was fought on native soil by the Belgian Resistance.

King Leopold had a far clearer understanding of the situation than his prime minister. On May 26, he confided to Roger Keyes, admiral of the British Fleet personally assigned to him by Churchill, "I can only hope to help my people by suffering the ordeals of occupation with them. . . . By opposing me, my ministers have forced two hundred thousand young Belgians to fight in France. They are cannon fodder. They will be dragged down with the collapse of that country, which I am sure is imminent."

Events proved him right. The myth of the "two hundred thousand Belgians" was soon dispelled, as was the hazy idea of a "safe place in Brittany." Meanwhile, the French navy suffered losses while waiting in vain at La Pallice, Le Verdon and Bordeaux for the "contingent of thirty thousand recruits" which Reynaud had proposed to transfer to North Africa.

Pierlot's "revised" text seems to contain only one valid point. Speaking of the forces he intended to muster, he said that they would be used "to serve the cause, the cause *which has become ours* with Germany's invasion." That is precisely what King Leopold did from May 10, having been prevented from acting earlier because of Belgium's neutral status. The king had done everything in his power to serve his country well.

In addition to Paul Reynaud's accusations, the officious French Agence Havas added its own criticisms of the king. Supplementing its usual press statement, it also broadcast the following dispatch over the radio. This suggests that there had been some powerful outside interference in the writing of that text. Pierlot and his associates, undoubtedly under pressure from the French premier, almost certainly had prior knowledge of it. After a biased summary of the situation with regard to Belgium's military operations, the dispatch went on to say:

"Leopold's surrender, which we know has grave consequences on the military situation in Flanders, has certainly made this agency revise its earlier opinions. Information received from Belgian political refugees in France who are in close contact with the Belgian government indicates that, contrary to our belief, the king's betrayal of his country should not be judged solely from a military standpoint. It is in fact a premeditated crime.

"It appears that Leopold III had been pursuing a policy which for some years had been purely his own. He did this either directly or indirectly through his ministers, whose powers he abused. And thus, since the beginning of the war, the king has forbidden his ministers to leave the country, and particularly to come to France, in order to prevent any personal contacts being formed. He also tried to impose press censorship to paralyze Belgian public opinion, which was favorable to the Allies.

"Thanks to a few ministers who resisted the attempts to silence public opinion, he was not able to enforce these measures. Furthermore, *before* assuming command of the army in 1914, Albert I made a formal appearance in Parliament to show his intention of resisting the aggressor and of presiding over the Royal Council. Despite the ministers' request, Leopold III refused to go to the Palais de la Nation, and he did not get in touch with his government. In vain did the Belgian ministers ask him to speak out against the aggressor over the radio, to denounce the invader. The king never said one word.

"It is the king who was against any policy that allowed the government of Belgium to consult with the French authorities about the evacuation of those people under threat of invasion. The king wanted to keep all the men who represented moral and economic power within the country, and thus they were more exposed to the danger of capture by the enemy.

"He also made his ministers remain in Brussels. They were forced to follow his instructions and did not leave the city until the last moment, two hours before the bridges were blown up. When they reached Ostend, they were still in two minds. Most of them left. Four went to General Headquarters, where they begged the king to accompany them to France and restore the command of the army to the general staff. They also suggested that he give precedence to his duties as head of state over those as head of the armed forces. The king refused.

"This could still have been regarded as an act of supreme heroism. The four ministers: Pierlot, the prime minister, Spaak, minister of foreign affairs, General Denis, minister of defense, and Van der Poorten, minister of internal affairs, informed their colleagues that the king wished them to remain with him. The government split up and most of the other ministers went to Sainte-Adresse for a few days. All communications between them ceased.

"At General Headquarters, Pierlot, Spaak, Van der Poorten and Denis immediately tried to persuade the king to leave with them if it ever became necessary. They even reproached the king for not following General Weygand's instructions. Leopold replied that the army was too exhausted to retreat in good order, but the ministers did not feel this to be true—morale was good and the army was in excellent fighting condition.

"The atmosphere became more dramatic. The ministers endeavored to make the king face his responsibilities and repeated their criticism of his behavior several times. General Denis reminded the king of the military regulations which he, the king, was about to transgress. A surrender in mid-battle was definitely against all regulations, and his action would dishonor the nation. The position was very clear.

"It was quite by chance that the ministers learnt that the enemy was only six kilometers away. They left Bruges on May 25, after a last audience with the king who still remained obstinately determined. Prime Minister Pierlot made one last effort to stop the king from ordering the surrender, but Leopold's refusal was brusque and final. He said he was determined to make peace in order to keep some degree of independence. In the end Pierlot warned the king that he was about to violate the Constitution he had solemnly sworn to uphold. The ministers then set off for England, which they reached after a lot of hardship. It is easy to see now why German propaganda said they had been captured and shot.

"While the members of the government were in conference on the night of May 26, the king asked them for a blank signature which could be used to countersign the appointment of another minister. It should be pointed out that, according to the Belgian Constitution, the signature of only one member of the government was needed to allow the king to overrule the entire Pierlot Cabinet. 'That was just one more deception before the final crime,' stated one important Belgian politician.

"The ministers, however, did not fall for this ruse and refused to give the king the all-important signature. A few moments later, Leopold ordered the cease-fire, with the full support of General Van Overstraeten and Henri de Man, who had been in charge of Queen Elisabeth's charity work in the army since the beginning of the war."

———

"He spoils his case who tries to prove too much" goes the old tried and tested proverb. It certainly applies to this malicious indictment, so laced with lies and deceit that it says little for those who had a hand in it (I shall return to it later). On that tragic day, May 30, 1940, when the French army was on the verge of collapse, just as Leopold had predicted four days earlier (Lille surrendered the next day after putting up a brave struggle), that radio broadcast left such a strong impression of a "criminal king" that many of my compatriots still believe it to this day. In 1924, when Hitler was in a prison at Landsberg, he made a good analysis of this particular phenomenon. Dictating *Mein Kampf* to his accomplice Rudolf Hess, who had been arrested with Hitler and was acting then as his secretary, the future master of the Third Reich had the following to say about deception:

"There is always some credibility in any important lie, for the guileless masses are more easily taken in by a big lie than by a small one. Most people tell small lies and are too ashamed to tell larger ones. They are therefore unable to imagine that others might have the gall to distort truth so outrageously."

It is tempting to believe that the anonymous authors of that Havas dispatch, broadcast in France on May 30, 1940, were influenced by these words. The text emphasized the statements made two days earlier by Reynaud and Pierlot. Very shortly after, Spaak also corroborated it by allowing the "treason" charge laid on Leopold to pass without comment.

———

Perhaps my readers are thinking, "This is a despicable affair, but since it is a Belgian one, what right has a Frenchman to meddle in it?" The answer is simple and based on two points.

Firstly, I do not believe that any national boundary can prevent a man from defending someone whom he believes has been the victim of unjust and shabby treatment. Secondly, the shameful accusations made against King Leopold III originated in France through Frenchmen. They were voiced by a French politician who was then head of the French government. They were subsequently exaggerated on French radio, as much by the French Havas press agency as by the Belgian ministers, who were party to a political gambit to direct the anger of the French toward the king and away from their army. I think these are good enough reasons to justify this public reparation by a Frenchman to a king who was so dishonorably treated by his detractors that he ended up a prisoner of the enemy, though he only wanted to share the fate of his army and stay among his people.

———

One final word. About ten years ago I published in the Paris weekly *Carrefour* an account of what took place at Bruges provincial palace on May 28, 1940 between Leopold and von Reichenau, commander of the German VIth Army, who had "come at Hitler's orders to be at the king's disposal and to extend the Führer's good wishes." I related the event just as it had been described to me by an eyewitness, Colonel Rombauts of the Belgian army. I became so interested in the affair that I began to search for more evidence on the Eighteen-Day Campaign. I knew only a little through hearsay, and naturally my Belgian friends were reluctant to discuss the matter because of the fierce verbal attack on their king, and by inference, their country, on May 28, 1940. I had decided to write a book about this incident when my friend Robert Aron asked me to refrain since he had just begun a work on the same dramatic episode, so little known to the French. Since Robert Aron is more of a historian than I am, I felt his book would be better than mine. However, this unassuming man who, I chanced to learn, had won the "Ruban Rouge" in the Great War, an honor less freely given then than now, unfortunately did not live to see his task completed. This is why I resolved to write this book, for the sake of revealing the truth, which for long has remained hidden from the French people, at least. My only regret is that many of the politicians, some French, some Belgian, whom I have taken to task, are no longer with us. The same goes for some generals, who seem to me to be of the "career" type, as General de Gaulle scornfully put it. It reminds me of a disillusioned comment made by an English military commentator: "The career soldier does not like war for two reasons:

the first is that he may lose his life; and the second is that he most often compromises his military career during wartime."

However, I am sure there are still some of their friends left to refute any criticisms which may seem too extreme.

REMY

*May 8, 1976*

# THE SON OF THE "ROI-CHEVALIER"

What kind of man was this king who took command of the Belgian army to repel the enemy at the first sign of aggression against his country? What had he done before to try to save his people from disaster? What were Belgium's commitments to France and England, who declared war on Hitler's Germany on September 3, 1939?

A brief answer to all this would be that since childhood, Leopold III had always tried to follow in his father's footsteps.

———

Leopold was the eldest son of a king who was given the title "Roi-Chevalier" in his own lifetime for his unfailing loyalty and his steadfast courage. Leopold became heir to the throne on December 23, 1909, at the age of eight, when his father, Albert I, succeeded Leopold II. Who would have thought that this modest, self-effacing king, Albert I, would play a significant and much-admired role in the Great War in August 1914? When the German Imperial Army violated the agreements that Prussia had made in 1839, and invaded neutral Belgium for the first time, Albert displayed great inner strength by demanding to assume command of the army, as was his constitutional right. From the start he revealed a good strategic mind and set about evacuating Antwerp to prevent his troops from being surrounded. He then thwarted the enemy's designs on Calais and Dunkirk by setting up an impassable barrier along the Yser River. While his government took refuge at the port of Sainte-Adresse in the provinces, Albert set up General Headquarters at La Panne, a narrow stretch of territory which the Germans had been unable to capture. There, he shared the life of his soldiers.

He predicted that even if the victory so dearly wanted by the Allies was won, the actual conflict would have severe repercussions throughout the world. And so in October 1914, he appealed to His Holiness Pope Benedict XV to use his influence with the Viennese court and begin peace talks. Three years later, he asked Prince Sixte of Bourbon-Parma, a relative of Empress Zita, to propose a plan for ending this divided peace to Emperor Franz-Josef. However, French diplomacy was very hostile to the Catholic Austro-Hungarian Empire at that time, and thus a plan which could have succeeded failed. Had it been put into effect, hundreds of thousands of lives would have been spared and untold suffering avoided in the Western world. No doubt, it could also have prevented the outbreak of World War II twenty-two years later.

Circumstances forced King Albert to devote himself to the war effort. In September 1918, he led a combined force of General Gillain's Belgian forces, General Degoutte's French forces and General Plumer's English forces. He fought in the front line, from which General Foch expected decisive results; he seized the Flanders ridge on September 29; he waged war from October 14 to 18 on the Torhout-Tielt front and relieved Bruges. On November 22, accompanied by Queen Elisabeth and his children, he triumphantly entered the reconquered capital, watched by a deliriously happy crowd. The following month he personally supported the law that gave Belgium universal suffrage. He made an economic treaty with the Grand Duchy of Luxembourg, and in 1925, relinquishing its neutrality, Belgium signed the Pact of Locarno with France, Great Britain, Poland, Czechoslovakia, Stresemann's Germany and Mussolini's Italy. According to the treaty, France, Belgium and Germany agreed to maintain the territorial *status quo* and the inviolability of their boundaries as laid down in the Treaty of Versailles. Germany agreed to abide by Clauses

42 and 43 of the treaty, which concerned the demilitarized
Rhineland zone. In the event of conflict, France, Belgium, Ger-
many, Poland and Czechoslovakia agreed to seek arbitration.
The signing of the Pact of Locarno won Germany a seat in the
League of Nations, and it seemed that Europe was at last entering
an era of peace. In 1928, on Albert's initiative, Belgium set up the
National Foundation for Scientific Research, which ensured that
several institutions endangered by the recent devaluation of the
Belgian franc would continue. It also allowed many scientists to
pursue their research. Frequently consulted in matters of arbitration, Albert sought relaxation in his favorite sport of mountain-
climbing. On February 17, 1934, while on a climb at Marche-les-
Dames in the Ardennes, he suffered a fatal fall. All Belgium
mourned his death. His son, Leopold, was then thirty-two years
old.

—

By courtesy of the Belgian *Revue Generale*, I have reproduced here
an interview with the son of the "Roi-Chevalier" on the occasion
of the centenary of the birth of Albert I.

"I was very close to my father. We felt great affection for each
other, and I admired him immensely. The qualities I liked best
about him were his kindness, his moderation, his integrity, his
respect for people, his freedom of thought, his tolerance and also
his exacting morality, his simplicity and his wonderful stability,
which allowed him to overcome life's difficulties with serenity.

"His taste for simplicity has often been commented on. It is
true that he embodied simplicity itself. He liked neither the pomp
nor the ceremony to which he was subjected, but bore them like
a duty inherent in his position. He lived without pretension at
Laeken, and he lived in even simpler style with his family at La
Panne during World War I.

"He was sincere and truthful, and was irritated by all false pre-
tences. He abhorred boastfulness and vanity, and detested

gossipers and flatterers even more. Real human contact was precious to him; that is why he loved talking to ordinary people in the street. If he was not recognized he was all the more delighted. This is the reason he enjoyed the company of the guides who climbed with him. With them he could be simply a mountaineer and nothing else. Apart from the time spent with his family, mountaineering was his greatest joy.

"We were a real family. My mother and father had fallen in love at first sight, and their love for each other never weakened. It was an undemonstrative and tacit love, but it was the very heart and joy of their lives. It is wonderful for children to grow up in an atmosphere of such perfect harmony.

"After the tragedy at Marche-les-Dames, my mother seemed utterly broken and lifeless. She did not return to life until I myself was fated to lose a loved one. I returned from Switzerland, terribly upset by a death [of his first wife] less than a year and a half after that of my father. My mother came to me and said she would begin to live once more: she felt needed again.

"My affection for my father brightened my childhood. He was interested in us—in our games, in our problems and in our development. How many times did he and I go for a walk together in the park at Laeken that he loved so much! We talked about anything and everything. I used to look forward to those times, for we were close and alone.

"As for family life, I remember that after a visit to England at the beginning of World War I, I came back to join my parents at La Panne. In spite of the tragic times, the years spent there were in many ways the best of our lives. We lived in a simple little villa without ceremony or display. We would go for walks along the deserted beach. Visitors were few and far between. Sometimes there would be high-ranking officers, politicians or famous artists at the house. I remember meeting Joffre, Foch, Haig and Pétain. I met Verhaeren, Ysaye, Saint-Saëns and Emile Claus, as well as Admiral Keyes, whom my parents thought a lot of. I particularly remember it as a family home.

"Despite the grim situation, my father and mother were happy during the war. In fact it afforded them the opportunity to give their best: he in the trenches with his soldiers, she taking care of the wounded.

"My father was essentially a peace-loving man forced into war. He was convinced that a country must be prepared to defend itself if its cause is just. I shall never forget what he said to me, particularly because of the circumstances then. It was at Antwerp in 1914, when we were setting off for England. He was very solemn, for the moment was tragic; no doubt he thought we would not see each other again for some time, if ever.

"He said, 'You should not neglect the army. Belgium must always have a strong army.' It was like a final wish. I was twelve years old, and I have never forgotten it.

"When war was declared, he immediately became commander in chief of the army. He soon found it necessary to reshuffle the high command, and took sole responsibility for this courageous and onerous task.

"He had received solid military training from the Military School which he joined at a very young age. Service in the ranks also put him in contact with all classes of society and gave him a deep understanding of human nature.

"As commander in chief he demanded courage and physical fitness as well as competence and the ability to adapt to changing situations from his high-ranking subordinates. The weighty decisions he made when faced with basic alternatives are being appreciated more and more: the early battles, the withdrawal to Antwerp, the retreat from Antwerp to the Yser and the order to hold it at all costs.

"During the entire war he remained unswervingly loyal to one principle, to save the lives of his soldiers. That is why he wanted to retain central command of the Belgian forces, and condemned as foolish or lethal the offensives on some fronts.

"The Allies were often infuriated by my father's refusal to compromise on these matters. Although he was both loyal and faithful to them, he nevertheless took full responsibility for his own decisions. The events that followed proved him right. He lent tremendous assistance to the Allied cause, but he also respected the honor and lives of his soldiers, making sure that futile sacrifices were not made.

"Perhaps that is the reason my father, who became known to Belgians and the world as the "Roi-Chevalier," was able to resume his peacetime activities so easily. Peace was his real world. We know how scrupulously he devoted himself to it. He realized the importance of the actions of a dedicated monarch, and he met with his ministers or presided over the cabinet whenever important decisions were at stake. That was very important for him.

"Besides this, he wrote numerous letters to his ministers. setting down his thoughts, his comments and if necessary his criticisms. In his constitutional duties, he exerted a personal influence, which will become even clearer when certain papers about his reign are published in the future. He devoted all his attention to public life, and had great respect for worthy officials, particularly those who were totally dedicated to the nation.

"He was a well-informed man. He rose early and so found time to read all newspapers and magazines, including the foreign press. He made notes on whatever he read. He answered letters that he thought deserved a personal reply. He read and spoke several languages. His reading material not only consisted of newspapers; he liked to consider himself something of a bibliophile, with interests ranging from literature to technical and scientific material. My father was a dedicated man. He insisted on accuracy and exactitude.

"He had a little library in his dressing-room. One day he showed it to me, saying, 'Do you see those books? I read them while waiting for your mother to get ready to go out to dinner or to some function.'

"If he had time between appointments or before sitting down to dinner at home, he would pick up a mathematics book and practice solving the problems.

"My father adored the railways and he knew the Belgian network as well as any expert. Whenever we traveled together, he made sure that I knew all the stations on that line, and he liked to check that we were on time. He timed the delays and knew that those forty seconds or two minutes would be made up on such-and-such section of the line where the gradient was such-and-such. He taught me to recognize every type of locomotive.

"Sometimes, riding our bicycles in the park at Laeken Château, we would climb the embankments of the Brussels-Ostend line in the hope of spotting the Flamme 10 engine, famous at that time.

"I can remember once in 1910, when the czar of Bulgaria, who was also a railway enthusiast, came to visit us. He insisted on chartering an engine and carriage in which he and my father rode from Brussels to Ostend in only one and a half hours.

"Our father was very concerned about the moral and educational development of his children. He sent me first to Eton, for he thought highly of English educational methods, particularly those of that school, a veritable seedbed of statesmen. Then he wanted me to go to the Military School. For mathematics I was tutored by an eminent professor from Liège University. He also wanted me to have a good general grounding, and being an admirer of French culture, he arranged for a French officer brought up in the traditions of that army to guide me in my studies.

"Much has already been said of my father's interest in sports. He loved walking, which he did every day. He had flown in a balloon. At the start of the war, he went up in planes with our best pilots and flew over enemy lines; he had always been interested in flying and followed the Wright brothers' attempts closely.

"He liked the motorcycle, which suited his temperament. For seven years before I had a car, I rode with him on his motorcycle because he thought it was good practice. He often left Laeken at three in the morning on his motorcycle to arrive at the Ardennes before dawn and spend the day in the solitude of the forest. As for cars, I think his favorite was a little two-seater Ford, with Swiss plates that ensured anonymity.

"He liked to meet people who had participated in some sort of adventure of a sporty or technical nature. Charles Lindbergh was received at Laeken after he crossed the Atlantic; so was Professor Picard, first explorer of the stratosphere, whose exploits had been enthusiastically followed by my father.

"He adored travel and went to Russia at the age of nineteen for the coronation of Czar Nicholas II. In 1908, a few months before Leopold II died, he went to the Congo, which he revisited later.

"His visits to the Congo were like field trips. My father wanted to see for himself the real state of the colony, to acquaint himself with the national parks and particularly to get to know the Congolese people. The diary he kept during his last visit there is a remarkable and lucid document.

"As a young man he had been to Mexico and the United States. In 1919 and 1920, together with my mother and myself, he was jubilantly received in Brazil and the United States. For their silver wedding anniversary in 1925, my parents went to India and the Himalayas, any climber's dream. He visited the Middle East and what is today Israel, a nation he admired.

"I should also mention another of his passions, the movies. He had neither time nor opportunity for movies in Belgium, for it was difficult for him to enter a theater unnoticed. So he used to make up for this when he went abroad: in Paris once, he saw four movies one after the other.

"However, nothing was dearer to him than mountaineering, and one of my greatest joys was to accompany him on a climb. He had a villa at Hasslihorn on Lake Lucerne—he admired Switzerland for its democratic spirit—and he would set off from there. He also climbed in the Dolomites. Some of the guides were among his best friends; they were simple, sincere people totally dedicated to their work. Mountaineering cost my father his life, but it also gave him the most profound rewards: the solitude of the peaks, the dependence on one's own effort, the contact with nature and the triumph of the will.

"There are so many more things I would like to say! His respect for others was so strong that he was even afraid of overinfluencing his own children. Each human being should be himself, he thought. That is why he was not eager to command, and why he found it so difficult to forgive those who had deceived or used him. He prized loyalty above all, and made it his guiding principle.

"Loyalty was his yardstick in giving out trust and friendship. My father was always wary of politicians who appeared to defend the crown rather too strongly, for he doubted their sincerity. Others, who were politically opposed to him, won his friendship because of their loyalty. I am thinking of Emile Vandervelde, who said to him one day, 'Whatever happens, I shall never lie to you.' That is why on February 17, 1934, Vandervelde wept.

"This man then was my father, and his memory remains with me always: a man of deep faith, a man who detested intolerance, a man who was famous throughout the world, yet so simple at heart, a man who never for a second forgot his duty to the nation, very timid and very brave at the same time, a man who needs no legend to make us remember him and the great example he set. A man who for me was also—and above all—my father."

# BELGIUM'S FOREIGN POLICY

In his address to the nation on May 10, 1940, the day on which Belgium, after a lapse of a quarter of a century, was brutally invaded for the second time, King Leopold III made the following statement: "I have put myself at the head of the Belgian army as my father did in 1914, with the same trust, the same faith."

He had never forgotten the advice of his father, Albert I, on a similarly dramatic moment twenty-six years earlier at Antwerp: "You should not neglect the army. Belgium must always have a strong army." Ever since the tragedy at Marche-les-Dames that had brought Leopold to the throne at the age of thirty-two, he had devoted himself wholeheartedly to what he considered his sacred duty.

On October 14, 1936, Leopold referred to Hitler's denunciation of the Pact of Locarno, coupled with what he called " 'the bolt from the blue' reoccupation of the Rhineland." He demanded that his ministers take appropriate measures to reinforce the Belgian army immediately, stressing his own fears about the likelihood of a second German invasion.

The king had every reason to compare the remilitarization of the Rhineland by the new master of the Third Reich to a "bolt from the blue." It had been a big gamble, as was later revealed when the Wilhelmstrasse archives were seized after the collapse of Hitler's empire. This operation, known as "Schulung," would have been averted had France taken a strong stand in support of the statement made by the president of the cabinet, Albert Sarraut, when he said, "We will not allow Strasbourg to be at the mercy of German guns."

In General de Gaulle's familiar words, this was merely empty oratory, a weak retaliation for the humiliation François-Poncet, the French ambassador to Berlin, had suffered the same day. He was summoned by von Neurath, the Reich's minister of foreign affairs, and was given to understand in short order that some detachments of the newly formed Wehrmacht had begun to reoccupy the Rhineland. Simultaneously, Hitler was ranting to a frenzied assembly, "The Locarno Pact is dead! As from today the sovereignty of the Reich has been reestablished in the demilitarized zone!"

The French government only lodged a timid protest with the League of Nations, whose apathy had led to the occupation of Austria conducted under the name "Anschluss" (union), followed by the annexation of Bohemia-Moravia the next year. In the meantime, the French Popular Front won the elections that followed the "Schulung" (a word that could be translated as "training") operation and was spreading confusion that verged on sabotage in our arms factories. The disastrous effects of this would be felt by the French soldiers four years later. What help could Belgium have expected from France, which, like Spain, seemed poised on the brink of civil war?

———

The sad state of affairs in France was no doubt taken into account in Paul-Henri Spaak's address to the foreign press in Brussels on July 20, 1936: "I have only one wish and that is for a foreign policy that is wholly Belgian." Spaak had nothing more to add when he heard the king make the following statement to the cabinet on October 14, 1936, regarding Belgium's position in the international arena:

"Our geographical position necessitates the maintenance of a military force capable of dissuading any neighboring country from using our territory to attack another nation. This is our mission, and by fulfilling it we will contribute greatly to peace in Western Europe. Through it Belgium will also earn the respect and eventual support of all countries interested in maintaining peace. On these points I believe the Belgian people unanimous.

"But we must not commit ourselves beyond that. Any unilateral policy would weaken our position externally and would foster— rightly or wrongly—internal dissent. An alliance, even a purely defensive one, could not achieve its aim because, however promptly an ally's support may be given, it could only come after an invasion, which in itself would be devastating. In meeting that initial attack, we shall, to all intents and purposes, stand alone.

"Unless we ourselves are prepared to undertake a system of defense capable of resisting the enemy, Belgium will be subjected to a fierce invasion right from the start and will be immediately ravaged. Allied intervention would certainly assure final victory, but in the ensuing struggle Belgium would be so devastated that the 1914–18 war would pale by comparison. That is why, as the minister of foreign affairs said recently, we must pursue a policy that is "wholly Belgian."

"This policy must be resolute in its aim to place us outside the area of conflict of our neighbors and to fulfill our national ideal. It must be maintained by a reasonable military and financial effort, and it will unite the Belgian people, who are motivated by an intense, deep-rooted desire for peace.

"Let those who doubt the feasibility of such a foreign policy consider the fine and determined example set by Holland and Switzerland. Let them remember how Belgium's scrupulous adherence to neutrality weighed heavily in our favor, and that of the Allies, during the last war and the subsequent settlements. Our moral standing within this country would have been considerably weaker and the world would not have afforded us the same sympathy, if the invader had found a reason for aggression because of our alliance with one of its adversaries. I repeat, therefore, that it is only to protect ourselves from war, from whichever quarter, that we have a military force, and it is important that the public has our firm assurance on this point."

King Leopold's inveterate critics insinuate that after this statement, the monarch had to "oppose certain ministers in order to ,impose his point of view." It is tempting to say that nothing could be further from the truth, but the jumble of false allegations is too difficult to untangle. Among the ministers present then was the head of the Socialist party, Emile Vandervelde, whose entry into politics dated back some fifty years. He was registered as a member of the Belgian Workers party in 1885 and soon became its most popular leader. In 1894, he was elected member of parliament for Charleroi and constantly reelected since, he rose to become head of the Socialist party. As president of the Second International since 1900, he had undisputed influence. In 1914, the year Belgium was invaded, he had accepted the post of cabinet minister in the national coalition government, and through it had won the friendship of King Albert. It was he, as minister of foreign affairs, who had signed the Pact of Locarno on behalf of Belgium. When he headed the opposition, he became a member of the government once again, as minister without portfolio. This spirited fighter was respected by one and all.

When the king sat down again, Emile Vandervelde leaned toward him and said, "I could have sworn that that was your father speaking. . . . What you have just said must be spread beyond these four walls; the whole nation must hear this!"

He endorsed that statement very explicitly on December 16 in the Chamber of Representatives, when he said: "The king's speech was addressed exclusively to his ministers, and those ministers are unanimously in favor of the speech being made public. I participated in that decision, and I wish it to be known to all that I do not regret it for a moment."

———

King Leopold had every reason to say that Belgian public

opinion was unanimous. The Socialist senator of the Walloons, François André, was one of the few opponents to his plan for peace because, he said, "I mistook independence for neutrality, and in my mind neutrality was somewhat suspect and cowardly." Three weeks before the Wermacht invaded Belgium, André gave a *mea culpa* in his speech to the cabinet: "Shocked by the recent events that have sullied human conscience, I have come to recognize my error, and for the past eight months I am sure that it was our young king who saw the situation clearly. As an old republican I now give him my thanks."

The vote that followed the king's speech on October 14, 1936, reflected similar opinions. One hundred and thirty-one senators approved the government's policy, which was what the king had outlined. There were only three dissenters, all Communists, and two abstentions.

From this it is evident how little truth there was in the Radio-Paris broadcast on May 30, 1940, which stated that Leopold III had implemented "a policy which for some years had been purely his own," by manipulating his ministers "whose powers he abused." Spaak, whose views at the end of May 1940 seemed to confirm this, wrote in the London *Daily Telegraph* in May 1941:

"The Belgian Government has, always, in accordance with the Constitution, assumed the whole responsibility for Belgium's foreign policy and, since 1936, the policy adopted has been increasingly endorsed by an enormous majority in Parliament. It is, therefore, a gross misrepresentation of the facts to hold King Leopold responsible for this policy."

It seems likely that Spaak—in whom modesty was never a strong characteristic, and who could be reckoned among the king's most virulent opponents—wanted the British to give him credit for the policy he had implemented as minister of foreign affairs. He did not see fit to mention that his policy corresponded exactly to the one stated by Leopold on October 14, 1936, to the government, of which he was a member. One should also bear in mind that Spaak took credit for that policy at a time when, presumably, his powers were no longer being "abused," something which, according to Radio-Paris, had been inflicted on him and his colleagues.

———

I believe that a remark made by the king shortly before the conflict that Hitler was about to impose on the world almost certainly contributed to his censure by members of his former government. To Pierlot and several of his ministers—including Spaak—in the presence of the burgomaster of Brussels, the director of the National Bank and the head of the Christian trade unions, Leopold stated categorically that "the government's methods are bad." After reminding them of the important responsibilities that the government must fulfill in its role as trustee and servant of the nation, he concluded, "The most important reform is to change the mentality of the men in power." So that none might misunderstand, he added, "I refer to that of the ministers."

It happened that before the war I was director of an organization that financed most of the French movie productions, which put me in touch with a number of performers. It was the first time I had come across such forms of pettiness, squabbling over whose name should appear first in the credits, who should be the star, how large should each name be written on the screen. Such extreme egotism, I thought, could never be topped, but I was wrong. After the liberation of France, when I had the honor of being in General de Gaulle's immediate circle, I realized that the egotism of actors was nothing compared to the unbelievable conceit of men in politics. The young king's cutting remark to Pierlot and the ministers could never have been uttered in France without an immediate constitutional crisis taking place. General de Gaulle himself, who had no qualms about criticizing his ministers in private, would never had dared to do such a thing, even at the time when he held supreme power in the Elysée. Millerand, reputedly guilty of a similar but far less serious crime than the king, that of "lèse-majesté" (that is to say the assumption of certain rights by those elected by the people), was forced to resign. He was politically banished by Edouard Herriot, head of the brand new left-wing cartel, for a speech he made at Evreux as president of the republic, indicating his wish to confine Parliament's functions to legislation and administrative control. His speech was much more moderately phrased than that of King Leopold, but the president of the republic, when all is said and done, is only the top-ranking civil servant, whereas royalty carries a somewhat superior quality. Since Pierlot and his associates could hardly have asked their sovereign to step down, the criticism they were subjected to in public that day must have been hard to swallow.

—

Vandervelde recalled that far from having "imposed his point of view" on his ministers, King Leopold was unanimously urged to publish the speech he made to the cabinet on October 14, 1936, through which he came to play an important role in international affairs.

In a joint communiqué issued on April 24, 1937, the French and British governments acknowledged Belgium's plan of defending its borders against all aggression, from whichever quarter, as well as preventing the use of its territory as a base for aggression against a neighboring state. In the same text, the two governments absolved Belgium from the mutual aid clause of the Pact of Locarno and from agreements made in London on March 19, 1936. Both governments confirmed that they would continue to abide by the conditions imposed in the said agreements. The releasing of Belgium from its obligations was a mere convention, for the Pact of Locarno was worth less than the paper it was written on following Hitler's reoccupation of the Rhineland on March 7, 1936.

Anxious not to seem dilatory compared to Paris and London, the leader of the Third Reich also recognized the inviolability of Belgian territory on October 13, 1937. Two years later, Hitler forestalled the British and the French by being the first to congratulate Grand Duchess Charlotte on the occasion of the first centenary of Luxembourg's declaration of independence. He sent a telegram in which he hoped that "the Grand Duchy remain free and independent for many years to come." A few months later, he invaded Luxembourg and quite simply annexed it, placing Belgium in the nebulous "Lotharingia" region, which he proposed to reorganize after his final victory.

---

A desire for independence should never be confused with the wish to maintain neutrality at any price. When Leopold acceded to the throne he believed he was following the example of his father, who had been concerned with safeguarding his country from aggression since 1930. As he knew only too well that an eventual attack would come from the east, the fortifications at Namur and Liège were reinforced and modernized, and strong defense lines along the strategic canals built. By placing a few fortifications along the border with France, he appeared to be maintaining a balance between east and west, and ensuring that Belgium's neutrality would be respected. The government had asked the king to publish his statement of October 14, 1936, since it was anxious to overcome some Belgian hostility to the measures undertaken for national defense. The king considered those measures essential for the nation's security as well as a safeguard for Belgium's independence.

Pierlot himself defined that policy to the House of Representatives on June 8, 1939: "Should war ever break out between other countries, we have neither promised to intervene nor not to intervene. Our hands are not tied. We must judge our responsibilities accordingly, taking into account that country's principal interests."

This could not have been more explicit, nor could it indicate greater support of the policy advocated by the king. Yet Pierlot was to change his tune when Great Britain and France declared war on Hitler's Germany on Sunday, September 3 of that year. Concerned that the harsh language of the press might give the

Nazis further pretext for aggression, the king spoke to the nation over the radio the very next day. After reminding them of the importance Belgium attached to "the exercise of freedom in all its forms," he gave this warning to the people: "At this critical time, when a word, an act, a carelessly written article could jeopardize this country's interests, I ask each of you to exercise the most rigorous control necessary for a neutral country when expressing your feelings." Three days later, Pierlot endorsed this by saying: "In a free country, public opinion, and the press in particular, has the ultimate right to sincerity. It has the right to express its opinions— within the limits of public interest. It is impossible to claim we are at peace while the press speaks in the language of war." This indicated that the government was prepared to impose censorship if necessary, and the prime minister explicitly said so. However, he did not consider it wise to mention this when, two days after he had gone over to Reynaud's side on May 28, 1940, he heard the Havas dispatch on Radio-Paris, saying that King Leopold attempted "to impose press censorship to paralyze Belgian public opinion which was favorable to the Allies." From this, we see the source of the information, which according to Havas had been received "from Belgian political refugees in France who are in close contact with the Belgian government." This was the government of which Spaak, as minister of foreign affairs, was still a member. In his speech to the press on October 27, 1939, he had said that Belgium's neutrality necessitated "certain ground-rules." Neither Spaak nor Pierlot thought it expedient to correct the statements in the Havas dispatch.

———

Even if France and Great Britain, in their joint communiqué of April 24, 1937, had absolved Belgium of its obligations in the Pact of Locarno, Belgium, as a member of the League of Nations (from which Germany had withdrawn in 1933), was still committed to the mutual aid clause that bound all its members. Let us therefore examine the conditions in which that help was to be given.

It would certainly not be in the form of armed intervention: no sanctions were brought against Japan after its invasion of Manchuria, nor against Italy for its aggression in Ethiopia. In both cases the League of Nations admitted it was powerless to intervene. The League had been born out of the last of President Wilson's famous "Fourteen Points" of January 8, 1918. In order to justify its existence, the League had condemned some acts, but it was severely criticized for only making verbal reproofs and not taking action over the Sino-Japanese war, the foreign intervention in the Spanish civil war, the "Anschluss" invasion and the cutting up of Czechoslovakia. It also proved incapable of stopping the slicing up of Poland, although it took credit for expelling the Soviet Union for its unjustified aggression against Finland. At that time, World War II was already into its third month.

Moreover, the Geneva Assembly had adopted a resolution on September 29, 1938, specifying that military intervention according to Article 16 of the covenant was not obligatory. It also put precise economic and financial restrictions on the nature of the intervention. The British delegate, Count de La Warr, had made it clear from the outset that if conflict occurred, each nation should judge how far its particular situation allowed it to participate in any plans envisaged by other member nations of the League.

Despite these conditions and restrictions, the king's critics nevertheless maintained that if he had given the Allies free passage into his country, Belgium could have prevented Poland from being crushed, and thus changed the course of events in the war. They supported their claim by quoting General Gamelin, who on September 1, 1939, had regretted that he was unable to send his troops into Belgium to force the Wermacht to release its hold on the Polish front. It would appear that this commander in chief of the Allied ground forces was quick to change his mind. Eight days previously, in a letter to French Prime Minister Daladier, he had said that France "could only give limited support to Poland at the start of operations," and added that an offensive in which they were sure of "being the initiator" could not be considered until 1941–42. Even supposing the second opinion to be correct, Gamelin specified that, having taken General Georges's opinion into account, the recommended intervention could not take place until after the seventeenth day following general mobilization. The "Blitzkrieg" in Poland, which had begun on September 1, was practically finished by September 14, when Warsaw was surrounded. Coming in for the kill, Stalin took eastern Poland on the seventeenth, putting an end to all further resistance, which by then was only sporadic.

Besides, was Belgium ever ordered by France or England to open its borders when they declared war on Hitler's Germany? It is impossible to find any evidence of such a demand. So we can safely say that the allegations made against Belgium—among them, regrettably, was one from Churchill, who said that Belgium had failed to recognize its "obligations"—are just trumped-up charges. On the contrary, it can be said that Belgium's armed neutrality made it easier for the British Expeditionary Force to land, and at least it partly helped the mobilization of the French army by placing its own army in battle position. Any action which would have given the Wehrmacht a pretext to invade Belgium would have been highly prejudicial to the immediate interests of the Allies. That was the objection made to General Gamelin, commander in chief of the Allied ground forces, by General Georges, his deputy. Churchill himself said in his memoirs that circumstances had forced France and England to declare war "under the worst possible conditions," and General Ironside, chief of Imperial Staff, went even further when he made the following statement to the foreign press on April 5, 1940:

"The Allies should be grateful that they could take advantage of a seven-month delay to prepare their armed forces. I shudder to think what would have happened if the Germans had attacked from the very beginning, when we were virtually without an army. . . . It is only in the last two weeks now that we can really say we have overcome this barrier."

King Leopold and Belgium cooperated in the most effective way, through their determined attitude and skillful diplomacy, to gain that seven-month delay for France and England.

# AN IDEAL BATTLEFIELD (FOR OTHERS)

The fearful example of Poland—devastated, crushed, and decimated in less than four weeks—was an ominous but valuable warning for Belgium.

The Polish government, relying on the pledges made by Great Britain on March 31, 1939, fifteen days after the Wermacht took Prague, was later to shrug its shoulders at Hitler's denunciation of the nonaggression pact by which he was bound in Warsaw. Being further backed up by promises of French military intervention given by General Gamelin, chief of staff of the French army, the Polish government refused to negotiate with the Reich about the "free city" status of Danzig and the construction of the exterritorial "corridor" to the Reich. On August 23, 1939, under Stalin's watchful eye in Moscow, a treaty was signed between Joachim von Ribbentrop, a former salesman of sparkling wines, and Viatcheslav Mikhailovitch Scriabin, the Russian minister of foreign affairs. Scriabin had changed his surname, which was that of the famous Russian composer, to "Molotov" (meaning "hammer"), because it sounded more "proletarian." Exactly eight days later, at five o'clock in the afternoon, General Gerd von Rundstedt, the commander of Army Group A, received a brief coded message, "Y.1.9.0445," which meant he was to launch an attack on Poland the next morning at 4:45.

When the French politician Pierre-Etienne Flandin expressed concern over what resistance Poland could offer against the inevitable German attack, General Gamelin said on August 27, "I know the Polish army well. Its troops are excellent and the leadership well able to handle the task. The Poles will hold out for at least six months, which will give us time to go to their aid through Rumania."

The promises of intervention made to Poland by General Gamelin, who became commander in chief of the ground forces after war was declared on Germany, were in fact confined to Operation Sarre, a plan drawn up on July 24, 1939. General Prételat, commander of Army Group 2, was entrusted with its execution, and on September 7, it was begun as a patrol operation. Under the command of General Réquin, the 4th Army penetrated about a dozen kilometers into German territory without much difficulty. They entered some abandoned villages and suffered some losses from booby traps hidden inside the houses. The 3rd Army under General Condé successfully took the wooded projection of the Warndt. It had been decided that as from Sunday, September 17, they would attack the "Westwall"—better known to the Allies as the fortified "Siegfried" Line. However, because of news from Poland, General Gamelin became cautious and put his troops on the defensive, a decision approved by the Franco-British Supreme Council. On October 16, after a few rearguard skirmishes, the French troops evacuated the villages they had occupied and the Germans reoccupied them, dismantling those booby-traps that had not torn our soldiers to pieces. With a rather cowardly sigh of relief, the rearguard was beginning to believe the misleading aspects of this "phony war."

———

It took five hours of shilly-shallying for the French leaders to decide to enter the conflict that Great Britain had just begun. Marcel Déat, former militant Socialist who had now become head of the "left-wing pacifists," proclaimed his refusal to "die for Danzig." Many joined his protest, with the exception of the Communist party, whose murmurs of dissent about the German-Soviet pact were soon stifled by the party's rigid discipline.

The sad inadequacy of the Allies in the face of the Polish tragedy, together with internal events in France, must have led
Belgium to wonder how far it could count on the effectiveness of
the agreements—always supposing they would be honored—which
France and England had signed on April 24, 1937. The wisest
thing, surely, was to depend on Belgium's own neutrality and to
reinforce the army and defense systems as far as possible to show
its determination to remain independent. Leopold set about this
task quickly, establishing a series of lines of resistance in the Liège
area supported by four strong fortifications. These were extensions
of the defense centers on all main roads to Luxembourg and
across the Limburg waterways. Publication of the king's statement
to his ministers on October 14, 1936, resulted in the extension of
military service from twelve to eighteen months.

The treaty signed in London between Belgium and Holland on
April 19, 1839, meant that although Belgium retained Antwerp, it
lost Maastricht, thus breaking its line of defense along the Meuse.
To remedy this breach in the east, the Albert Canal had been
constructed. One hundred and twenty-nine kilometers in length,
it connected the Meuse and the Schelde (Escaut) rivers between
Liège and Antwerp. In the angle formed between the canal and the
Meuse, the Eben Emael fortress was constructed, and positioned
to the fore of Liège, it seemed impregnable. However, the king
foresaw that in case of a German attack, the best line of defense
that could be jointly set up with French and British troops was
between Antwerp and Namur. The king used his prerogative as
commander in chief of the army to order the building of a strongly
fortified system consisting of many barriers and over three hundred
structures capable of resisting heavy artillery. This fortification
was called "Position KW" from the initials of Koningshooikt and
Wavre. The warning that had preceded the Munich Agreement
concerning the Sudetenland in 1938 gave the king the opportunity
to improve the measures undertaken for general mobilization.

Hitler was not deceived. On November 19, 1940, he justified his
violation of Belgium's neutrality by accusing Leopold of having

made his country a fortress, which was directed against Germany, thus protecting England and France. That was perfectly true, but the master of the Third Reich failed to recognize that his policy had forced the Belgian nation and its king to make a tremendous effort, which, considering that country's resources, far surpassed anything the French or the British had been able to accomplish in the same period of time.

———

On October 27, 1939, in a broadcast to America, Leopold confirmed his wish to keep Belgium independent and neutral, saying that peace was a matter of life or death to his people. Then he added these words, which apart from being his own opinion, also echoed the hopes of the Belgian people:

"We have no ambitions for territorial expansion. Neither had we any part whatever in the happenings that brought about the conflict today dividing Europe. If we become involved in the fray, it is on our soil that the issue would be fought out, and in view of the small size of our territory, that would spell utter destruction for Belgium, whatever the issue of the war.

"We fully know our rights and our duties; we await the future with steadfast serenity and a clear conscience, which nothing can perturb. We are prepared to exert our entire strength in order to uphold our independence.

"Exactly twenty-five years ago, day for day, the Belgian army, under the command of my father, King Albert, arrested after a hard battle the progress of a cruel invasion. If we were attacked— and pray God this may not happen—in violation of the solemn and definite undertakings that were given us in 1937 and were renewed at the outset of the present war, we would not hesitate to fight with the same conviction but with forces ten times stronger. Once again single-minded notion would support its army. But we cannot believe that the belligerents would fail to respect our neutrality. We trust in the word they have given us and have proclaimed before the world just as they may rely on our loyalty, from which, following the example set by my beloved father, I am resolved never to swerve as the sovereign of a free and gallant people."

A week later, the king was informed of significant reinforcements to the German divisions already assembled between Clèves and Trèves. Belgian intelligence discovered that the German officers there had detailed maps of Belgium. In Berlin, von Ribbentrop stated that the concentration of troops was justified because of "the considerable numbers of French and British troops now gathered to support Belgium, and besides, Belgium's new positioning of its forces is clearly directed against Germany." Meanwhile, the German ambassador in Brussels was showing signs of nervousness. Faced with this state of affairs, on October 30, the king asked his aide-de-camp and military adviser, General Van Overstraeten, to go to the palace of Lieutenant Colonel von Pappenheim, the German military attaché in Brussels, to give him the following letter:

"In a conversation between the German ambassador and Mr. Spaak, it was mentioned that the minister of foreign affairs for the Reich had justified the concentration of German troops in the lower Rhine region on the grounds that large contingents of French and British forces were gathered there to support Belgium, and that Belgium's new positioning of its troops was clearly directed against Germany. What I am about to say now is neither an excuse nor an explanation. I ask you to consider this as nothing more than a friendly communication that His Majesty feels you have a right to know.

"It is correct that for a month now, we have been reinforcing our positions along the German border. The reason is simply that during the first weeks of war, most of our available forces were in the south, but as soon as the campaign in Poland came to an end, we foresaw that the bulk of the German army would move west. Since then, we have proportionally set up a series of defenses in the east, in strict conformity with our policy of neutrality.

"I give you this warning in all sincerity. We have assigned more than half our troops to this mission and have put all our energy into organizing a powerful defense system, which is already in a satisfactory stage of completion.

"I also wish to draw your attention to Belgian public opinion, by which I mean that of most of the nation, not of a few people, or of various cliques or certain newspapers. If even a single German soldier were to set foot on Belgian soil, the whole nation would rise to a man against you. We are an independent nation, and we will not be drawn into this war, by either side, against our will."

When Leopold spoke of "various cliques" and "certain newspapers," he was referring to two political parties with which Lieutenant Colonel von Pappenheim must have been acquainted, since they more or less openly supported Nazism. They were the Rexisme party, founded and led by Léon Degrelle, in which there were twenty-one members of parliament, and the Vlaams Nationaal Verbond—VNV for short—a Flemish separatist movement with seventeen members of parliament, led by Staf De Clercq. The pro-German propaganda paper of the Rexisme party, *Pays Réel*, was freely on sale; and De Clercq's *Volk en Straat* concentrated on undermining the morale of the army, and was distributed by propagandists who had infiltrated the army to encourage the men to mutiny.

—

Following that communication, the German military attaché in Brussels, if he had known about it, would certainly have given General Van Overstraeten a copy of the letter General Gamelin sent to the French premier on September 1, 1939, confirming their talks that day. Premier Daladier had asked Gamelin, commander in chief of the French army, if he could find a satisfactory means of going to Poland's assistance. Although Gamelin's deputy, General Georges, had already stressed that such intervention could not take place until the seventeenth day following the order for general mobilization—that is to say, at a time when Poland's fate would already have been sealed—Gamelin had recommended that French troops should enter Belgium. The following letter shows the views of the man, whom Joffre had appointed chief secretary to his staff in 1914.

"I believe it is my duty to confirm in writing my own point of view, which I had the honor of relating to you personally, regarding the neutrality of Belgium and Luxembourg (and, therefore, Holland).

"Of course, I understand the French government's point of view, which was clearly stated in recent talks held with those three countries. As we have pledged to respect their neutrality, and thus cannot enter their countries unless asked to do so, France cannot take a moral standpoint, nor any other attitude. She can but abide by her agreements.

"But, nevertheless, we must recognize the fact that Belgium's current position is playing entirely into the hands of the Germans.

"With regard to an offensive action conducted by France against Germany, although we have a strongly fortified area along the one-hundred-twenty-five-kilometer front between the Rhine and the Moselle, we would have a front more than double the length between the Moselle and the Meuse (especially if we can go through Maastricht in Dutch territory). There, our attacking position would be much more favorable, for the fortifications are weaker—in some places they are still on the drawing-board—and we would have better targets. Belgium could provide useful bases for our air force to strike at the provinces in the lower Rhine, the centers of industry, and later the larger towns. Only by this route can we give strong, effective and quick assistance to Poland. Merely by extending our front line, we would be able to mobilize more troops. Moreover, the neutrality of Spain, and especially Italy, would leave us sufficient troops to assemble a powerful front along this route without even having to wait for England's support.

"I might add that even from a defensive point of view, in the case of a later attack on us by Germany through Belgium and Holland, it would be in our best interests to use Belgian forces to defend the important positions: the area south of the Albert Canal, Liège, the Meuse, and even the territory beyond the Meuse, which is easily defended as there are positions from Liège as far as the Moselle in the difficult zones of Malmédy, and if possible, the area boxed in by the Our and Sauer rivers. This arrangement would allow us to make the most of the Belgian air bases and would keep the war away from France, especially from our rich northern provinces. On the other hand, if the Belgians do not ask for our help until they are attacked by Germany, for without doubt they do not have the means (either in numbers or in military strength) to defend their front successfully against the enemy, we will have to shoulder the burden of a retreating army, a difficult task by motor transport and modern aircraft.

"We could have done such plain speaking to a man like King Albert, who has proved himself. Is there anyone in Belgium now who would listen to us? I do not mean immediately, but when the time is ripe. I don't know, but it is unfortunate if there is no one in Belgium today who is aware of Belgium's fate or who does not doubt the possibility that if Germany were to win the war, Belgium would certainly become part of the Reich. I thought I would let the French government know what the command feels on this matter."

—

"Plain speaking" indeed, which in fact meant, "We shall *use* your territory so that our air force can have a convenient base from which to attack the Ruhr, which, among other advantages, will prevent the destruction of our rich northern provinces," together with a hidden innuendo that "Belgium will suffer the devastation which we hope to spare France." The mention of King Albert—with an implied slur on King Leopold—is strange. The "Roi-Chevalier" had proved himself because the German army under the "Schlieffen plan" invaded Belgium without warning at dawn on August 4, 1914. King Albert, who was as committed to his nation's independence as his son, "proved himself" by becoming a soldier-king. It was to maintain its independence and the inviolability of its territory that Belgium called on England, France and Russia to drive the enemy out of its territory. General Gamelin was making a grave error if he imagined King Albert would have allowed the French army to penetrate Belgium to ward off a possible German attack before August 4, 1914. Besides, Gamelin immediately contradicted himself when he wondered if there was "no one" in Belgium who would listen to his "plain speaking," and specified, "I do not mean immediately, but when the time is ripe." Surely at the moment Daladier received that confused letter, the Wehrmacht had already begun to attack Poland at dawn. His word "immediately" would have been much more to the point.

This former member of Joffre's general staff was only correct on one count: that Belgium would certainly have lost its independence if Hitler had won World War II. But if, as happened, Hitler was defeated, then Gamelin, who cheerfully contemplated violating not only Belgium's neutrality but that of the Netherlands and Luxembourg as well, was plainly wasting his time.

———

"We had many reasons to fear a German invasion," said René Blum, who in 1939 was a member of the Luxembourg government. "Like Belgium, we had vivid recollections of the 1914–18 occupation, and from 1937, we concluded some agreements with the French staff to be quite clear what preventative measures we were allowed to take as a neutral country. Germany needed our iron ore, which we would have liked to refuse them. . . . We told Germany that since we were a strictly neutral country, we would have to supply France and Belgium with equal quantities, and so we were able to limit the damage somewhat.

"From a military standpoint, our situation was laughable: we only had one volunteer corps consisting of two hundred and fifty men, recruited specifically for parade duties. They could shoot, but had never received any formal training. Our artillery consisted of three old cannons, all over one hundred years old, which we fired from time to time to salute the Grand Duchess. As for defense, the French general staff advised us to place some booby traps at our frontier posts, and showed us how to make them. The Nazis immediately picked that as a bone of contention, saying it was a flagrant violation of our neutrality. In the meantime they were building landing stages along the Moselle River. What would they have said had they known the French were urging us to prepare for an imminent attack and were laying an underground telephone cable and transmitting station for use by either of us in a case of extreme urgency! A few days before we were invaded, an emissary arrived from the French high command. He advised us to padlock all the level crossings along the railway. When I protested that padlocks would not stop the German tanks, he replied that while they looked for the key, the sentry could raise the alarm on the telephone!"

At the War Council on April 25, 1940, General Weygand stated that the French command had entered the conflict with "outdated armaments and plans."

———

Holland, like Luxembourg, had little reason to doubt the possibility of a German invasion. King Leopold and Queen Wilhelmina had made a last attempt to stop the war—on August 28, 1939, they approached Poland, Germany, Great Britain, France and Italy to negotiate a peaceful solution to the Danzig affair. They did not know that on the same day, the German SS had initiated a plan, Operation Himmler, whereby they donned Polish uniforms and made a pretended attack on a German broadcasting station at Gleiwitz on the German-Polish border in order to make Poland appear the aggressor. The plan was expedited the night of August 31, while in similar disguise, some other "Polish" troops attacked German border-posts at Pitschen and Hochlinden, leaving several dead bodies, kindly supplied by the administrators of the concentration camps who had selected a few of their inmates for that purpose. Since the die was cast at dawn on September 1, the only thing Belgium and Holland could do to dissuade the Germans from attacking was to reinforce their military position in the east. Although their joint plan was a diplomatic failure, it nonetheless demonstrated the perfect solidarity of the two countries, each concerned with preserving its neutrality.

———

In November, Belgium and Holland saw the storm-clouds gathering over Germany as well as over the Allies. In the latter days of October, they learned of significant movements of German ground troops concentrated along the Belgian and Dutch borders. On the other side of the Rhine there was a forced press campaign against Belgium and Holland, both accused of accepting too eagerly the strict blockade measures advocated by the British, whose Royal Navy now lined their shores. Similarly, using different arguments, the Nazis had accused Austria before "Anschluss," Czechoslovakia before the Sudetenland affair, followed by the entry of German troops into Prague when the ink of their violent articles against Poland was barely dry. The repetition of this ploy by Dr. Josef Goebbels, the "wolf in sheep's clothing," grand master of Hitler's Propaganda and "Information" Service, was not very reassuring.

Viscount Davignon, Belgian ambassador in Berlin, said on October 27, that he had it on good authority that Hitler had decided to send the Wermacht into Belgium without delay. The "good authority" was the German Resistance, which was considered to be one of the most reliable sources of information. Even after more than a third of a century, few people know of the existence of such a movement in Germany. It can boast of a large number of heroes, whose actions were even more commendable, since the Gestapo was far more efficient within Germany than in the vast stretches of territory occupied by the Wermacht. Worse still for them, they must have known that the only way they could rid their country of Nazism was if Germany was defeated in battle. The speech that Leopold broadcast to America on October 27, in which he said how his father had prevented "a brutal invasion," must have cut Hitler to the quick.

"Up to now we have fought with restraint, but unless a way is found to peace, our soldiers will want to fight with drawn knives!" said the German ambassador in Brussels, von Bulow-Schwante, to Baron Pierre van Zuylen on November 3. He voiced strong apprehensions that French and British forces would soon invade Belgian territory. "We cannot believe such a thing," replied van Zuylen. "France and England entered this war to protect the smaller nations. They could not attack them without being dishonored and thus give the lie to their entire cause in the eyes of the world. Besides, it seems to me that the forces in the west are fairly balanced, and any aggression against Belgium would put our army in the opposite camp, which would not be to the aggressor's advantage." Von Bulow-Schwante replied that a plea for peace by the neutral countries would obviate these dangers, and he hoped this would be done as soon as possible to avoid the worst.

—

The German ambassador in Brussels seemed sincere. Or was he perhaps aware of the military talks which had begun at the Allies' insistence from the end of September 1939, in which Holland had staunchly refused to partake for fear of jeopardizing its neutrality? The Dutch government had already given another reason. "What possible advantage could there be in military talks at a time when England is not ready for war, France is in chaos and the Germans are rearmed?" wrote Van Kleffens, Dutch minister of foreign affairs, in a letter to *The Times* in England.

Those talks were also risky for Belgium. The Allies had an

answer. "Everything points to the fact that sooner or later the Germans will invade your territory, just as Emperor Wilhelm II did in 1914. The pledges of assistance we made to you two years ago still stand, but how can they be effective if we haven't agreed beforehand on the military arrangements which must be decided by common agreement?"

The argument was valid; so much so that had Hitler known about these exchanges, he would surely have invaded Belgium immediately, on the pretext that it had violated its neutrality. In fact the Reich had such a tight espionage network in Belgium that the king had to ask the government to pass new laws in March 1940, since there were no existing ones capable of protecting state security. A senator and a deputy immediately objected to this measure, which they claimed was a first step toward authoritarian rule in Belgium. The objection was taken up in the Havas broadcast on Radio-Paris the following May 30. At the same time that Leopold was taking these measures to control espionage, he also had to contend with subversion from Nazi-sympathizers, who operated quite openly when Belgium was invaded. Member of Parliament Staf De Clercq, who put his Flemish VNV party at the disposal of the invader during the occupation, stoutly denounced the sanctions that would affect his subversive propaganda in the army. He was arrested on May 10, 1940, when the Wermacht invaded Belgium, but was released two days later by order of the cabinet, which feared accusations of authoritarianism.

It was therefore necessary to hold military talks between France and Belgium in absolute secrecy. Although the king was careful to see there was no written record, he gave General Gamelin all the details of his defense positions. In his book *Servir* (*Serving*), the ex-commander in chief of the Allied ground forces defined the scope and results of those talks:

"As soon as I was allowed to enter into talks with Belgian general staff (at the end of September 1939), I felt they wanted to take up the agreements we had made to support the Belgian army along the Liège-Antwerp front under any circumstances. I replied that the promises made in those former agreements related to a situation when they requested our assistance at a time of political tension, but this was no longer the issue. We would, with Britain's agreement, consider as a first step the bringing of our forces to the Meuse, from Givet to Namur—the Dyle Valley—and Antwerp, but only on two conditions. One, that the Belgian army should be in a state of permanent general mobilization, sufficient to allow it to withstand any sudden attack, and two, that Belgium should immediately undertake the organization of a front which I would occupy. It was understood that the Belgian army would hold the Louvain-Antwerp line on that front. Finally, the Belgian front on the borders of Luxembourg, Germany and Holland would serve as cover for our forward thrust. The troops that joined our forces would be under French command until such time as it was possible to regroup them and send them back to the main body of the Belgian army."

Recognizing that the Belgians' refusal to sign anything stemmed from the fear that a "leak" would allow Hitler to allege that Belgium had broken its vow of neutrality, Gamelin adds, "However, I still managed to send written communications to Headquarters and the king, and the Belgians always let me know they agreed to my propositions."

He goes on to say that the Belgians' assent made it possible to reach a firm agreement at the beginning of November 1939, which was approved by the English generals, and which Churchill confirms in his memoirs was ratified by the Supreme Council on the seventeenth of that month.

———

In fact, the suggestion made by the German ambassador in Brussels had come from Berlin. The king had proof of that when Queen Wilhelmina, who had the same hunch, suggested on November 6 that they revive the plan they had previously put into effect on

August 28. Even if the plan was a diplomatic failure, since it did not prevent the outbreak of war, at least it had the important effect of confirming the solidarity between Belgium and Holland. The king accepted this proposal and left for The Hague that night, accompanied by Spaak and General Van Overstraeten.

The two sovereigns, attended respectively by the minister of foreign affairs and military advisers, soon reached agreement on the terms for a joint declaration. But although the Dutch advocated giving the declaration immediate and widespread publicity, the king, supported by Spaak and General Van Overstraeten, objected on the grounds that publicity would inevitably cause the enemy to take up positions even more entrenched than now. This view did not shake the Dutch at all. They refused to discuss the smallest points—not even an exchange of views—on military matters, for fear that it might furnish Hitler with an excuse to invade their territory. Having succeeded in toeing the narrow line of neutrality during World War I, they hoped to repeat the same performance.

While King Leopold was still on his way home, the Dutch government issued the following communiqué to King George VI, Lebrun and Hitler in the afternoon of Tuesday, November 7, 1940:

"During this anxious moment for the world, before a violent war is unleashed in Europe, we are convinced it is our duty to raise our voices once more.

"The warring parties declared some time ago that they would not refuse to consider a reasonable and trustworthy plan for an equitable peace. We feel it is difficult for them in the present circumstances to meet to define and reconcile their points of view. As sovereigns of two neutral states on good terms with our neighbors, we are prepared to offer them our services. If they are willing, we are ready to effect whatever they wish to suggest by whatever means we are able, in a spirit of friendly cooperation, in the hope of eventual accord.

"Such is our mission as we see it, for the benefit of our countries and in the interest of the whole world. We hope that they will make use of our services, so that a first step may be taken toward establishing everlasting peace."

—

This latest plan of King Leopold and Queen Wilhelmina was as unsuccessful as the previous one of August 28. An "anxious moment for the world," they had called it. The first words of Jacques de Launay's foreword to his book *Les Grandes Décisions de la Deuxième Guerre Mondiale* (*Great Decisions of the Second World War*) seem to justify those words:

"The world war 1939–45 lasted 2,174 days. Fifty-five million people died, that is to say 25,298 victims per day, of whom 40 million were white. Half the Jews living in Europe in 1939 were exterminated.

"The number of civilians killed, 28 million, is greater than that of the military: this is a characteristic of a total war.

"Not a single problem that existed in the world in 1939 has been resolved, apart from the elimination of German nazism, Italian fascism and Japanese militarism. However, the conflict hastened the evolution of certain phenomena: decolonization and the formation of two rival power blocs facing the third world. Paradoxically, the migration of 20 million people—the largest exodus in history—has provoked a resurgence of nationalism.

"That war cost $7.36 per second. The total amount spent on it would have been sufficient to raise the national per capita income of all the underdeveloped countries by 2 percent for a period of ten years.

"Thirty-five million war-wounded are scarred for life by that cataclysm; our entire generation has been deeply affected by those events."

Jacques de Launay only makes passing reference to the abominable concentration camps, which crushed to their very souls millions of men, women and children. Monstrous crimes against humanity were committed, for which generations to come will bear the burden. When we ask, like him, "Who? Why? How?" we can only regret that the steps taken, against all hope, by Queen Wilhelmina of the Netherlands and King Leopold of Belgium were not successful.

—

On December 19, 1939, at the meeting of the Chamber of Representatives, Spaak showed great respect for the king's unceasing efforts toward peace.

"It is not enough for me merely to accept what the king has done as part of his duties. I wish to thank him publicly for the wonderful effort he has made during the last few years to spare our country from the horrors of war. I want to thank him for the sound advice he has continued to give to successive governments; the firm spirit in which he fulfills his thankless duties; and the example he has always set those around him, an example which rightly earns him our respect, admiration and affection. Only those who do not want to understand could have doubted our king or attributed to him some ulterior motive."

By this rather obscure last sentence, the Belgian minister of foreign affairs was publicly denouncing a reference that had just appeared in a Belgian magazine called *Le Flambeau*. According to the article, Queen Wilhelmina's and King Leopold's renewed intervention had been inspired by the king to serve Germany's interests. The editor of that journal, having fled to France, tried five months later to take his revenge by publishing a "manifesto" on June 1, 1940. Supposedly expressing the indignation of members of universities and institutions of higher education in Belgium, it denounced "ex-King Leopold's horrendous betrayal." Let it be said that this libel against the "unworthy son of Albert I" did not get more than three signatures, one of them, presumably, being the author's. Another member of the officious assembly of Belgian ministers who was present in Limoges on May 31, 1940, went even further. Like a second Fouquier-Tinville (the head of police during the French Revolution who sent many victims to the guillotine), he said, "I do not accept any claims in favor of the king; I do not admit to any extenuating circumstances; I say that in those circumstances he had a very precise and necessary role to perform. He failed to do it; let him be executed." Strong words worthy of that notorious executioner, but when the time came for him to be on the receiving end, he cut a pathetic figure with his own head on the block.

———

At the same meeting in Limoges, Spaak was not the last to become turncoat. Unlike some of his more vehement colleagues, Spaak could not bring himself to admit that the king's "betrayal" had been "long premeditated," although he agreed that the king "betrayed" his country. Given that it is difficult to premeditate after an event, the minister of foreign affairs presumably wanted to cover his tracks, recalling his statement to the Chamber on December 19, which might have suggested his complicity in the crime. Spaak reproached the king (in what sounds more like praise) for having foreseen "with a foresight which today seems almost uncanny" the military operations that were about to take place. The choice of the words "foresight" and "uncanny" would suggest that the first duty of a commander in chief of an army, which Leopold was, was to lack discernment. I shall pass over "the senseless ideas on war" which Spaak accused the king of in the same speech. Six months earlier he had praised before the Chamber the king's unceasing efforts to spare Belgium from the horrors of war, his strength of spirit and the example he set to all, then suddenly he denounced the king for a "complete lack of moral sense."

We shall always remember that accusation, which, when spoken by such a new opponent to the king, has a very special flavor. There is one further point. Not a single member of the audience at Limoges, which included Pierlot and General Denis, minister of defense, contradicted Spaak when he said that the king had "too scrupulously followed the orders given him by the French high command." Furthermore, the Havas dispatch on Radio-Paris the previous day had claimed that its information came from "Belgian political refugees in France who are in close contact with the Belgian government." Concerning the visit paid to the king at GHQ by Pierlot, Spaak, Van der Poorten and Denis on May 25, Havas said, They "reproached the king for not following General Weygand's instructions." How could the agency have known about that if it was not through one of those ministers, and more particularly, through Spaak? According to Spaak, it was he, who on May 28 dictated to a "young Belgian boy scout" the first draft of the statement Pierlot broadcast on French radio that evening. It appears that it only took Spaak twenty-four hours to disapprove of the king's relationship with the new general, the only one there was, which even for a politician is a remarkable acrobatic feat.

—

On Tuesday, November 7, 1939, before Leopold had even returned to Brussels, his panic-stricken government was preparing to issue the general mobilization order and to call on Great Britain and France to act on their promises of assistance. The concentration of German divisions between Clèves and Trèves looked more and more threatening, while attacks by the Nazi press were reaching their most frenzied.

My friend Colonel Paillole, in his remarkable book concerning the activities of the Special Services of National Defense during the years immediately before World War II and the occupation of France, painted a frightening picture of the extent the German espionage system had penetrated France. Belgium had no cause to envy us on that score, and it would not be surprising if enemy agents knew of the exchanges between General Gamelin and General Delvoie, military attaché to the Belgian embassy in Paris.

Those exchanges committed to paper by the commander in chief and dated November 10, gave details of how the Allies were dealing with the operations in support of the Belgian army. General Gamelin had not abandoned his pet theory, and Belgium's territory still seemed to him the ideal battlefield both militarily and because the rich northern provinces of France would be spared. Indeed it would not be surprising if he had divulged secrets, which passing from ear to ear eventually became known to the agents of the Abwehr.

Under those circumstances, the question still remains whether the frenzied Nazi activity had been provoked by Holland's broadcast of the text signed by Queen Wilhelmina and King Leopold. According to telephoned information from the Belgian ambassador in Berlin, the attacks in the Nazi press had preceded the publication of The Hague's transmission. But at seven o'clock in the evening, it became known that the Dutch government was also in a state of alarm.

The next morning, Wednesday, November 8, the news from Brussels became even more alarming: three Panzer divisions were assembling along the border. News from Holland was no better. Were these two countries to suffer the same fate in such a short space of time after the invasion of Poland?

In this tense and anxious atmosphere, The Hague informed Brussels on Thursday, November 9, that Queen Wilhelmina had just sent a telegram to Hitler congratulating him on his escape from an assassination attempt, which according to Berlin had taken place the day before. But such a small peace-offering could not prevent the storm-clouds from gathering along the frontiers of the two countries, which were clinging desperately to their threatened neutrality. In the afternoon of that Thursday, November 9, a message from Colonel Goethals, Belgian military attaché in Berlin, said that according to the usual "sources" of his Dutch colleague, Major Sas, the Wermacht was mobilizing for an attack, the objective and timing of which the informer did not know. During the evening they became even more anxious, when it was announced that Hitler was about to make a decision.

—

The situation worsened on Friday, November 10. In a reply to General Delvoie, who had visited him the previous day, General Gamelin said the following:

"Taking into account the new situation and the experience of Poland in the war, we must face the enemy with a continuous front, a wall that advances by road at night, and by day turns to face the attack. Even the light armored divisions must march under the protection of anti-aircraft guns to avoid attack.

"In other words, the Allied troops' advance shall be very methodical, at the speed of the foot-soldiers, from battlefield to battlefield and searching for anti-tank mines in each one. Since the German army is already in battle formation and taking the initiative, according to the rules of strategy we cannot send isolated divisions to the Albert Canal. If this operation follows the rules, the troops on the right should at a certain time reach Namur, those on the left should reach Zeeland, with the front moving through Wavre-Louvain-Lierre-Antwerp. Then, depending on the situation, we shall know what kind of defense to give the Albert Canal and the Liège-Namur line. It would be dangerous to bring the Allied troops forward to defend Luxembourg, or to support you on the Ourthe River. We must be prepared for the fact that the Germans will soon form a large pocket in the Ardennes."

We would see in May 1940, how quickly "the wall that advances by road at night, and by day turns to face the attack" was broken. (Imagine how spirited the soldiers must have been to face an attack with their legs well rested after a night's walk!) What is really astonishing is that General Gamelin was surprised by the Panzer divisions' surge through the Ardennes, when six months before he had stated he was prepared for the fact that the Germans "will soon form a large pocket" there.

Anyway, his reply just as it stood was accepted by General Denis, the Belgian minister of defense. "If we are attacked," he said, "it is essential to ensure the triumph of our combined forces. It does not make much difference whether the battle takes place fifty kilometers to the front or to the rear: in either case, our country will be destroyed." Refusing to view matters in that light, King Leopold thanked General Gamelin for his communication, saying he appreciated its "forthrightness and trust," but reiterated his hope that the measures taken by his army were "such that, should intervention from Allied powers be sought, the army would already be protected from any surprise ground attack." Could this have been a premonition? The surprise attack on the morning Belgium was invaded came from the sky. The Eben Emael fortification, the key point in the entire first line of defense, was destroyed almost immediately.

London and Paris sent their confirmation that the agreements in the joint declaration of April 24, 1937, would be upheld. This, together with the measures taken along the Belgian border, allowed a breathing space before the catastrophe, which seemed unavoidably imminent.

But Brussels and The Hague were soon dismayed by a speech, whose author appeared to be provoking Hitler to act immediately. Winston Churchill, First Lord of the Admiralty in Neville Chamberlain's government, stated that if Hitler allowed winter to pass without mounting an offensive in the west, "the first round" would be won by the Allies. Meanwhile, a dispatch from Baron de Cartier, Belgian ambassador in London, indicated that British opinion, which had at first been in favor of Belgium's and Holland's neutrality, had completely changed: "The idea gaining popularity here is that if the Germans invade Belgium and Holland, and we are forced into war on their side, there would actually be more advantages than disadvantages for France and England, and it would answer their immediate interests."

Had the theories supported so persistently by General Gamelin and turned down by Daladier become common knowledge across the Channel? General Ironside, chief of Imperial Staff, was against it, as seen in the statement I quoted before where he congratulated himself on the respite (due mainly to Belgium's staunch neutrality) the Allies had gained since the opening of hostilities. But Churchill had too much of a fighting spirit to accept the unfolding of this "phony war." Churchill, who succeeded the feeble Neville Chamberlain on May 10, the day when war really began in the west, was blissfully ignorant of the plight of the British Expeditionary Force, which was evacuating with difficulty from the beaches of Dunkirk, abandoning all its supplies. He sent the following message on June 4, to General Hastings Lionel Ismay, minister of defense in Britain's War Cabinet. General Ismay had to read it twice, to make sure he wasn't dreaming: "It would be marvelous to act in such a way that the Germans would not know where the next attack was coming from, instead of being forced by them to surround this island by a wall with a roof on top!" Two days later, reviewing standing orders, he summarily urged the the leaders of general staff to suggest immediately, "some measures suited to a vigorous, bold and relentless offensive along the entire coast occupied by the Germans." He defined its objective as "spreading terror along the length of these shores." As I was able to see at firsthand the extreme vulnerability of England in July 1940, I too, like General Ismay, would have rubbed my eyes in disbelief at such a message. I would have been proved wrong, of course, for above all else, it is a strong will that wins wars. But sometimes, the cost is high to the allies of the country that is directing the fight.

On receipt of Baron de Cartier's information, General Denis, Belgian minister of defense, commented as follows on the trend in London:

"At this moment, both France and Britain are militarily well-equipped in terms of total strength and fortification. The reequipped Dutch army has been positioned along the fortified lines now covered by flood-waters, and the large contingent of Belgian troops is firmly entrenched. The warning we gave on November 11 has shown how calmly and resolutely our countries will defend their neutrality.

"Perhaps in October the British feared that Holland would be rapidly occupied and also suspected that Belgium would be invaded. At this moment they could justifiably cherish their hope of reaching the Albert Canal and the Meuse River in Belgium. In Holland they could at least reach the mouth of the Schelde and the Meuse, as well as the coastal positions of Helder and the Friesland islands.

"Should such a hypothesis prove correct, then Britain and France would hold the major part of Belgium, Germany the major part of the Low Countries, apart from the coast which is most important for submarine activity. The advantages gained by the British and French in such a situation are undeniable.

"From a military viewpoint, we have the addition of Belgian and Dutch troops, air bases in a convenient location for use against the industrial targets of the Reich and a sound sea position a short distance away from German military ports. From an economic point of view, there is a tightening of the blockade and the addition of Dutch and Belgian colonial resources.

"Furthermore, as a result of declaring and waging war, the consequences of the blockade—which is actually very tight now—would be felt far more quickly beyond the Rhine. This is because Germany would soon need replacements for its armaments, and because of the increase in demand for materials it does not possess in sufficient quantities: petrol, rubber, non-ferrous metals, etc.

"No doubt the Germans would gain some convenient air bases closer to England in Friesland, Groningen and Drente, but that would be poor compensation compared to the advantages gained by the British.

"In conclusion, I think I can wholeheartedly agree with de Cartier's opinions concerning the motives which might explain Britain's change of tack with regard to Belgium and Holland."

Now that is what is called being objective! Thinking strictly from a military point of view, General Denis made a summary of the price to be paid by the people of Belgium and Holland whose countries would be transformed into closed battlefields in which "as a result of declaring and waging war," the outcome would be decided. What would remain of those two countries once victory had fallen to this or that side? The ruin and suffering sustained in 1940 and again four years later, in the brief ten-day battle at Arnhem, can only give us a vague idea.

# "MY GRAND MANEUVER
IN THE NORTH"

I had the honor of befriending Colonel Sir Claude Dansey, deputy to General Menzies (chief of the Intelligence Service), who sometimes confided in me. He told me how during World War I he had made the acquaintance of a young German naval officer called Wilhelm Canaris. When Canaris's cruiser the *Dresden* was sunk by the Royal Navy in March 1915, he managed to flee to Spain, where he received "Intelligence" training, and later took command of the Abwehr. Sir Claude said of him, "I have always had great repect for him, as he really is a gentleman. We have so many things to talk about."

Uncle Claude, as Colonel Dansey was affectionately known, was never able to realize his wish of meeting him. Canaris was implicated in a plot against Hitler that ended in von Stauffenberg's assassination attempt on July 20, 1944, and he died in appalling circumstances at the Flosenburg concentration camp one month before the collapse of the Nazi regime that he had hated so much.

He was one of those Germans I mentioned earlier with a strong moral conscience, which became very evident on the day the invasion of Poland unleashed World War II. For someone like Canaris, the only hope of creating a new Germany, free from the yoke of Nazism, lay in the military defeat of his own country. As he held the highest state secrets, it was within his power to hasten that defeat before Germany was totally destroyed by the war. However, this officer, whose spirit had been molded by the strict

71

discipline of the German navy, could not bring himself to act alone. Besides, he was closely watched by Himmler's diabolical partner, SS Reinhard Heydrich, head of the dreaded *Reichssicher-heitshauptampt*, which gave him a firm hold on all police and security activites in the Nazi machinery.

One of Canaris's closest associates was Colonel Hans Oster, who also detested Nazism, but went further than him in seeing it as his duty to hasten the Wermacht's defeat. "Maybe I'll be branded as a traitor," he said, "but I think I am a better German than those who meekly follow Hitler. I have only one aim and one duty, and that is to rid Germany and the whole world of the Nazi curse." Even if it is unlikely that Canaris actually asked him to give the Allies information that could change the course of the war, it is certain that Oster was encouraged by his superior's attitude. He was sure that Canaris could "cover up" for him if there was a leak about his activities which might make the SS suspicious. This is exactly what happened.

Colonel Hans Oster had developed a close friendship with Major Sas, military attaché to the Dutch embassy in Berlin. Oster used Sas as a neutral go-between, knowing that Sas was on friendly terms with Colonel Goethals, military attaché to the Belgian embassy. No doubt Viscount Davignon received his information from Goethals, and thus could claim he had access to a very good source. This same source had told Major Sas that on the advice of Hitler's astrologer, Swiss-born Ernest Krafft, the Führer had decided to switch the invasion of Holland and Belgium from dawn, Tuesday, November 14, 1939, to Sunday, December 10. Apart from astrological influences, there was also the bad weather, which had turned the fields and paths into a mud-bath, and the reinforcement of Belgian defenses on the eastern front, which certainly influenced that decision. In the meantime, a Luftwaffe plane chased by the French had crashed on Belgian soil. Belgium, anxious to demonstrate its neutrality, stated it was prepared to safeguard the wreckage until the cessation of hostilities.

The number of Nazi divisions along the Belgian border had

again increased and, according to general staff, now stood at fifty or sixty. Alarmed by this, Holland proposed to Leopold that they once again attempt a peace settlement, this time asking the king of Italy and President Roosevelt to join in. The idea never got off the ground, but it made Belgium consider a new possibility; if Hitler should attack only Holland, what position should Belgium adopt? It was probable that Great Britain might feel threatened by the installation of air and submarine bases in Holland, and would certainly, together with France, ask Belgium for free passage for the Allies. This would give Hitler the opportunity he was waiting for, to invade Belgium without seeming to renege on his agreements.

The problem was even further complicated by the Dutch government's refusal to listen to any approaches made by Belgium on military matters, clinging to the illusion that it could thus avoid the horror of a German invasion. The only positive step the Dutch took was to declare that if the German troops now positioned along its borders should make a move, it would call on the Allies.

—

The fateful day of Sunday, December 10, passed without incident. Both The Hague and Brussels wondered whether the source Major Sas put such faith in was really so reliable. But it would have been a mistake to suppose that Hitler had merely been bluffing.

During a conversation held on December 30 in Rome with the Belgian Princess Marie-José (wife of the heir-apparent Prince Umberto), Count Ciano, Italian minister of foreign affairs, said that a German attack on her country seemed very likely. Ciano arranged with her to relay to King Leopold through a reliable person some information he was about to receive. On January 9, 1940, she was asked to say, "Only the most rigorous preparations can avert the storm." A similar note was received the next day from Monsignor Micara, apostolic nunciate in Brussels, and confirmed in a message on January 13 from Viscount Davignon, Belgian ambassador in Berlin. Once again Colonel Goethals's source had issued a warning. Pope Pius XII himself intervened to inform them that an attack would take place "very shortly." Wednesday, January 10, proved to be a nerve-racking day for Brussels as well as for The Hague, London and Paris.

Major Reinberger was commander of the 7th Division of the German airborne troops under General Kurt Student. He was temporarily serving as liaison officer to the 2nd Luftflotte, headquartered at Munster, and was charged with the delivery of secret instructions to Cologne, some of them bearing the signature of General Student. On the way to the railway station, he spent some time with his fellow officers and helped himself rather too freely to the bottle. To his horror he realized that he had missed the train to Cologne! The documents were of a most urgent nature. What would General Student say, this tough soldier who had distinguished himself as commander of a fighter squadron in .the Great War and who was renowned for taking his orders very seriously?

Seeing his friend's unfortunate predicament, Major Hoenmann, a pilot in the reserves, offered to take him in his little plane to Cologne, an offer Reinberger gratefully accepted. Were the snow and fog to blame? Or had Hoenmann also drunk too much? Anyway, instead of landing in Cologne at the Luftwaffe air base, they landed at about 11:30 in the morning of Wednesday, January 10, in the neighborhood of a little Belgian town called Mechelen-aan-de-Maas, or Mechelen-sur-Meuse. The town is situated on the Dutch border near Maastricht and was then held by the 32nd, 33rd and 34th regiments, comprising the 13th Division of the Belgian army, plus the 21st Artillery Regiment and the 14th Battalion of the Engineer Corps.

Their forced landing caused some damage to the plane; both its wings were ripped off while passing between two trees, and the plane had landed with its engine deeply embedded in a hedge. Hoenmann was still in shock when three Belgian soldiers arrived on the scene. The two Germans were led to the command post of Captain Rodrigue, while one of the men went to look for him. Their papers were seized and placed on the officer's desk.

A thick icy fog lingered over the morning of Wednesday, January 10. To protect the men from the cold, a cast iron stove glowed warmly in the room where Reinberger—who was seated there with his companion—pretended to fall asleep. Seizing an opportunity when the guard was not paying any attention, he leapt from his chair, grabbed the papers and stuffed them in the stove. At that very moment Captain Rodrigue arrived. He snatched the papers from the fire and managed to put out the flames, burning his hands in the process. Furious, the Belgian officer exclaimed, "It is always the same with you Germans. We treat you correctly, and you play a dirty trick like this!" Saying this, he put his revolver down next to the papers, whereupon Reinberger leapt up and threw himself on it, and Rodrigue had to tear the weapon from his hands. Then Reinberger had a hysterical fit, banging his head against the wall to try and knock himself unconscious; he rolled on the floor and moaned, "I have committed an unforgivable crime! I wanted your revolver so I could kill myself!" Leaning over Reinberger, Hoenmann said, "You must excuse him. . . . It's bad trouble he's in—he's an officer in the regular army!"

A brief look at the partly charred papers so amazed Rodrigue that he immediately got in touch with his regimental staff.

—•—

On January 11, General Van Overstraeten noted in his log, "The veil has been torn away." He had just read the "General Orders for Operations of the 2nd Luftflotte," which I have reproduced below. (Brackets indicate where the paper was destroyed by fire.)

"The German army in the west will carry out its offensive between the North Sea and the Moselle, aided by the air force, through the Belgian-Luxembourg territory in order to. . .the most important parts of the French army and its. . . .The area around Liège and. . .surrounded . . . . Besides, our intention is to take over Dutch territory, with the exception of *Vesting Holland*. . .with a grouping of troops (10th A.C. and 1st C.D.). The 8th Air Corps and some of its troops must support a disembarkation operation made by the 7th Airborne Division on the first day of attack. In close cooperation with the VIth Army (mainly positioned close to and west of Maastricht), it must support the progress of the ground forces attacking the defense lines covering the Meuse basin and destroy the Belgian army west of that area. . . . The fighter planes must gain air supremacy over the VIth Army's zone of attack.

"The combined battle formations of the Luftflotte 3 shall take on the French air bases to prevent them from intervening in any battles fought on land. Next, the Luftflotte shall prevent French armies in the north from advancing toward the northeast. . . . The 10th Air Corps, together with the Kriegsmarine, will concentrate on fighting the British naval forces. . . ."

The instructions signed by General Student directed the 7th Division of the airborne forces to land on the west bank of the Meuse beyond Namur. Their mission was to prevent the blowing up of the bridges between Dinant and Annevoie and to form a bridgehead at Yvoir. This operation was scheduled for Wednesday, January 17.

———

The king asked Hayoit de Termincourt, public prosecutor of the Supreme Court of Appeals, to investigate the supposed forced landing of the German plane as well as the nature of the documents seized. This eminent magistrate proclaimed without a doubt that the landing had been accidental and the documents were authentic. By this time their contents had already been made known in Paris and London.

Their authenticity was confirmed when the German military attaché asked to talk to his two compatriots. Permission for the meeting was granted with the proviso that it took place in the presence of a Belgian officer. Pretending to look for a pencil, the attaché asked the officer to bring him one. The officer agreed, and even took his time about it, since microphones were concealed in the room. The visitor was heard to express concern as to whether the documents had really been destroyed. Reinberger replied, "When they were retrieved from the stove, only a few pieces remained, no bigger than the palm of my hand."

It was not until the Nuremberg trials that we learned from Field Marshal Keitel—who was on trial as a war criminal—that Hitler had been informed of Reinberger's escapade on the night of Friday, January 12, and had it not been for the extreme cold on the nights of January 13 and 14, he would have launched his offensive immediately. Keitel said at Nuremberg:

"When he was told about the incident, Hitler flew into a frenzied rage, the worst outbreak I have ever seen. The Führer went into a trance, he was frothing at the mouth, he struck the wall with his fists, vowed he would have the guilty parties executed and roared terrible oaths about incompetence and treachery among the general staff. Göring, forced to bear the brunt of his fury, had not even recovered from it the next day. When Kesselring went to visit him, he found him more depressed than ever."

The hapless wives of Major Reinberger and Major Hoenmann, who were in no way connected with those events, were both thrown into prison, and General Helmuth Felmy, commander of the 2nd Luftflotte, was sacked for his subordinate's mistake. Hitler chose Kesselring to replace him.

———

The king, as commander in chief, did not await authentification of the documents before first, ordering the army to take the necessary measures, and second, informing the French, British and

Dutch authorities of their contents. But it was not until the evening of Saturday, January 13, after receiving Count Davignon's message from Berlin, that Spaak asked the French and British ambassadors, in the presence of the Dutch ambassador in Brussels, if their governments were prepared to act on the joint declarations signed on April 24, 1937. He specified that any intervention by French and British forces on Belgian soil would depend on the eventuality of a German attack. That night, at 00:30, Bargeton, French ambassador in Brussels, sent the following message to his minister:

"We have just returned from a meeting with Spaak, who called us a moment ago. He asked me to tell you immediately that according to information he has on hand tonight, the Belgian government considers it likely that Belgium will be attacked at dawn today, Sunday.

"The Belgian government has finalized all military measures against such an attack. If an attack should take place, it will immediately call on France and England for assistance as stated in the 1937 declaration. The Belgian ambassador in Paris has already been informed of what he should do in such a situation."

———

The same Saturday, January 13, 1940, while Spaak was conferring with the French and British ambassadors, the king summoned Sir Roger Keyes, admiral of the British Fleet, well known for his daring attack on the German submarine base at Zeebrugge on April 23, 1918, during the Great War. The admiral had been a great friend of King Albert and now extended that friendship to King Leopold. This factor had prompted Churchill, First Lord of the Admiralty in Neville Chamberlain's government, to ask him to liaise between the king and the British prime minister.

Leopold, who was educated at Eton and whose first cousin was George VI, knew the English well. He remembered how his father, caught unawares by the sudden German attack, had not been able to call in time on Great Britain, France and Russia—his Allies by force of circumstances—to come to his aid in defending the integrity and neutrality of his country. "Do you not think," said Leopold to Sir Roger Keyes, "that the time is right for Great Britain to confirm its readiness to honor its pledge, should Belgium be forced to appeal for help, according to the agreements signed by England and France? Could I ask you to inquire privately of your friend Churchill whether it would be wise for my government to make an official request for help?"

Sir Roger Keyes thought this an excellent idea and decided to return to London immediately, particularly in the face of threats resulting from the Mechelen affair. Unfortunately, thick fog prevented his plane from taking off. He called Churchill by telephone, and the latter, whether sincerely or not, interpreted his request in a completely different way from what Leopold had intended when he first asked the admiral to intervene. On Monday, January 15, the British government gave its reply through the prime minister, a reply that worried Spaak, who saw the king's initiative as an "unconstitutional act." Sir Roger Keyes was clearly mortified when he brought Leopold the following message, which had been dictated over the telephone by Neville Chamberlain himself:

"We are ready to accept invitation to British troops to enter Belgium and understand French attitude is the same.

"We are asked to give guarantees to Belgium which go further than anything we have promised to France and which we might not be in a position to carry out at the end of the war.

"Subject to the above we are ready to promise as follows if such an invitation were given at once:

"1. If Belgium thereupon becomes involved with the Allies in hostilities against Germany, we will not open peace negotiations without informing Belgium and we should expect them to do the same.

"2. We will do our utmost to maintain the political and territorial integrity of Belgium and her colonies.

"3.  If after the war Belgium is in need of financial and economic assistance, we will include her in any assistance we may be able, in conjunction with our Allies, to render in these respects.

"The king will realize that the value of the invitation will be seriously discounted from the point of view of Belgium as well as ourselves unless the invitation is given in sufficient time to enable British and French troops to secure a strategical advantage of position before any German attack begins."

Understandably, Lord Keyes, who had Belgium's interests at heart, was very embarrassed to find that the mission he was entrusted with had provoked such a response, especially as it had been a private inquiry for information. In fact, the British government was subordinating its promise of assistance made in conjunction with France on April 24, 1937, to the right to enter Belgian territory at once. According to the terms of that agreement, aggression by a foreign nation was the only condition whereby Britain could intervene in Belgium.

General Gamelin was informed of the British reply at eight o'clock in the morning that Monday, January 15. He immediately requested an audience with Daladier, who received him with Champetier de Ribes and Alexis Léger (his literary pseudonym was "Saint-John Perse"), respectively secretary of state and secretary general of foreign affairs, and Coulondre, former French ambassador in Berlin. After the talks, Daladier summoned Le Tellier, Belgian ambassador in Paris, to inform him that the French army "had taken all necessary measures for immediate entry into Belgian territory." He then added, much more brutally than London, "You must formally say yes or no, if we can enter Belgian territory. If the answer is no, we are back to the *status quo ante*. Let it be understood that in the case of any danger in the future, we have the right to decide and do what we think best. We shall await your answer until 2000 hours."

One does not wear kid gloves when issuing an ultimatum. No doubt Daladier—who did not mind being called the "bull from

Vaucluse"—thought that his tone in addressing a friendly nation was in keeping with his "image." Over and above his role as premier, he was playing those of minister of war and minister of foreign affairs, which is quite a lot for one man, even if he is "made of steel." He also said he had good reason to refer to the *status quo ante*, in other words, the situation that existed prior to the question posed by Admiral Keyes in the circumstances I have outlined.

The *status quo ante* referred to the pledges of assistance signed by France and Great Britain on April 24, 1937, with regard to Belgium's "determination, publicly confirmed, to defend its frontiers with all its might from all aggression or invasion, and to prevent Belgium from being used as a base for any foreign aggression, either as a passage or a springboard for land, sea or air operations."

Daladier's unreasonable request, like that of the Chamberlain government, not only tried to force Belgium to abandon its neutrality (thus playing right into Hitler's hands and bringing Holland into the war), but also tried to compel Belgium to go back on its word and its ideal, which had been the basis for the *status quo ante*, now brandished as a threat by the "bull from Vaucluse." This was completely unreasonable and illogical.

———

The Belgian government replied:

"If this situation ever occurred, the king's government would be taking on a tremendous responsibility by involving its people in a war which may be avoided, simply because of its knowledge that Belgium might be attacked.

"Our attitude, which does not conflict with our faithfulness toward our agreements and our main interests, is also in keeping with the agreements and interests of France and England. From the standpoint of justice and the treaty, the entry of French and British troops into Belgium should not precede the actual violation of our territory.

"To sum up, either Germany will abandon its plan to attack, thus freeing Belgium from the trials of war whilst it continues to protect the French border, or Germany will commit a fresh act of aggression. In that case, any support from French and English troops in the name of justice will be morally acceptable and, with the Belgian army, our combined forces will increase the chance of success."

This serene reply served as a reminder to Paris and London that their agreement of mutual assistance was based on Belgium's insistence on defending its borders with all its might "against all aggression or invasion," and on preventing Belgium from being used as "a passage or a springboard for land, sea or air operations." If Belgium had submitted to the French and British governments' requests, it would have perjured itself.

Although the wording of this reminder was very tactful, it was most displeasing to its recipients. In very bad faith, Paris, of whom Belgium had asked nothing, accused Belgium of having sent out an appeal for assistance, thus causing the French army to make useless marches back and forth. In more poetic language, Churchill compared Leopold's kingdom to the victim of a crocodile which, in the hope of being eaten last, grovels shamelessly before the monster. The worst part was that the First Lord of the Admiralty, forgetting that the main points of the documents seized at Mechelen had been communicated to him under oath of secrecy, now made public mention of them by underlining their importance. Meanwhile, Leopold and his government were striving to give the impression that they did not know of Hitler's plans to attack. To prevent any reaction from the Reich, Viscount Davignon was asked to make the following statement on Wednesday, January 17, to the German government:

"We are most surprised by the excitement caused by our military measures. Please note that these measures are a result of the documents that fell into our hands after the landing of the plane you mentioned in yesterday's dispatch. These documents caused us both pain and surprise, for they revealed Germany's plans for a fully considered offensive. Nevertheless, we remain determined to preserve our neutrality, and will only call on the Allies in the case of aggression. But, because of the above-mentioned documents, it is essential that Germany reassures us by its actions, so that our confidence may be restored."

———

Major Sas's usual source informed him that the note had thrown Hitler into an unbelievable fury. The source confirmed that preparations for attack by Wehrmacht divisions along the Belgian border had been halted all day Wednesday, January 17. The order to invade Belgium had been postponed indefinitely.

Two and a half months later, General Ironside, referring to the state of unpreparedness of the British troops at the beginning of hostilities, said, "It is only since the last two weeks that we can really say we have overcome the obstacle." By avoiding the worst in mid-January, Belgium's firm diplomacy secured an additional two months' respite for the French and British.

———

On March 20, 1940, the "bull from Vaucluse" vacated the premiership to make way for Paul Reynaud. True to the dictum that small men often have aggressive characters, the new head of the French government immediately subscribed to Churchill's suggestion. Churchill, forgetting the lesson he had learned twenty-five years before in the Dardanelles, persuaded Reynaud to mount a campaign that would deprive the German war industry of iron ore from the Swedish mines of Kiruna, which was carried via the Norwegian port of Narvik. From April 8, 1940, the French navy and the Royal Navy mined Norwegian waters. Reynaud at once proclaimed that "The iron road has been cut!" In retaliation, Hitler immediately ordered his troops to disembark at Oslo, Larvik, Kristiansend, Stavanger, Bergen, Trondheim and Narvik, while the Wehrmacht invaded Denmark.

During the night of April 9 to 10, Spaak was notified that the French ambassador and the British chargé d'affaires in Brussels, both bearers of an identical and urgent communication from their governments, wished to be received without delay. The minister of foreign affairs was told that Paris and London were worried about "the alarming news from the Dutch government," and wanted Belgium to open its borders immediately to the French and British forces "to assure its own safety."

When asked to elucidate upon the "alarming news," both Bargeton and Aveling declared they knew nothing about it, and for a very good reason. For at the same hour, the Dutch minister of foreign affairs was also visited by representatives of France and Great Britain, who referred to the the "alarming news from the Belgian government." Bargeton told Spaak that according to what he had been told, the Allied troops would only go as far as the defensive lines between Antwerp and Namur. This showed clearly that Belgium's east side would be immediately open to a German invasion, which would certainly be brought on by Allied intervention.

—

As soon as news of Germany's operations in Norway and Denmark was received, the French War Council met in the Elysée Palace, chaired by President Lebrun. Admiral Darlan, bitterly reproached by Paul Reynaud for his lack of foresight, replied with the suggestion that French troops immediately enter Belgian territory. This proposal was eagerly supported by Gamelin, as we can well imagine. Reynaud hesitated for a while, arguing that the Wermacht was superior, but Gamelin brushed aside any doubts that needed resolving. The new premier was anxious about the effect of a German initiative on his newly-formed, three-week-old government. That same day he set off for London to bring the British round to his point of view. The specially convened Supreme Allied War Council agreed to the suggestion, and went as far as deciding to issue an ultimatum to Belgium, should Holland be under threat of invasion and Belgium refused to allow Anglo-French troops into its territory. General Gamelin himself stated the terms of the official report of that meeting:

"The French and British governments shall make representations to the Belgian government, insisting that the Allies be invited without delay into Belgian territory before Germany attacks Belgium. It should be pointed out that this would give the Allies the best chance to render effective assistance, should there be a German invasion. The communication shall stress the heavy responsibility that Belgium will shoulder if it fails to make this offer. The French ambassadors should support this combined diplomatic move—the terms of which were agreed at the end of the meeting—by a simultaneous approach to the Belgian general staff, a move which has been approved by French high command."

General Gamelin went on to write another note that same day, April 9, 1940, to Daladier, minister without portfolio in Reynaud's Cabinet:

"It would be to our advantage not to mention our intervention in Holland and Luxembourg: on the one hand—specifically to keep it a secret—we can gain no advantage by revealing these two problems in advance; on the other hand, our entry into Belgium will pave the way for our entry into Holland and will be the first step toward it. As for Luxembourg—apart from protecting the industrial basin of Longwy—it is only of secondary importance to the conduct of this war, but initially, Luxembourg can cover our entry into Belgium."

The next day, Wednesday, April 10, 1940, in his headquarters at Vincennes Palace, General Gamelin gave a sumptuous luncheon in honor of General Weygand, commander in chief of operations in the eastern Mediterranean, who was passing through Paris.

If World War II had broken out four years earlier, General Weygand, former chief of staff under General Foch who became chief of staff of the Allied armies in March 1918, and played an important part in directing operations in France resulting in a final victory, would have been named commander in chief of the French and British forces in 1939. But Weygand had retired in 1935, at the age of sixty-eight. Seventeen years earlier, he had prevented the Red army from entering Warsaw. He then replaced General Gouraud as high commissioner in Syria and the Lebanon and became member of the Supreme War Council and director of the Center for Advanced Military Studies. He became chief of army general staff in January 1930, and vice-president of the Supreme War Council and army inspector general in February 1931, all of which—according to current talk—made him "a born generalissimo." "If France is in danger, call Weygand," Foch liked to say. This remark resulted in Daladier recalling Weygand into service in 1939, and asking him to take over command of operations in the eastern Mediterranean at Beirut. To give Reynaud his due, he did try on Thursday, May 9, the very eve of the German offensive, to make Weygand commander in chief of the army, thereby replacing Gamelin. But just like the time he tried to make Colonel de Gaulle undersecretary for war, he came up against Daladier, who refused point-blank to discharge the present commander in chief, Gamelin, from his duties. The disagreement between the two men was so violent that Reynaud put his case to Lebrun. Had the latter not reminded Reynaud of his position, a ministerial crisis would have occurred at the very moment the Wermacht was moving west. It should be noted, however, that even if Reynaud had succeeded in overruling the "bull from Vaucluse," General Weygand could not have changed any of Gamelin's arrangements, since the die had long been cast.

On April 10, 1940, General Gamelin, in honor of Weygand, assembled a dazzling group consisting of General Georges, his deputy, General Doumenc, chief of staff of the armies, General Koeltz, deputy chief of staff, and Colonel Petibon, his private secretary, Colonel Simon and Lieutenant Colonel De-leuze, Commander Christian de l'Hermite and Captain de Montjamont with their adjutants, and Captain Roger Gasser, Weygand's chief secretary. They dined lavishly on sole, Bresse chicken *mascotte, foie gras* with truffles, salad, cheeses and *profite-roles* dripping with chocolate. The food was served with White An-jou, Beaune 1933 and Monbazillac 1929. Throughout the meal Gamelin did not make a single allusion to military matters or to current operations. Then, he declared abruptly, "When will the Germans decide to attack so I can begin my grand maneuver in the north?"

His exclamation was followed by deathly silence, and conversation was resumed on another topic. One month later to the day, Hitler granted Gamelin his wish by simultaneously invading Holland and Belgium, combined with a general attack on the west.

———

On Wednesday, April 10, 1940, while Gamelin was enjoying the chicken and *foie gras*, the Belgian government breathed a sigh of relief: there were no disturbing signs along the German borders and, according to The Hague, the same went for Holland. On Thursday, May 11, the following communiqué issued by the cabinet was given to the press:

"The cabinet has heard the minister of foreign affairs outline the external situation. The government has again expressed its unanimous desire to persevere in its policy of independence and neutrality, which it has followed since the beginning of the conflict in Europe."

I have it on good authority that this statement caused Reynaud considerable anger, and he even threatened that Belgium would regret its refusal to allow French and British troops into its territory when it was not being attacked by the Wermacht. This threat voiced by the little man riding on his high horse was similar to what he had declared to Bargeton, French ambassador in Brussels, when the latter was asked to call on Spaak during the night, "I shall stamp on those who stand in my way!" It is to our regret that Reynaud did not think of transporting his government inside the walls of the ancient citadel at Sedan; for if he had repeated such a threat to the 7th Panzer Division of the Wermacht, he might have intimidated Rommel and Guderian and thus changed the course of the French campaign. Reynaud was doubtful whether the Belgian government had acted in complete agreement with their king, and devoted himself from that time on to making fierce attacks on Leopold, the first effects of which were soon evident.

—

Before his luncheon on April 10, General Gamelin summoned the Belgian military attaché. He asked General Delvoie how his government would react if he promised that the French army would march only as far as the Albert Canal. Such a plan would obviously suit Gamelin, who was sure that Belgium would be equally satisfied. When the French War Council heard about this later, it was most surprised to learn that such a daring proposal had been made by its commander in chief.

Back-pedalling, General Gamelin—who had meanwhile consulted with General Georges—realized that he could not fulfill such a promise and fell back on the excuse that the British could not move further forward than the Dyle Line. General Vuillemin, commander in chief of the French air force, caught the ball on the rebound by questioning the ability of the French army to enter Belgium given the unpreparedness of the French air force. His minister, Laurent-Eynac, who was there, echoed his views.

This double setback riled Gamelin, who pulled out all the stops to argue that it was impossible for the French and British governments to appear to be giving up when they had already promised Belgium some preventative measures. But General Vuille-min stuck to his principles, causing the War Council to split into two camps over this controversial issue: if Belgium refused to agree to allow French and British forces to enter, which those around the table that day knew would be the case, France would avoid "provoking German reaction until its air force is prepared." Thus the advocates of intervention at any price were able to save face.

Did General Vuillemin's stolid stand cause Gamelin to reconsider the real state of the troops, for which he was responsible? It would seem so from a note he sent General Georges on April 19, 1940:

"The fixed positions of our large units along the Belgian border do not allow us to begin maneuvers in Belgium without some prior reorganization. Not only will that reorganization delay our maneuvers, but the enemy will also be alerted and the Belgians will be anxious. It will also exhaust and irritate those troops that have to be moved.

"It seems to me possible to effect a positioning that will allow the first units to be moved quickly, and which will not disrupt the organization of our defenses during a general alert. I therefore wish you to issue some instructions to this effect."

So the head of the army, who had never ceased to advocate armed intervention since the beginning of the conflict, and against Belgium's will if necessary, now wondered whether there was any value to the condition made by the French and British governments after the message from Lord Keyes. If King Leopold had given in to this unwarranted demand made in mid-January 1940 and had immediately invited France and Great Britain to send troops into Belgium, no effective aid would have been forthcoming, while Belgium would have had to face a German invasion through the violation of its policy of neutrality. Apart from the risks this would bring the Allies, we can well imagine the reaction of the people, who would have rightly felt betrayed. No wonder then that less that a month after this note to General Georges, France suffered a crushing defeat, followed by the inevitable surrender of the Belgian army.

On Thursday, May 9, 1940, a little before ten o'clock at night, two men met in a street outside Berlin. "Well, what's the news?" asked Major Sas, military attaché to the Dutch embassy, of his friend Colonel Hans Oster.

Since the big alert in January, when the Mechelen incident made Hitler postpone, indefinitely, his invasion of Holland and Belgium, Oster and Sas had met several times. "That pig," as Oster referred to Hitler, "has not given up, quite the contrary!" said the associate of Canaris. His information made Colonel Goethals, Belgian military attaché, specify on March 27 that the Wermacht had added another 49 divisions since September 1, 1938, when the number had totaled 108. On April 5, returning from a visit to the Königsbrück camp, Oster described the morale of the German soldiers, "The troops are eager and enthusiastic, and their equipment is in perfect order. The divisions formed this winter are said to be the equal of the older divisions." It was learned from Oster that 136 divisions were required to launch an offensive in the west, the rest being split among Norway, Denmark, southern Austria and various training camps. Among the 136 divisions were ten Panzer and seven mechanized divisions.

Ten days earlier, Oster had told Sas that the date set for the offensive was Sunday, May 5. Bad weather forced Hitler to put it off until Friday, May 10.

"This is it," he told his friend on the night of Thursday, May 9. "There are no counterorders. That pig has set off for the front."

Soon after, Sas went to his colleague Goethals and a message was sent to Brussels. At 23:30, the king informed the army general staff. At his order a state of general alert was immediately declared to all units.

———

The state of affairs was different in France. That same Thursday, May 9, Lieutenant Pierre Duchatelle of the 1st Regiment of Moroccan Sharpshooters, who had been fighting the enemy during the winter of 1939–40 in the Sierck-Montenach area and was currently assigned to fortification work on the north border, left Feignies with a valid pass. And he was not the only one. And yet, according to E. W. Winterbotham, a British coding officer who played an important role throughout the war since May 1, 1940, the French military attaché in Berne had been telling GHQ that firsthand information indicated that the Wermacht would launch its attack in the west between the eighth and tenth of that month, centering on Sedan. From ensuing events, it appears that this very important piece of information—which must have emanated from anti-Nazi elements in Germany, had gotten left at the bottom of a drawer at Vincennes.

# FRIDAY, MAY 10, 1940

It was just half an hour before the morning sky began to pale that Friday, May 10. The Belgian soldiers of the 7th Infantry Division who were defending the eighteen-kilometer front along the Albert Canal—coming from Brabant, they had only just relieved the 5th Division, and almost a fifth of their number had still not yet returned from leave—saw a myriad of bright lights in the sky hurtling toward the sea. They were not meteorites, but the Luftwaffe's squadrons, whose cockpits reflected the rays of the sun, still invisible at ground level. They were flying at an altitude too high for the antiaircraft guns, and behind them trailed long parallel streams of whitish vapor. Before these thin trails had even vanished from the sky, huge swarms of mechanized insects followed in a continuous and seemingly endless stream. Abruptly at 4:15 A.M., like a flock of starlings that scatter at some mysterious signal, the planes dispersed, then one after the other tipped their wings and plunged with a terrifying screech toward their targets. Postponed twice, the German invasion of the west had now begun.

At 12:20 A.M., French GHQ had informed Vincennes (General Doumenc, chief of staff of the ground forces, had his staff at Montry, a small place in the Crecy-en-Brie canton in the Meaux district, where GHQ was located, but General Gamelin had set up his headquarters at Vincennes Palace) of "considerable artillery movement on the German border." At 1:30 A.M.,

Lieutenant Colonel Poydenot—deputy to Colonel Petibon, Gamelin's private secretary—received the following message from the French minister of defense and war: "Our ambassador in Luxembourg reported to the minister of foreign affairs at 0030 that information received from the German community indicates that some of the Germans in the Grand Duchy have been assembled and armed tonight. There has also been significant artillery movement on the German border. According to unconfirmed rumors here, the German army has entered Holland."

Lieutenant Colonel Poydenot reported this information to his superior, and also the 1:40 A.M. message from the minister of defense, which was recorded by Commander Berthelot of the 2nd Bureau at army staff:

"General Laurent, our military attaché in Brussels, reports that since eleven o'clock the sound of motors in unspecified activity has been heard along the Dutch-Belgian border. Very worried about movements near Aix-la-Chapelle and the Luxembourg border. Ammunition has been distributed to the Belgian infantry and Brussels remains calm."

General Laurent's message ended with this significant coda: "Be prepared."

At 3:18 A.M. the political undersecretary of foreign affairs telephoned Lieutenant Colonel Poydenot to say that he had the following information from a "confirmed" source:

"1. The Belgian authorities have been informed that Germany has ordered a general offensive on the western front to take place at dawn this morning, probably at around 5 A.M.

"2. Dutch and Belgian general staffs have received information that the Germans will cease all preparations by 2100.

"3. The impression of the Belgian general staff is that preparations have subsided. The Belgians do not think there will be any offensive, but ask us to remain on the alert."

At 3:25 A.M. General Doumenc, chief of staff of the French armies, tried to ring General Gamelin, but Colonel Petibon flatly refused to awaken his chief as he felt that "the state of affairs did not necessitate waking up the commander in chief." General Doumenc therefore decided to take the necessary measures on his own authority.

At 4 A.M. the political undersecretary of foreign affairs once again telephoned Lieutenant Colonel Poydenot: "Toward 3:30, I spoke to our minister in Luxembourg, who informed me that an incident concerning some "tourists" had taken place at the Luxembourg border, resulting in the death of two members of the Luxembourg police. The Grand Duchess has evacuated to a place closer to the French border, and our minister has the impression that the government is preparing to do the same."

At 4:30 A.M. Vincennes GHQ heard the news that Luxembourg had just been invaded by the Germans, who had crossed the border at Echternach; the Grand Duchess had fled to a place of refuge at Longwy. A quarter of an hour later it was reported that some shots had been fired in the region around Saint-Jean-les-Deux-Jumeaux and La Ferté-sous-Jouarre, where General Georges's headquarters was located. The former area was the headquarters of General Vuillemin, commander in chief of the air force. At 5 A.M. word was received that Holland had been invaded (the Germans crossed the border at Roermond), and five minutes later came the announcement that The Hague had been bombed. Then at 5:07 the Germans crossed the Belgian border and were heading toward Eupen. When General Pujo heard at 5:10 that some German parachutists had landed on Les Bondons—General Georges's residence at La Ferté-sous-Jouarre—he rushed over, only to find that it was a false alarm. At 5:15 the enemy occupied "all the roads in Luxembourg." At 5:20 the Luftwaffe was launching massive air attacks with bombs and mines around Dunkirk and Calais. The same happened at Nancy, and the air bases at Frescaty, Toul and Bitche were seriously damaged. At 6:40 A.M. General Georges gave the order for General Condé to enter Luxembourg, and General Billotte, commander of Army Group I, to enter Belgium. Meanwhile, Colonel Petibon had finally decided to wake General Gamelin. When he was dressed and ready, he received Captain Beaufre, who had been sent by General Doumenc, whose headquarters was at Montry in Seine-et-Marne, not far from those of General Georges and General Vuillemin.

Captain Beaufre had often visited the commander in chief at Vincennes and was surprised to find him in such good spirits early in the morning of Friday, May 10, 1940. Usually a rather subdued person, General Gamelin "was striding up and down the corridor, humming softly, with a satisfied and warlike air about him," a sight Beaufre had never seen before. His overt satisfaction that day was due to two reasons.

Gamelin's strong "republican" convictions, in the radical sense of the word, had always assured him Daladier's firm support. Paul Reynaud, a left-wing Republican from the former "National Bloc," who had just replaced the "bull from Vaucluse" as premier, was not so pleased with Joffre's former chief secretary. This was perhaps because he, Reynaud, had become the self-appointed champion of the daring plans of a young colonel called Charles de Gaulle, whose career had been helped along by Marshal Pétain for some time. Rumor had it that the governmental declaration read by the new premier on March 23 to the Assembly, had been secretly redrafted by his protegé, a staunch advocate of armored vehicles, whose revolutionary views disturbed the conservative general staff. On all counts Reynaud's dry and imperious statement was disliked by the deputies, who only granted him a slim majority of one vote. Edouard Herriot, president of the Assembly, openly murmured, "Even so, I'm not so sure that he even had a majority!"

Reynaud had immediately indicated his intention of entrusting Colonel de Gaulle with the important post of undersecretary for war. Like Churchill, Reynaud had established a War Council for the purpose of coordinating operations, and the position of undersecretary was in effect that of supervising the commanders in chief of the ground, sea and air forces. Since Gamelin reacted so violently against this plan, he must have told Daladier that it would relegate him to the back seat. When Reynaud's emissary came to sound out his views at Rue Saint-Dominique, Gamelin thundered, "If de Gaulle comes here, I will leave this office; go downstairs and telephone Daladier to tell him he can have my job!" Finally, it was Paul Baudouin who was appointed, and on May 18 "the bull from Vaucluse" left his office without fanfare, to be replaced by Paul Reynaud, who gave Daladier the very provisional position of minister of foreign affairs.

The day before Friday, May 10, when Captain Beaufre had been surprised by the commander in chief's sprightly good humor, Paul Reynaud had to give way in a cabinet meeting with his radical Socialist ministers, after his unsuccessful proposal to replace Gamelin with General Weygand. This was a considerable victory for Gamelin, and well-informed people declared that it would result in a ministerial crisis, which would certainly strengthen his position.

When Gamelin received the news at dawn of the simultaneous invasion of Belgium and Holland, he saw everything in a rosy light. He saw the startling confirmation of his former predictions, and he had just ordered the immediate implementation of his "grand maneuver in the north," to which he had alluded one month before, during the splendid luncheon in Weygand's honor at GHQ. This maneuver called "Dyle-Bréda" was the masterpiece of his "War Plan 1940," in which he stated:

"Only the Luxembourg-Belgium-southern Holland battlefield is suited to a long, decisive battle without the use of systems of fortifications. For the French counterattack against the Germans, who will have taken the Albert-Meuse defense system in front of Liège, troops at the Albert Canal can turn north and the Meuse troops can immediately take up position between the Ardennes and the Moselle."

Army Group I, consisting of five armies, thirteen army corps, and forty divisions—about 600,000 men in all—began to move on the morning of Friday, May 10, 1940. Gamelin, in the corridors of his stronghold at Vincennes, where he had received General Doumenc's envoy, no doubt believed that the Wermacht would be caught in the "trap" he had laid during those long, grim months of this "phony war."

—

Charles de Gaulle was summoned to GHQ five weeks after Reynaud's failure to make him undersecretary for war. There, he found Gamelin "not only confident of his own plans and the worth of his troops, but also satisfied and even impatient to see them put to the test." Gamelin was sure that he would prevail in the confrontation with the enemy, whose imminent attack he predicted would be mainly centered on Holland and Belgium, to try and cut off the British Expeditionary Force from the French forces. Gamelin gave his visitor the "impression of a scientist in a laboratory testing and measuring the results of his strategy." De Gaulle left him after being promised the command of a 4th Armored Division yet to be formed. It was, nevertheless, a flattering position for an officer of his rank, and he expressed his satisfaction to the commander in chief, but did not conceal his reservations about the French army compared to the numerous and massive German Panzer divisions. Gamelin replied, "I understand your satisfaction. As for your anxiety, I do not think it is justified."

What were Gamelin's reactions during the course of that Friday, May 10, 1940? No record remains, but I should think his early morning optimism must have faded by the hour as the news became more and more alarming, especially since he could not get a clear picture from the dispatches or telephone information received at Vincennes GHQ. The news was even worse the next morning, when it was confirmed that the key Eben Emael fortress had fallen, which all had agreed was practically impregnable, and on which the right flank of the Belgian 7th Infantry Division depended. And on top of all this, there were General Student's gliders.

For several months, 382 men of the Wermacht airborne troops, destined to be transported by forty-two gliders, together with the pilots of these, had been undergoing intensive training under Captain Koch. The Germans, taking into consideration the risks of dispersing and the difficulty of regrouping under enemy fire, had given up their plan to use paratroopers.

At 3:50 in the morning of May 10, eleven gliders carrying some eighty "pioneer attackers" flew into the attack. One of them landed on top of the fortress, crushed one of the four antiaircraft machine-guns and completely surprised Major Jottrand, the commander. The enemy spread out bands of white material painted with a black swastika to indicate the areas to be destroyed by the Junker 87 bomber planes. These bombers gained an awesome reputation under the name "Stuka," a contraction of *Sturzkampf-flugzeug,* or "flying apparatus for nose-dive combat." At the same time, all the accessible defenses in the fortress were attacked with explosives and flame-throwers directed at every possible opening, while the enemy pushed ahead of them any prisoners they caught to form a protective shield.

In perfect synchronization, the other gliders landed on the left bank, held by the three regiments of the 7th Infantry Division, whose mission was to protect the bridges at Vroenhoven, Veld-wezelt and Briegden. The sudden appearance of these unknown machines, which seemed to be making a forced landing, momentarily had the Belgian troops dumbfounded. They soon fell into disarray when Captain Koch's men surged out of the planes and and immediately opened fire. The Belgian troops were rapidly overcome by the Germans, who began destroying the bridges, cutting telephone cables and throwing explosives into the canal.

The 7th Infantry Division was stretched along an eighteen-kilometer front. Constantly harrassed by the diving attacks of Stuka fighters, they were unable to stop the enemy from strengthening the bridgehead set up by Captain Koch on the left bank of the canal with machine-guns parachuted in in sections during the morning. By the middle of the day, the German troops were joined by forward contingents of the 4th Panzer Division, which had crossed the Meuse at Maastricht.

During the night of May 10 to 11, all hell broke loose in the underground chambers of Eben Emael. The explosion of the ammunition ignited the oxygen cylinders and the barrels of limechloride left behind by construction workers, resulting in the defenders being asphyxiated under their gas-masks. The situation became unbearable by the morning of Saturday, May 11, when the bulk of the 4th Panzer Division, followed by the 16th, fell into line. Sad at heart, Major Jottrand had to resign himself to the destruction of the remaining armaments in the fortress after having alerted the 3rd Corps of the Belgian army with whom he could still communicate, thanks to a deep telephone cable. His surrender was received by First Lieutenant Mikosch, commander of the 51st Pioneers of the Wermacht.

On the night of Saturday, May 11, the Belgian 7th Infantry Division was almost finished. An air attack to cut off the bridgehead held by most of General von Reichenau's VIth Army cost the Belgians, French and English twenty-eight out of thirty-nine bomber planes, and not one of them succeeded in hitting a single bridge.

---

General Gamelin would have been surprised to learn that his "War Plan 1940" played directly into the enemy's hands. The mission of the German Army Group B under General von Bock was to draw the French troops and the British Expeditionary Force into Belgian territory, there to be attacked by von Reichenau's VIth Army, while General von Küchler's XVIIIth army took care of Holland. There were also the parachutists, often dressed in Belgian or Dutch uniforms, to create confusion behind the lines already disorganized by continuous air attacks. The Germans attacked in strength, facilitated by their large numbers and their resources. However, this did not, for instance, deter the Belgians of the 5th Company of the 2nd Grenadiers (whose commander had been killed) from thrice repelling the enemy at Kanne Bridge, which they had successfully blown up. In all the Belgian lines that day, there were many heroic deeds, but performed at the cost of numerous lives. One of the men in the 6th Company of the 18th Regiment asked his commander on the morning of May 11, "Lieutenant, we are surrounded by the Germans, who are barely thirty meters away; can't we surrender?" Second Lieutenant Ausquer replied, "You shall see how a Belgian officer surrenders to the Germans!" And with a submachine-gun he ran out of the trench and let fly a hail of fire at the enemy. A moment later he fell, his body riddled with bullets.

—•—

The Belgian people gave an enthusiastic welcome to the vanguard of the French 1st and 9th armies and the British Expeditionary Force, which entered Belgium at 9:30 A.M. on Friday, May 10. Racing at full speed through Flanders, the 1st Light Armored Division was preceded by the 7th Army under General Giraud, marching toward Bréda. In the south, General Blanchard's 1st Army took up position between Wavre and Namur, covered by General Prioux's mechanized cavalry corps. Further south, General Corap's 9th Army was also taking up positions. When the British Expeditionary Force passed by, Belgians lining the streets recognized the 12th Lancers who had fought at Waterloo, and just about a century later, at Mons. The army was heading for the KW defense line between Louvain and Wavre, which was full of antitank ditches, flooded in part, covered with barbed wire and concrete tetrahedrons and scattered with mines and felled trees. Since May 10, the 1st Ardennes Division had to confront General Guderian's XIXth Panzer Corps there. Unaided, the 5th Company, led by commanding Captain Bricart, who still mourned the death of his commander, had succeeded in holding the 1st Panzer Division in check. They were so successful for a while that when the Germans finally gained the upper hand, they destroyed their documents that would prove the Belgians' inferiority in numbers and arms, since they had held the Germans at bay for so long. Above all, the courageous Ardennes fighters had prevented the advance of three Panzer divisions for a whole day. No wonder they cursed the skies when there was no sign of Allied planes, particularly as the roads were full of enemy tanks and mechanized vehicles, which had been halted in their tracks and were unable to move.

—

But the enemy was too strong, despite the immense courage shown by the Belgian, British and French troops. At Gembloux, where the first tank battle in military history took place, the French had the advantage, and only lost by dint of shortage of arms and petrol. Learning that the Eben Emael fortress had been destroyed, General Prioux, whose orders were to cover Blanchard's 1st Army in the trench at Gembloux with his cavalry corps, informed the latter at 14:00 on Saturday, May 11, of the difficulty in executing the "Dyle" maneuver and asked permission to fall back on the "Escaut" (Schelde) plan. Approving this, Blanchard informed General Billotte, who immediately called General Georges: "General Blanchard is in favor of the 'Escaut' plan. I shall personally go to the 1st Army to ask General Prioux to undertake the 'Dyle' plan, to which we must adhere." Unwittingly, he had facilitated the accomplishment of the Ardennes maneuver anticipated by Hitler. Also, the Belgian army's retreat, which began on the evening of Saturday, May 11, occurred just three days before Hitler's own prediction. After forty-eight hours of combat, General Michiels, Billotte's superior at general staff, reviewed the situation as follows:

"The Belgian army was covering an arc of territory extending from Antwerp through Liège to Namur, all the way along the Albert Canal and the Meuse. Some advance demolition units were at the border, adequately reinforced by detachments along the French border. The Belgian army was preparing to defend the strengthened positions where fortifications were constructed. Surprised by an unannounced and unprecedented attack, troops in the Eben Emael fortress and neighboring divisions were engaged in full combat under very difficult conditions. Through as yet unexplained circumstances, the bridge at Maastricht and the three bridges at Vroenhoven, Veldwezelt and Briegden (on the Albert Canal) fell into enemy hands. This event, which had far-reaching consequences, coupled with the lack of any support from the Allied air force until the following noon, decisively influenced the outcome of that battle. After a thirty-six hour struggle, despite desperate resistance and several counterattacks by the 7th Division, the Germans made a breach in our defense. Armored divisions poured through and threatened our entire position along the Albert Canal and at Liège on the other side, in spite of the intervention of our reserves and mechanized troops. The French and British troops had neither the time nor the opportunity to take part in this battle. Their participation, which had been foreseen on the third day, was aimed at falling into battle formation along the Meuse, south of Namur, and on the Namur-Louvain line. Simultaneously, the front of the mechanized column of the French 7th Army was launching an offensive in Holland near Bréda-Tilburg, and a group of light divisions was advancing in Belgian Luxembourg toward Marche, Neufchâteau and Arlon. Gradually, during the night of May 11 to 12, our defense troops on the Albert Canal and the Meuse retreated, protected by a network of demolition and rearguard troops positioned up at Tongeren and the Gete River, where fierce fighting took place on May 13 to assure safe passage for the divisions. From May 12, our army regrouped to gain a better position along the strong defense line from Antwerp to Louvain, extended up to Wavre by the British army and the French 1st Army and supported at Namur by one of our army corps. Meanwhile, the Germans were attacking the Meuse front at Houx, which was defended by the French 9th Army, and infiltrating the

Yvoir River valley at Givet. After two days, this army—disorganized and broken on its right around the region of Sedan—beat a retreat under enemy air force attacks.

# THE FIRST WEEK OF BATTLE

Since May 10, General Denis, minister of defense, had been at GHQ at Fort Breendonck, situated between Brussels and Antwerp—which the enemy soon transformed into one of the worst areas in "the concentration camp universe," to use David Rousset's striking phrase—to confer with the king. They studied the situation together with the aid of a map, and Denis was asked to inform the government of the situation. He visited the government again on the eleventh, and from then on it became a daily occurrence. On Sunday, May 12, the king left for Casteau, north of Mons, for a meeting called by General Gamelin. Daladier was present, together with General Georges, General Billotte and Lieutenant General Pownall, chief of staff representing Lord Gort.

After announcing Gamelin's decision to wage a decisive battle on the Antwerp-Namur-Meuse front, General Georges spoke of the necessity of close coordination between the French, Belgian and British troops, suggesting that General Billotte be put in charge of coordination. "I subscribed to this plan as it seemed indispensible," said Leopold, who decided to "conform in the interests of the war by placing the Belgian army under the orders of the commander in chief."

This meant that General Billotte's overwhelming responsibilities were now extended to cover five armies—with the possibility of a sixth if the Dutch joined in—plus the British Expeditionary Force. In fact the leader of Army Group I would have to face General von Bock's Army Group B, as well as Army Group A commanded by General von Rundstedt, who, with his deputy General von Manstein, had personally had a hand in planning the campaign in the west.

During the morning of Friday, May 10, Generals Huntziger and Corap, commanders of the French 2nd and 9th armies, had crossed the Belgian border with their cavalry to start a delaying action in the Ardennes and to cover the position of the massed troops. The next day, General Corap was forced by the enemy thrust to withdraw his forward troops on the left bank of the Meuse. Their three hundred or so tanks and submachine-guns were captured by seven Panzer divisions, totalling 2,270 armored vehicles on wheels or tracks, which had advanced at von Rundstedt's order. It should be noted, however, that despite the enormous inequality in strength, the French retreat was achieved in perfect formation. In the afternoon of May 12, all the bridges on the Meuse had been blown up behind the French troops.

But during the evening of that Sunday, May 12, taking advantage of a breach at the Houx lock downstream from Dinant, the 7th Motorcycle Battalion of the 7th Panzer Division under General Rommel crossed the Meuse and established a bridgehead. During the night of May 12 to 13, a French reconnaissance plane spotted a huge mechanized group at the confluence of the Meuse and the Semois. "What speed! How bright!" exclaimed the airman. Convinced of the overwhelming superiority of their Luftwaffe, the Germans drove through the night with headlights ablaze.

Further south, matters were worse still. The brave resistance put up by the Ardennes light infantry—who had stopped three armored divisions of the 19th Panzer Corps—was finally broken, and General Kleist's five Panzer divisions pressed relentlessly forward on May 13, supported by the dive-bomber attacks of twelve JU–87 squadrons. Toward six o'clock in the evening, near Sedan, after only one German tank had crossed the Meuse, panic gradually spread from one French heavy artillery regiment to the other units, so that they blew up their own cannons, destroyed the telephone communications and retreated by road.

By midnight, the 19th Panzer Division sappers had already re-established a route over the partially blown-up bridges south of Sedan. The French 71st Infantry Division seemed on the verge of collapse, just like the 55th Division that had disappeared, leaving five hundred dead on the battlefield. Along the road, an officer from general staff saw some artillery soldiers riding at a gallop, fleeing from the battlefield. He wrote, "We pass through swirls of smoke from a convoy of petrol trucks that has been bombed from the air and is burning on the road. Elsewhere an artillery group has been attacked while marching. On the road and all along it a series of huge craters and numerous dead horses indicate the severity of the attack." Such scenes were to become commonplace between France's northeast border and the Atlantic during that five-week period.

On Monday, May 13, Leopold felt that his army, which had been badly shaken by the force of the enemy's attack, needed to hear the voice of its leader. He addressed his soldiers:

"For three days, the Belgian army, savagely attacked in an unprecedented surprise move and caught by a vastly equipped army backed by a powerful air force, has been carrying out a most difficult maneuver. The success of that maneuver is of the utmost importance to the general conduct and outcome of the war.

"This maneuver requires all of us, leaders and soldiers alike, to give an extraordinary and continuous effort at a time when we are utterly demoralized by the sight of the destruction wrought by a pitiless invader.

"However difficult these trials may be, you must overcome them with courage. Our position improves by the hour. In the decisive days to follow, you must summon all the energy and make all sacrifices necessary to stop the invasion.

"As on the Yser in 1914, the French and British troops expect it of us; and the safety and honor of this country demand it."

Quite apart from the firm example the king set to his troops, I would like to comment on three points from this order of the day.

Firstly, by evoking "the sight of the destruction wrought by a pitiless invader," the king commiserated with the plight of most Belgians, whose possessions had been destroyed in the battles. Quite a contrast with Denis's offhand remark: "It does not make much difference whether the battle takes place fifty kilometers to the front or to the rear: in either case, our country will be destroyed." Denis had said this when he approved the reply given to General Delvoie on November 10, 1939, by General Gamelin, whose dream was to use Belgian territory to fight it out with the Wermacht! For the king, every inch of land was important because it was a piece of national territory, which if abandoned would bring infinite suffering and hardship.

Secondly, by saying that the outcome of the war depended on the success of the difficult maneuver being carried out, King Leopold showed remarkably clear thinking, which Spaak called "an uncanny foresight" at Limoges on May 31, as though it would be better to lull ourselves with comforting words in the face of danger or to blind ourselves to the facts like an ostrich burying its head in the sand.

Thirdly, "our position improves by the hour," shows that the king was reassured by his talks at Casteau the previous day, when it was decided to place the coordination of the Allied effort under General Billotte, although it appears that he had not yet heard of the tragedy on the Meuse. Was his allusion to Yser some sort of premonitition about what would follow? Only the king himself knows.

———

At three o'clock in the morning, Tuesday, May 14, Captain Beaufre arrived with General Doumenc at General Georges's "northeastern" headquarters, to which the chief of staff of the ground forces had been urgently summoned. Beaufre wrote this disturbing account of the scene that took place:

"The atmosphere is like that of a wake. Georges gets up hurriedly and stands in front of Doumenc. He is very pale. 'Our front has been breached at Sedan! There were certain inadequacies . . .' He falls into the armchair, choking back a sob. He was the first man I saw cry in this war. Alas, I was to see many more. It made a very deep impression on me.

"Doumenc was surprised at this greeting and immediately replied, 'General, this is war! During a war, such incidents always happen!' Then Georges, still very pale, explains the situation: two mediocre divisions have given ground after a disastrous air attack. The 10th Corps has reported that its position has already been penetrated, and the German tanks reached Bulson at around midnight. Georges sobs again. All those present remain silent, overcome by the scene.

" 'Come, come, General,' says Doumenc, 'all wars have such routs! Look at the map. Let's see what we can do.' He speaks loudly in that hushed atmosphere, and I begin to feel better. In front of the map, Doumenc sketches a new maneuver. 'We have to stop up the gap, "seal it up," as we used to say in 1918.' . . .''

—

"Seal it up." By using an expression familiar to Foch, General Doumenc had hoped to help General Georges overcome the grief which had rendered him incapable of action. In charge of the army's motorized transport during World War I, Doumenc had made a decisive contribution to the victory at Verdun. He had organized the constant flow of food and arms convoys along the road connecting Bar-le-Duc to Verdun via Rosnes and Souilly, which came to be known as the "Holy Road." Such a technician must have seen that the huge exodus of refugees, flowing like lava from Belgium south toward France, would hamper the armies' movements and transform any retreat into a shambles which even a good leader's superhuman energy could not control. It was estimated—probably well short of the truth—that some five million men, women and children on various forms of transport or on foot, crowded the roads between May 10, 1940, and Saturday, June 22, 1940, when the armistice between France and Germany was signed in a railway carriage at Rethondes, where Germany had signed its surrender twenty-two years previously. To give you some idea of the road situation in May 1940, when General Doumenc tried to console General Georges, I shall quote from Pierre Duchatelle, the young lieutenant in the 1st Regiment of Moroccan Sharpshooters, who had quietly gone on leave on May 9. When he heard the next morning in Paris that this was the end of the "phony war," he turned back immediately to rejoin his unit. On May 11, he was entrusted with bringing the "rolling-stock" of the companies, together with the baggage and supply cars, plus an ambulance and a stock of ammunition for the anti-tank and submachine-guns to Gembloux. He advanced laboriously:

"Great crowds of refugees fleeing the German advance, in indescribable disorder and in conditions beyond belief. Their numbers had steadily swelled, due to the Belgian army's retreat and the French light armored divisions being thrown back west as far as Holland since May 12 and 13, after many ordeals. Until May 14, I walked continuously without sleep, stopping only to persuade staff officers posted at crossroads to make way for us. We progressed a step at a time amid a jumble of every conceivable type of vehicle loaded with the more fortunate refugees. Our advance was frequently halted by attacks from Stuka planes, which dived at us with that sinister wail of sirens, strafing anything that looked military to them. We were forced to lie flat on our bellies with the civilians, whose corpses we hastily pushed to the sides of the road. I was very astonished to see a large cart drawn by two horses with several people in it surrounded by their baggage: it had stopped stock-still like a wax statue at Grévin

Museum, the driver frozen in a natural stance, and neither he nor the passengers bore any trace of wounds. I had to touch the driver to make sure that he was dead, as dead as the passengers and the two horses. . . . They had all probably been killed by the bomb blast and frozen into this position. It was an uncanny sight."

Just one small detail should be noted, apart from the fact that Lieutenant Pierre Duchatelle set off on foot from Maubeuge to Gembloux, where his battalion awaited the ammunition (since the convoy was on horseback, that is reasonable). "But," he told me, "all I knew about Gembloux was that it was a small town northwest of Namur, and I had no map until I picked one up in Belgium, and that at the back of a postal almanac. . . ." General Gamelin's order of the day at midday, May 10, had said, "The attack we had foreseen since last October took place this morning." Lieutenant Duchatelle's simple lack of a map of Belgium explains a lot of things.

———

Responding to the king's appeal, Belgian soldiers undertook some brilliant rearguard action on May 13 at Haelen, Tienen and Réthy; but news from the Ardennes front the following day, May 14, was disconcertingly bad. General Billotte looked worried when he was received by the king at Breendonck GHQ. Rumors from Paris said that Vincennes GHQ was anxious—desperate in fact—but reassuring news arrived that evening. Realizing that the enemy was to move into the Ardennes, General Gamelin had asked General Georges to send all his reserves into battle to stymie the attempt.

Pierlot, also summoned to Breendonck GHQ, did not hide from the king the alarming situation in Brussels, created by the rumors of refugees crossing the capital in ever-increasing numbers. During the night of May 13 to 14, an alarm was raised by a burst of gunfire from a park in the heart of the city where soldiers claimed they had seen parachutists landing. People in Brussels fled in terror from their houses toward the French border. Another rumor spread that palace guards were seen shooting at parachutists who had landed on the terraced roof of the Electrobel Company near the equestrian statue of Leopold II. Pierlot added, "I had to issue a statement over the air to announce that, contrary to what was being rumored, no parachutists had landed in Brussels either yesterday or last night."

At four o'clock in the morning on Wednesday, May 15, General Billotte called General Georges on the telephone: "The 9th Army is on the verge of a calamity. I suggest we hand over the command to General Giraud, a born leader of men, who knows how to apply the necessary psychological shock to galvanize his troops into action. There is no reason to blame General Corap, who I suggest be put in charge of the 7th."

Another telephone call was made three and a half hours later, which necessitated Churchill's valet waking his master. "We are beaten," Paul Reynaud said to the British prime minister. After a moment's silence, the French premier continued, "The front has been breached near Sedan. They are pouring through it with tanks and armored vehicles."

"Well!" replied Churchill, when he had recovered from the shock, "We know from experience that an attack runs itself out after a certain time. . . . I tell you this because I remember March 21, 1918. You will see, in five or six days, the Hun will have to halt for supplies: then we shall make the counterattack. I learned that long ago, from Marshal Foch himself."

While this conversation was taking place, King Leopold at his GHQ was informed by the Belgian 7th Army Corps headquarters besieged at Namur that Blanchard was preparing to retreat. To the question, "What positions should we adopt?" the king replied, "Let the mobile forces rejoin the armies in battle. The permanent positions should continue to resist as before." That same day, May 15, General Michiels, chief of staff, noted, "It looks as though the French 1st Army has been broken up in the northern and southern outskirts of Namur."

At the king's request, General Denis went to Brussels to fetch Pierlot, with whom the king wished to discuss the worsening situation and, especially, Holland's announcement that it was preparing to lay down its arms. Ever mindful of preserving Belgium's independence and the integrity of its colony, the Congo, Leopold asked the government to intercede with the French and British governments while there was still time and obtain formal confirmation of the guarantees as stated in the appeal he sent out on May 10. The following official report of that meeting with the prime minister, in the presence of General Denis, was issued at GHQ:

"After indicating that the French front between Namur and Sedan seemed to be in trouble, the king asked the government what it proposed to do.

"Pierlot replied that his summons to GHQ had postponed decision until the king indicated how they should act. He said that it was increasingly difficult for the government to remain in Brussels, for the tense atmosphere there prevented any effective work. He thought it desirable for the government to join the administrative services already installed at Ostend.

"The king pointed out that Brussels seemed the least exposed to bombing. He stressed the effect of the government and foreign diplomatic missions on morale in the capital. The ministers agreed and abandoned the idea of leaving Brussels that day.

"The king expressed his wish to remain in contact with the government. It was important that the government did not move too far away from him. The king and his army, as well as the British forces, might be cut off from the rest of the Allied forces following the breach at Sedan. The German troops might advance rapidly toward the Channel.

"The prime minister was dismayed by this prospect, remarking that it should be avoided at all costs by a maneuver to bring the army toward France. The king replied that the army's maneuvers depended entirely on the situation. General Denis added that they depended equally on the concepts underlying the operations and on the commander in chief's instructions.

"The king insisted once again on getting from London and Paris a written statement giving Belgium all its guarantees at the time peace would be signed. He drew the government's attention to the necessity of treating Belgium as a special case, as in 1914–18 under Albert I, by not involving it in a political alliance. Belgium was defending its independence; it was not bound to its guarantors' aims in this war."

———

I shall interrupt the story of the course of events that took place after May 10 to make a comment which I think is of interest: why did the Belgian government intend to evacuate the administration to Ostend right from the start? The king had informed the German command by telegram on May 10 that he had made Brussels an open city: that is to say it would be kept free of military operations. This meant in fact that Brussels was the city least likely to be bombed, as opposed to Ostend, which was in a strategic position. Perhaps Pierlot and his ministers' chief concern, justified by "the tense atmosphere" in the capital, was to be able to flee abroad at the earliest opportunity. That would also explain Pierlot's and Spaak's later persistence in trying to persuade the king to leave Belgian territory.

———

The king's insistence on getting a written declaration from Paris and London giving Belgium all assurances when peace was signed was based on the "Sainte-Adresse Declaration," evoked by Belgium in the king's appeal to the Allies on May 10, 1940; and this had been signed at the end of World War I. Calling on England,

France and Russia to repel the invader from its territory, Belgium had asked for a future guarantee of independence and integrity, specifying that it wished to leave the Belgian Congo out of that war. Being reminded of those guarantees, renewed by France and Great Britain in their joint declaration on April 24, 1937, did not appear to please Paul Reynaud. "The violence of his rebuke about our policy of independence and neutrality was quite unwarranted!" said Spaak, on returning from Paris to join Pierlot and Denis at the king's GHQ. Apparently ignoring Spaak's request, the French government continued not to give Belgium the assurances it wanted for the future.

—

The king summoned Pierlot, Spaak and Denis to his GHQ on Thursday, May 16, to tell them of the military situation which had once again deteriorated since the previous day. At about ten o'clock in the morning, the French military mission at Leopold's GHQ passed the king an instruction from General Billotte. In it he said that the difficulties facing the French 9th Army had obliged Army Group I, with the Belgian army and the British Expeditionary Force, to retreat to a position marked out by the entrenched camp at Antwerp and the bridgehead at Ghent, further upstream of the Schelde. General Billotte continued:

"I have the honor of requesting Your Majesty to order the right wing of Your Majesty's troops to retreat, together with the British Expeditionary Force:
—during the night of 16 to 17 to the Willebroeck Canal;
—during the night of 17 to 18 to the Dendre, downstream of Alost;
—during the night of 18 to 19 to the bridgehead at Ghent."

Attached to this was a brief sketch showing the depth of German penetration into the Ardennes: the Wermacht had reached Beaumont and Chimay, while Sedan had already been passed. By eleven o'clock that morning, the king's staff had received the orders for the maneuvers requested by General Billotte, and the ministers had been summoned to GHQ during the afternoon.

———

Briefing them on the overall military situation, the king concluded: "We therefore have two alternatives: if it can, our army will retreat toward France, thus abandoning our national territory; if the enemy's advance is so rapid that we are isolated from the Allied forces, the army will be pushed with its back to the sea and forced to surrender. The ability to maintain contact with the Allied armies depends entirely on the resistance the French army can put up against the Wermacht."

"After the king's statement," says the official GHQ report, "the ministers replied that everything should be done to prevent the army from being hemmed in on its own territory and cut off from the Allied forces. They considered surrender to be disastrous, both politically and from the point of view of morale, and thought that at least the government and a few soldiers should remain free so the country could still continue to exist and be able to participate when peace was signed.

"When the king pointed out that if the army abandoned Belgian territory, his command would be reduced to nothing, the ministers replied that the king, as commander in chief of the army, could always refuse any untenable orders imposed on him. Their opinion was based on the certainty that France would never give up the struggle, and the French army would resist, even if it had to retreat behind the Loire. Spaak recalled Mandel's prediction, 'The Allies will go on, catastrophe after catastrophe, to victory."

———

To take Mandel's prediction literally, it would appear that during the day of Thursday, May 16, the Allies were moving toward victory rather rapidly. Here is an extract from the communications log recorded at Vincennes GHQ that day:

0430—General Giraud, still at Vervins, has led the 2nd Armored Division as far as he can and at daybreak will clean up the Marles-Vervins-Montcornet area.

0630—General Dufour telephones, "This morning at 3:30, five good-for-nothings, one of them a general practitioner, two junior doctors and an officer of the 41st Corps (the only survivor of the 41st Corps) have fled shamefully to the rear. Orders to send them back to the front."

0640—General Dufour says that those moving toward the rear are people attached to the army: baggage-masters, supplies officers, commissariat officers (many from the reserves) and twelve thousand soldiers on furlough to Fismes (unarmed).

0645—Orders to stop everybody, and then move forward.

0720—General Gamelin decides to bring up urgently forty battalions of the state police to Paris.

0920—As a result of an error at the 4th Bureau, four *Somua* squadrons of the 1st Mechanized Infantry are at Soigny instead of Maubeuge. Precarious situation for the 1st Army. The 1st Infantry are in a bad position.

0925—There is no liaison to the left of the Charleroi Canal with the British who are retreating without having received any orders. There is a gap between the 3rd and 4th Corps and there are many shortages. General de La Laurencie is with his troops to encourage them. Given the exhausted state of the army, he intends to take up position on the Charleroi Canal.

1110—German detachments at Montcornet and Marle. Many people retreating toward the rear.

1150—Impossible to hold on to the Aisne. General Touchon is organizing cutting off the Aisne as far as the Ailette Canal. A thought: if the day passes without any mishaps, we hope to be ready tomorrow, but reinforcements are arriving very slowly and sporadically. The front will extend from Attigny to Chauny, which means twelve to fourteen kilometers per division.

1200—No news from General Giraud. The 9th Infantry is going toward Guise to form a blockade at the bridges.

1240—The king of Belgium is not happy about the idea of re-establishing ourselves on the Charleroi Canal. He does not want to endanger Brussels. Therefore maybe General Billotte will reposition on the Escaut (Schelde). General Doumenc intervened with the king, who stood by his order.

1310—Large armored column enters Montcornet and Dizy-le-Gros at eleven o'clock. General Tétu orders it bombed.

1325—There are some doubts about that armored column at Montcornet. Perhaps it is French, so we must cancel the bombing order.

1330—Too late. The planes have taken off.

1350—A large German column seems to be making for Laon. Up till now we are holding our positions. All the infantry divisions but one have met up on the fortified front. No excessive losses apart from equipment.

2000—Enemy attacks Dinant-Sedan area with 1,600 tanks.

2035—The 1st Armored Division suffered heavy losses during the action on the fifteenth; its units have dispersed and are unfit for action. Besides we cannot find the commander.

2210—Unable to contact General Giraud. The Germans have reached Marle.

2255—There has been a skirmish at Guise. The 9th Army does not know where to find General Giraud.

———

That Thursday, May 16, General Gamelin and Lieutenant Colonel Guillaut visited the minister of internal affairs for a meeting called by Paul Reynaud. Around three o'clock in the morning Gamelin arrived at Place Beauvau, finding not only the premier present but also Daladier, minister of defense and war for a few more hours. Also present were Langeron, commissioner of police, General Hering, military governor of Paris, General Decamp, Daladier's chief secretary, and General Ricard, second in command of army general staff. The conduct of the troops and the disorganization of command in the subaltern ranks were severely criticized. The previous day, when the 17th Battalion of Mountain Infantry of the 1st Mechanized Division was being blasted by German tanks at Montcornet, one lieutenant fled with some of his men toward Saint-Quentin, where he was ordered to go to a depot south of the Seine. It was evident that the announcement of the arrival of enemy armored vehicles was, in many cases, sufficient cause for panic.

Let us hope that General Gamelin was able to reply that in many cases, too, the French soldiers acted heroically when placed under a good commander who could set an example. That is indeed how young Lieutenant Jacques Robert, who later became part of my group, acted at Rethel, where he destroyed several enemy tanks. The same goes for my friend Second Lieutenant Paul de Lavareille and his men of the 97th Alpine Infantry, who admirably withstood the attack on the Ailette Canal referred to in the 11:50 message recorded at GHQ on May 16. But there was no doubt about the extent of the disaster: while it was still thought that French troops were fighting energetically on the Meuse the day before, the next day they learned that the enemy was only thirty kilometers or so from Laon. Enemy units were pressing toward Paris in strength, Army Groups I and II having already been separated and the latter's left flank exposed. At five o'clock in the morning, the ministry of internal affairs placed the military government in Paris within the army zone.

———

Toward the end of that morning of May 16, William Bullitt, United States ambassador in Paris, had just been shown into Daladier's office at Rue Saint-Dominique when the minister received a call from General Gamelin. His face became distorted, and Bullitt heard him shout, "No, that's impossible! You must be mistaken!"

General Gamelin had just informed him that a column of German armored vehicles had made a raid between Rethel and Laon, crushing all resistance in its path.

"Daladier," wrote the ambassador, "was breathing heavily. He manages to shout, 'We must attack immediately!' 'Attack?' replies Gamelin, 'With what? I have no more reserves.' Meanwhile Daladier's face seems to be getting smaller and smaller. I had the impression that the man was shrinking before my very eyes. The ominous dialogue concludes with this exchange, 'So, the French army is destroyed?' 'Yes, it is destroyed.'"

The same day, in a telegram to the State Department, Bullitt had said: "It seems obvious that unless some miracle occurs like at the battle of the Marne, the French army will be completely crushed." A little less than twenty-six years ago, the battle of the Marne had been preceded by an incident at Charleroi, like Sedan in this war, except that unlike Eben Emael, which was instantly put out of action by an unexpected enemy tactic, the Liège fortresses had held the enemy at bay long enough to allow Joffre to regroup his armies and gain victory.

———

In the afternoon of Thursday, May 16, Daladier, accompanied by Paul Reynaud and General Gamelin, went to the Quai d'Orsay to meet Winston Churchill, who had made a special trip from London. After hearing the commander in chief's brief statement of the situation, Churchill asked: "Where are the strategic reserves? Where is the bulk of the troops to undertake maneuvers?" Shrugging his shoulders, General Gamelin replied: "There isn't a single one left."

Through the window of the lounge where he was sitting, the British prime minister could see the foreign affairs department officials, their arms full of files, running toward a brazier blazing on the lawn. Rumor had it that in the panic of destroying the archives, the Treaty of Versailles too had been burnt.

———

There was similar panic at Vincennes GHQ. Staff officers were traveling continuously between Vincennes Palace, Montry and

La-Ferté-sous-Jouarre, moving with difficulty through the hordes of refugees, seeing the pitiful and useless barricades erected on the outskirts of the villages, while soldiers of all ranks and all armies watched listlessly from the bar terraces. Meanwhile, Colonel Petibon—who on May 10, had refused to wake his commander in chief for General Doumenc—was busy at the GHQ entrance. He had ordered embrasures cut into the large south portal to give a good welcome to enemy parachutists when they arrived. To complete this system of defense, he had a 75 mm. cannon pointed at the approach, a weapon which twenty-five years ago had been the wonder of its day, and ordered that his secretaries be trained to use it. Others hurriedly took down maps from the walls and parceled up files. Completely oblivious to the commotion around him, General Gamelin (according to an eyewitness), distressed and bewildered, wandered pitifully from the head of his staff to his adjutants, trying to cling to someone for hope, while no one dared approach him. Only six days had elapsed since Friday, May 10, 1940, when Captain Beaufre had been surprised at his jaunty air at 6:30 in the morning.

All this incredible rush at Vincennes was because they expected the Germans to enter Paris on Friday, May 17. It so happened that a colonel in the Wermacht, rather carried away by the thought of victory, was wounded in the French lines and his bag of documents seized. They revealed that the enemy was for the time being uninterested in conquering the capital, but had assigned Abbeville and Arras as the targets. This news was sent to GHQ at 9:40 by the 2nd Bureau:

"The enemy is deliberately avoiding Paris as it leaves Laon for Calais via Guise or the Somme, making a surprise attack in the Aisne region. Its goal is to isolate and destroy Allied forces in Belgium and to bypass the defenses below Laon. The enemy wants to maneuver into a position where it can threaten and destroy

England while sparing France; this operation is similar to those in Norway and Holland."

"While sparing France!" Such an interpretation by the 2nd Bureau was a case of wishful thinking, and it did not take long to disprove that idea. But even that supposition brought some respite to GHQ, where Colonel Petibon no doubt allowed his improvised gunners some rest.

One hour previously, General Gamelin, who for some reason had sprung back to life, issued a lively order of the day to his soldiers:

"The fate of our fatherland and of our Allies, and the destiny of the world depends on this battle. British, Belgian, Polish soldiers and foreign volunteers are fighting at our side. The British air force is as totally committed as our own. Troops unable to advance should die on the spot rather than give up the piece of national territory entrusted to them. As at all the crucial times in our history, our motto today is: conquer or die. We must conquer."

Gamelin had a good memory. On September 6, 1914, Joffre had said to his soldiers:

"At this moment when the fate of our country hangs on the battle being fought, let me remind everyone that it is not the time to look back; all our efforts must go into attacking and repelling the enemy. Any troops unable to advance must, at whatever cost, defend the conquered territory and die on the spot rather than retreat. In the present circumstances, no inadequacies will be tolerated."

But Joffre was Joffre, and he went on to win the battle of the Marne.

—

Entrusted with the command of the 7th Army, General Frère and General Touchon—commander of the 6th Army, originally assigned to cover the Swiss border—strove to "seal up" the breach made by the enemy. Still General Giraud was nowhere to be found and it was essential to reestablish contact with him. The sealing up operation necessitated transporting some twenty large units recruited from wherever there were men still capable of fighting, and involved mobilizing about five hundred trains and thirty thousand trucks. The Luftwaffe dive-bombers were delighted to see such a huge gathering adding to the general chaos. On Thursday, May 16, after nightfall, General Rommel's 7th Panzer Division crossed the Franco-Belgian border around Solre-le-Château, seized Avesnes and crossed Landrecies, arriving outside Le Cateau at dawn, after a fifty-kilometer march. Already disorganized, the 9th Army was unable to recover from the confusion this daring raid had thrown the rearguard into. The fatal blow came when they lost their leader, Giraud, who fell into enemy hands in the early hours of Sunday, May 19. It was not until the spring of 1942 that they heard of General Giraud again, when he made his sensational escape from the Königstein fortress, helped by the Alsace Resistance.

---

Here are some communications recorded at Vincennes GHQ on Friday, May 17:

0310—The operation prescribed for the 9th Army will not take place. No air support. Colonel de Gaulle will start at 0415. It seems impossible to stop him. Order: let it stand.

0450—de Gaulle's operation started exactly on time at Laon.

1650—de Gaulle has been ordered to go to La Fère to defend the bridges.

1655—Colonel de Gaulle asks if he should carry out the order or remain at Montcornet.

1700—General Touchon denies giving the order, so does General Roton. Who gave the order?

That "who gave the order" clearly demonstrates the utter

confusion at Vincennes GHQ. It was even worse at the front. A message received at 12:05 the next day, May 18, stated drily, "The 1st Armored Division has been partially destroyed by our own 47-type cannons in our defense position." Already one recorded the previous day at 12:45 had read, "Our air force has bombed a French column." But what was Colonel de Gaulle's operation all about? It should never have been carried out, given Vincennes GHQ's ineffectual "let it stand."

In his *Mémoires de Guerre* (*Memoirs of the War*), General de Gaulle wrote that he felt "driven to fits of fury" at the pitiful sight of the unending flow of refugees pushed back by the enemy's advance. Among them were thousands of soldiers. The enemy were in too much of a hurry to take them prisoner and merely shouted to them to lay down their arms in passing. Charles de Gaulle firmly resolved to bring this war to an end and wipe out the "blot on our nation." He confides, "Whatever I was able to do from then on was decided that day."

That day was Thursday, May 16, 1940. As I have already mentioned, he was unexpectedly placed at the head of the 4th Armored Division, which was still very much scattered. He received three tank battalions which he launched into attack at dawn on Friday, May 17. They swept over the foe to reach Montcornet, fighting until nightfall in and around that little village on the Aisne River, preventing the passage of the German convoys. Wedged in by the enemy on one side and the Serre River on the other, they could not advance without support. During the night, de Gaulle brought his tanks, which had advanced thirty kilometers beyond the Aisne, back to Chivres. He left the 10th Armored Division that had just joined them to battle the enemy and also threw in the 4th Battalion of Mountain Infantry which arrived that day. New reinforcements arrived: the 3rd Armored Division and the 322nd Artillery Regiment. Now he had one hundred and fifty tanks, with guns ranging from 37 to 75 mm. and an inexperienced crew. He had no radio to transmit his orders and only a skeleton commissariat. But the faith this excellent leader inspired in all the men gave them courage. On May 19, the 4th Armored Division, composed of odds and ends but moving with a single will, went into the attack. It went on to fight until the end of May, causing serious losses to the Germans and disrupting their movements. "Ah!" reflects de Gaulle (having been fortunate enough to know him rather well, I am more inclined to think he was cursing under his breath), "During those difficult days, I could not help imagining what a mechanized army I had always dreamed of having might have been able to achieve. If only it could have been there that day to turn toward Guise. The advance of the Panzer divisions was stopped dead, great confusion in their rear, the armies grouped in the north ready to join those in the center and east. . . ."

———

At 11:45 on Friday, May 17, at the king's GHQ situated just south of Ghent at Saint-Denis Westrem, Leopold received a "General Order No. 14," which was attached to a note from General Billotte, reversing the orders given the previous day. The "General Order" came from General Georges, commander of the Northeast front, who had recovered from his depression witnessed by General Doumenc and Captain Beaufre on Tuesday 14. It consisted of all the orders telephoned from La-Ferté-sous-Jouarre headquarters during the night:

"1. The enemy is directing all its effort toward the left flank of the Allied forces, particularly between Namur and Sedan. It has succeeded in setting up bridgeheads on the left bank of the Meuse, around Dinant and Mézières-Sedan.

"2. It is essential to prevent them from capitalizing on this early success and to prevent them from advancing toward Givet-Paris.

"To effect this, we should anchor ourselves firmly around Antwerp and at the Montmédy fortification. We must try to reposition ourselves along Antwerp, Charleroi, La Sambre, the east side of the Maubeuge projection and a second position at Liart, Signy l'Abbaye and Iner.

"3. The 7th Army, the Belgian army and the British Expeditionary Force shall initially form the northern pivot of the maneuver.

"Army Group I, in close contact with the British Expeditionary Force, will block the passage toward Sambre-Oise."

This order of the day reassured members of General Champon's French military mission, and more news arrived to rally the confident atmosphere caused by the cancellation of General Billotte's order to retreat. Known for his quality as a leader of men, General Giraud was to replace the hapless Corap at the head of the 9th Army, while the 6th Army, moving away from the Swiss border, supported him on the right to seal up the breach made by the enemy. Reading this order of the day over the radio, the commander in chief managed to emulate Joffre in inspiring courage and resolution in his men.

Alas, it was only a short-lived triumph, shattered that same night by Dr. Goebbels's triumphant announcement over the German-controlled radio station of German successes. According to Goebbels, the breach opened by the Wermacht in the Ardennes now reached a width of one hundred kilometers from Sedan to Maubeuge (the exact distance as the crow flies between the two towns). No doubt this was grossly exaggerated, but some Belgian liaison officers returning from Army Group I headquarters reported that General Billotte's entourage was becoming extremely pessimistic. There were whispers that this was the greatest defeat in the history of the French army, and some went as far as to say that German armored vehicles had been sighted at Avesnes. . . . As for the dynamic General Giraud, whom everyone hoped would boost the morale of the 9th Army, all attempts to reach him had been fruitless, and no one knew what had become of him. Only one thing was certain: contrary to the "General Order No. 14," General Billotte persisted in believing that the measures prescribed in his instructions given to the king the previous day were the only ones of any value and pressed General Georges to put them into action.

—•—

At 23:00 on Friday, May 17, a letter from Pierlot arrived at the king's private residence at Gavre Château. Here are some extracts:

"The government's main concern is for the Belgian army to remain with the Allied armies and not to become separated from them under any circumstances.

"This problem is closely linked to Your Majesty's own safety. Because of this the ministers have discussed Your Majesty's course of action in keeping with the principal interests of the country should the Belgian army be unable to retreat in order to avoid being surrounded. They unanimously advise Your Majesty to withdraw at any cost if there is a danger of your being made prisoner. Whatever the course of events, as long as the Allies continue their struggle, Belgium's existence must be affirmed by the retention and activity of the essential state machinery.

"Should the Belgian army isolate itself from the fate of the Allies, there would be a serious switch of public opinion in Belgium as well as abroad. Such a situation and its inevitable aftermath would place Your Majesty and this country in an untenable position with regard to the Allies. In countries abroad, where Belgium's moral reputation and Your Majesty's prestige are both very high, they would feel the keenest disappointment.

"Finally, taking the above into consideration, such an event and its results would make it impossible for Belgium to reestablish its state institutions. It would be the end of our existence as a nation."

Pierlot's letter was a perfect piece of argumentativeness: that is to say a strict form of reasoning which neither supposes nor allows any other implied proposition. French technocrats, who have become legion, make great use of it these days without bothering to verify whether their basic premises are true, which was not the case here. Rejecting the specious argument, King Leopold stayed where he belonged—sharing the fate of his army and his nation. None of the diplomatic actions following the collapse of Hitler's empire was "fatal" to Belgium, which had no need to "reestablish its state institutions," never having lost its existence as a nation or its prestige. Proof enough lies in the important role it has continued to play since the end of the war and the countless international organizations that have chosen Belgium as their base. That shows how one can be prime minister and still fail as a good prophet. But Pierlot did have the example of one of his predecessors, de Brocqueville, who, besides being prime minister some twenty-five years earlier, had also held the post of minister of war. This dates back to October 2, 1914, at Antwerp, where King Albert had set up his headquarters and had called a meeting of the national defense council.

Threatened by the enemy, the area seemed on the verge of collapse, and de Brocqueville stated that since all hope of saving it was lost, the government should leave Antwerp the next day. In confirmation of what he had said during the meeting, he presented the king with this note: "With the full agreement of the cabinet ministers, I take the liberty of urgently insisting that Your Majesty should not prolong his stay, and that he should place the interests of the state above the promptings of his personal courage."

It sounded just like Pierlot. And like the reply his son made twenty-six years later, King Albert had said that his place was at the head of his army, whose fate he intended to share. "But," cried de Brocqueville, "the king cannot run the risk of becoming a prisoner! The king is the country, he is the personification of Belgium." His insistence was in vain. King Albert stood his ground firmly, saying he would go to the barracks in Berchem if need be.

When the Antwerp retreat took place, the French and British governments tried to persuade King Albert to name one of his generals commander in chief of the army and seek refuge in England. They were met with a refusal framed in these terms: "The sovereign intends to retain the command of the Belgian army, whatever

THE FIRST WEEK OF BATTLE 129

its total stength." King Albert continued to abide by that resolution during the Germans' last offensive in March 1918, when they tried to cut the British and Belgian armies from the bulk of the French troops. Just as in 1914, the Allies triumphed. It is worth remembering that in 1914, an obscure French colonel called Aldebert dared accuse the commander in chief of neglect—the man who came to be known as the "Roi-Chevalier." In this man's eyes, the king was guilty because he ordered a maneuver that avoided the massacre of his soldiers. Twenty-six years later, Leopold became the object of a similar imputation. No wonder history repeats itself, since men do not change, especially if they are ministers. Here more than anywhere, the role makes the man.

———

That Friday, May 17, three thousand kilometers from Belgium, a telegram from the ministry of foreign affairs arrived at the high commission in Beirut. Once it was transcribed it was clear that it should only be decoded by the addressee, General Weygand. The message was brought to the residence of the commander in chief of operations in the eastern Mediterranean. It was about eight o'clock in the morning, and Weygand, who was busy getting dressed, asked Captain Roger Gasser, his secretary, to proceed with the deciphering. Gasser immediately went to the high commission, where he had some trouble obtaining the Quai d'Orsay code from the official in charge of ciphers. After giving in reluctantly to Gasser's request, he offered to help him. "I don't need anyone's help," said Gasser as he set to work.

On May 11, a telegram from GHQ had been sent to General Weygand. It reviewed the situation the day after the German offensive, ending with the words, "general impression favorable." A second telegram dated May 12 maintained this optimistic tone, even though it mentioned that the enemy had crossed the Albert Canal. "The Allies' maneuver is developing favorably," it said, with a conviction that was to deteriorate day by day. Hearing on May 16 that the Panzer divisions had reached Montcornet,

General Weygand wondered despairingly whether the French army, not having learned a lesson from the three-week collapse of the Polish army which had been severely criticized eight months earlier, was about to meet the same fate.

The affection and admiration Captain Gasser had for his old chief gave him a premonition of disaster even before he received the coded message for General Weygand. "It's just as I thought," he said when he passed the decoded text to Weygand, who was jogging on the Corniche while his car slowly trailed him. Reading the text, General Weygand sighed, "And yet I had prayed to God to spare me this cross." Then, recovering immediately, he looked back at Gasser. "When do we go?"

"Give me time to pack the bags, General!" replied his assistant.

Bearing Paul Reynaud's signature, the message read as follows: "The grave situation on the western front is worsening. I ask you to return to Paris without delay. Make the necessary arrangements to hand over your duties to the authority of your choice. It is important to keep your departure a secret."

The next day, Saturday, May 18, at 3:30 in the morning, General Weygand, accompanied only by Captain Gasser, set off for Rayak, where a Glenn-Martin plane awaited them. Before leaving Beirut, he was informed of the conversation about himself, which had caused a confrontation between Reynaud and Daladier on Thursday, May 9. During the afternoon of Friday, May 17, General Billotte's staff intercepted a German radio transmission: "From now on, the pressure is off Paris and on the sea." The enemy was so sure of victory that it no longer bothered to use code for its orders.

# "A TIRESOME SITUATION"

General Weygand had turned seventy-two on January 21 and undertook that trip in hasty conditions, which proved to be eventful and uncomfortable. He told us he was "sitting on a shaky garden chair" in the tail of the heavily loaded Glenn-Martin. It was piloted by Commander Pépin, whose fate was already sealed: a few days later, this brave French officer was brought down at the head of his group of fighter planes. Between the long legs of Roger Gasser—who was "perched on the gunner's seat"—the general could catch a glimpse of the sky.

Commander Pépin, having had some trouble in the takeoff from Rayak at 5:15 in the morning, counted on reaching Tunis in one hop to refuel, arriving in Paris the same night. But violent head winds around Benghazi caused him to return to the British base at Marsa Matruh, thus losing three hours. Because of this, his passengers had to spend the night at Tunis, leaving there early the next morning. Four hours later, after a chaotic journey, the Glenn-Martin landed at Etampes military base. Due to the weight of its cargo, the undercarriage collapsed, blocking the exit door. The turret dome had to be unscrewed so General Weygand could squeeze out of the plane. "Hurry, General! We could be attacked any minute!" It was Sunday, May 19, and the general was expected by Paul Reynaud at 14:30.

---

The previous night, Reynaud had announced his cabinet reshuffle over the radio. I had been relegated to the second reserves because of my four children, and my first request, asking to be enlisted as soon as war was declared on Hitler's Germany, had never been followed up. "Come, come!" said the grey-haired officer who received my application, "There's no hurry! Come back later and we'll see." Evidently my zeal must have appeared misplaced, and I thought he was right as the gloomy weeks of the "phony war" slowly dragged by after the excitement of mobilization. I was in Paris when the thunderbolt struck on May 10, and I immediately went to the Rue Saint-Dominique office, where an adjutant explained with typical military acidity that he had plenty of other fish to fry, thank you. Humiliated and feeling useless, I returned to my family in Vannes, but had to return to Paris on May 18. It was there that I heard Reynaud's broadcast.

His announcement, that he would now assume the post of minister of defense and war, left me utterly cold, and I was similarly unmoved to learn that Daladier was being transferred from Rue Saint-Dominique to the Quai d'Orsay, while Mandel was to go to the home ministry at Place Beauvau. But I remember thanking my lucky stars when I heard that Marshal Pétain had agreed to leave Spain, where he was French ambassador, to become minister of state and vice-president of the War Council. I did not know that General Franco, with greater perception than I, had done everything to dissuade him. He predicted that Pétain would have to bear the burden of the impending defeat and the French politicians responsible would hasten to "pass him the buck." That was the expression used by Commander Loustaunau-Lacau on July 30, 1945, in the proceedings against the conqueror at Verdun. Paul Reynaud showed his true colors when he suggested that it was quite erroneous to attribute this victory to the man he had called to his aid on May 18, 1940, dispatching General Pujo especially to Madrid to bring him to France.

On the same day that General Weygand arrived, General Gamelin tried to pass a military "buck" to General Georges. Gamelin gave Georges his "Personal and Secret Instruction No.

12," in which he said, "Without wishing to intervene in the conduct of the current campaign ordered by the commander in chief of the Northeast front, and while approving of all the measures taken, I think that at present. . . ."

In spite of the suggestion of approval, this was in fact a disguised attempt to name General Georges responsible for the series of failures suffered since May 10 by Gamelin's "War Plan 1940," which was clearly a disaster. General Georges was not deceived either, and on reading the above lines, sighed "He's put up an umbrella. . . ." It is very surprising that the man who had the honor of closely assisting General Joffre at the battle of the Marne (he let it be known that his own name could be linked to the victory) should forget the famous words of his chief, whose merit for the victory was contested by some people, "I do not know who won the battle of the Marne, but I know who would have been blamed if we had lost." The situation was reversed here, but the principle remained the same.

———

In the communications log at Vincennes GHQ, the following entries were recorded during the first part of Sunday, May 19:

0005—No communication since 2115. Highly irregular.

0100—Enemy mechanized columns converging near Amiens, one from Albert, the other from Saint-Quentin. At the rate they are traveling they could be at Amiens at dawn.

0545—Message from Army Group I: "Tonight's retreat is continuing slowly; the men are very tired; we are in the midst of making the last move behind the Escaut (Schelde), but the operation will not be completed by daybreak. The 9th Army did not hold out. The Germans are pressing toward Valenciennes." A tiresome situation.

The same morning of May 19, at Saint-André-lez-Bruges, where the king had transferred his GHQ, King Leopold welcomed Pierlot, Spaak, Van der Poorten (minister of internal affairs) and

General Denis, who had come to thank the king for keeping them with him when they announced they were going to set up headquarters at Bruges. (The previous day, when the ministers had shown their intention of leaving for Sainte-Adresse, where the government was moving, the king had opposed this, pointing out that their duty lay in remaining at his side with a skeletal staff of civil servants.) After dismissing the rest of them, the king gave the minister of defense a detailed account of the military situation, and judging by the way the king's remarks were heard, he felt that General Denis understood the gravity of the situation. The day before, Leopold had given his opinion to Spaak and Pierlot—revealing again that perceptiveness that Spaak later called "almost uncanny" at the meeting of ministers at Limoges on May 31—that there was a possibility the British troops might reembark. (In fact Lord Gort started actively preparing for this operation on May 20.) The king added that if that were to happen, the French army might be forced to surrender. Faced with this possibility, Pierlot and his ministers had once again pressed their king to leave Belgium with them. They even said that if the king refused, they would set up an autonomous government in France and would boycott any official actions carried out on national territory under enemy occupation.

"By what authority," replied the king, "can a prime minister in exile abroad prevail upon his people? What would our army think if its commander abandoned it?" A confused discussion ensued, which the king concluded with the words, "In any case, I cannot make an immediate decision. If in extreme circumstances my departure should be imperative, I could always go by plane."

———

On Saturday, May 18, the king was visited by the British officer responsible for liaison between the king's GHQ and Lord Gort's British Expeditionary Force. Without revealing his true intentions, the head of the British force expressed full satisfaction with the excellent coordination between the Belgian army and the Expeditionary Force. He complained that this was not the case with France, from which he had very little information.

Around noon, an officer from GHQ assigned to General Billotte came to the king with alarming news: four Panzer divisions were advancing at great speed between Le Cateau and La Fère, meeting only with weak resistance. Since no reserves were available, General Billotte was going to lead divisions of the 7th Army from the lower Schelde south, across the Belgian army's rearguard divisions. A German breakthrough seemed inevitable, bringing with it a breach in the French front at the Oise. The king saw only one solution: it was essential to defend the straits of Calais, which meant that the armies in the north would have to stand close together to form a bridgehead with its back to the sea. By nightfall the civilian population was showing signs of panic. On that day, May 18, German fighters had destroyed two Belgian squadrons, which left only three squadrons out of a total of 179 planes that the Belgian air force had at its disposal the day before May 10. It is true that among those planes were outdated models such as the Renard 31, whose top speed could not be compared to the Spitfire. When a British pilot was offered to test the controls, he had declined saying, "I'm sorry, but I'd rather use my bicycle as I'm in a hurry."

—

The Belgian army's retreat began as ordered by the French command. However, there was some strong opposition from some officers and men who, ignoring the general situation, could not understand why they should abandon such strong positions. It was generally disconcerting for the men who had fought so courageously; they felt their deeds had all been in vain when they began to retreat. Besides, defeatist rumors circulated among the civilian population by enemy secret agents had affected the troops and undermined their morale. To stop this, on May 19, Leopold ordered his cavalry corps to launch a counterattack to regain the positions from which the 5th Army had been driven. He also ordered the 1st Ardennes Light Infantry Division positioned on the Dendre—a tributary of the Schelde—to maintain liaison with the rearguard of the British Expeditionary Force. He addressed the leaders of the large units: "Confidence, order and discipline must be restored without delay, even if it means using the firing-squad to set an example. The army must be committed to standing firm against any attack the enemy may mount at this time."

This certainly sounds rather different from General Gamelin's "Personal and Secret Instruction No. 12" addressed to General Georges. Perhaps this note was the result of a meeting Gamelin had had the previous day, Saturday, May 18, with Doumenc, chief of staff of the ground forces, who was worried about the physical and mental strain General Georges might be put under as commander of the Northeastern Armies. Georges had not yet recovered from the wounds he received from Croatian terrorists at Marseilles on October 8, 1934, when he tried to help the king of Yugoslavia and Barthou, minister of foreign affairs in Doumergue's Cabinet. Doumenc said to Gamelin, "General, I think you may have to take over the actual directing of operations." "Do you think so?" replied Gamelin, "Just let me know when and where."

———

However, his fate was sealed at 14:30 on Sunday, May 19, when General Weygand walked into the office at Rue Saint-Dominique, vacated the previous day by Daladier. He was met there by Paul Reynaud and Marshal Pétain. As he had been Foch's man, General Weygand could not be Pétain's man, but at such a time, those considerations were not at all important. Besides, Marshal Pétain gave him a warm welcome that was scarcely his custom. "Believe me," said General de Gaulle, who was perhaps revealing some secret hurt to me, "I probably knew him better than anyone; he was completely cold." As I had the honor of seeing Marshal Pétain once, I think that remark certainly describes the way this prestigious and glorious old man looked to other people. On the other hand, he could arouse warm support from crowds, just as he had been able to capture the confidence of the soldiers in 1917, when the French army was on the verge of disintegrating. His fine features seemed to be carved out of marble, and were as cold; and after so many years, I still remember his icy blue stare.

Briefly informing General Weygand of the situation and the government's apprehensions about the conduct of operations, Paul Reynaud asked his eminent visitor to hurry to Vincennes for talks with General Gamelin, then to La Ferté-sous-Jouarre to meet General Georges. In his book *Rappelé au Service (Recalled to Service)*, General Weygand describes what took place at those two meetings on Sunday, May 19, 1940, the first at 16:00 at Vincennes GHQ and the second one and half hours later at "Bondons," the residence of the commander in chief of the Northeastern Armies.

The last time Weygand had met General Gamelin was on April 10, when the commander in chief had held a luncheon in his honor. Weygand found him "much changed," and saw on his face "traces of fatigue and anxiety." Without any recriminations, Gamelin told him "with calm and dignity" that it was natural that he should be replaced since he was beaten. Captain Roger Gasser, who was present during the exchanges between the two officers, felt Gamelin's "deep despondency."

General Georges came out to meet General Weygand in the garden of his residence. Weygand wrote, "I am shocked by the change in his features. He soon tells me that he can no longer sleep, not caring to hide his extreme exhaustion. To enter the office, I have to cross a large room where his closest aides are working. They stand up and bow with a sad look. . . ."

It was when General Weygand was in Marshal Foch's staff that he had learned to appreciate General Georges's "clear intelligence, accurate judgment, and strength and steadiness of character." When Weygand reached retirement age, Marshal Pétain, then minister of war, had asked him who he thought was the most worthy officer to put at the head of the army. Weygand had replied without hesitation, "Georges." The Doumergue government decided otherwise and chose Gamelin, with Georges as an aide "with no clear powers or responsibilities." His position remained "indeterminate" when Gamelin was named chief of staff for defense.

General Weygand concluded:

"When I arrived in France, the disconcerting circumstances in which General Georges had to carry out the direct command to our troops were well known to me. Although the commander in chief had conceived the disastrous maneuver and ordered its execution, he considered the battle in progress as "General Georges's battle," as he had delegated the command of the Northeastern Armies to him from January. I knew that General Georges had shown great strength of spirit when he accomplished his mission in those circumstances, this despite the serious injuries he had received at Marseilles when King Alexander of Serbia and Louis Barthou were assassinated. I was sure that, given his background and experience, he would soon become himself again."

At 19:00, Sunday, May 19, General Weygand returned to the office at Rue Saint-Dominique to meet Marshal Pétain and Paul Reynaud. The latter asked him to assume command of the French armies.

One of the greatest honors of my life is having had the benefit and privilege of General Weygand's friendship. The other was to have been the courier for this great warrior and saint, for the correspondence he sent to another great man and saint, President Salazar. On countless occasions I was able to judge (or, more accurately, glimpse) the perfect honesty and extreme modesty of this exemplary soldier. At the celebration of his ninetieth birthday, Marshal Juin reminded us of the glorious titles Weygand had acquired before World War II, and then said, "I salute, above all, General, how you were able after our defeat in North Africa, to re-form the army which I was given to lead to victory in Italy," a resurrected army that went on to further victories as far as the Danube. I am therefore certain that General Weygand spoke truly and honestly when he wrote these words about his acceptance of the offer made him by Paul Reynaud:

"Was this presumption on my part? When I ask myself—and since that date, I often have—I don't think I was wrong in acting as I did. I knew how dangerous the situation was and I realized that the French army, after the battle of Flanders, would have another much harder battle in front of it, and a decisive one at that. My confidence remained unshaken. I did not think it impossible to recover from our early failures. Our soldiers were the sons of those who had fought at Marne, Verdun, the battle of France in 1918, and their endurance and bravery had accomplished miracles. Our most experienced leaders had in their youth taken part in those great and terrifying campaigns. In spite of its numerical weakness, I had great confidence in the British army, which I had seen in action in the four years of the previous war. I knew the courage and tenacity of its soldiers and the reputation of its leaders. Distance had spared me the psychological shock of the early setbacks, and I felt capable of great energy. I hoped I would have the strength to pass on to all those who felt discouraged the faith and strength of will I felt. But my confidence was objective, and I realized we would have to go through hard times. I accepted the positions offered me by the premier out of a spirit of duty and total self-sacrifice."

———

While Weygand was resting in his apartment at 22, Avenue de Friedland, an officer from general staff who had returned from the Oise front after five days of vain struggle to reassemble the remnants of the 9th Army, was restoring some order to Vincennes GHQ. He reported these impressions to his companions:

"Complete chaos. Out of 70,000 men and many officers, not even the smallest unit has a commander. A stupid and haggard lot, complete mix-up of numbers, troops and services. Only about ten percent of the men still have guns. Not one automatic. A few 25 mm. cannons transported by car. Many noncommissioned officers and men travel in military or private cars. From the thousands that I sifted through, I was unable to form one company to defend the bridge at Compiègne. Yet the losses incurred have not risen: not one wounded among those thousands of deserters. It's not so much a question of morale, for the moment anyway: those men are bewildered, they don't understand what's happening, they are terrified at the sight of a plane. The services fell apart before the troops did, and it is they who spread confusion everywhere."

———

Night had not yet fallen when a dispatch-rider arrived at General Weygand's house with an urgent letter. It contained a copy of an order addressed to the commander in chief of the French ground, sea and air forces and chief of staff for defense. At GHQ the communication log recorded:

"2000—General Gamelin has been relieved of his command and General Weygand nominated as chief of staff for defense and chief of all operations."

At 19:25 the same person had noted: "Communication from General Billotte: 'The plan of operations has been carried out on the Schelde; a long haul, men exhausted, morale excellent. Everyone is in position on the Schelde; the attack will be launched at the agreed time. The 1st Army will cover the right flank; it is holding the Valenciennes-Cambrai front which is still occupied by the French but has already been penetrated by some elements of the enemy.' "

# MONDAY, MAY 20

At nine o'clock in the morning of Monday, May 20, General Weygand went to Vincennes GHQ. The situation prevented him improving on a chain of command that had proved disastrous: General Doumenc—chief of staff of the ground forces, whose duties were to prepare and draw up the orders—was operating forty kilometers away, while General Georges, assisted by General Roton, was at La Ferté-sous-Jouarre. To reorganize this hopeless state of affairs would only have made the situation worse. Weygand limited himself to replacing Gamelin's private secretary by Colonel Bourget—his own chief of staff in Beirut who was by chance on leave in Paris. He asked him to put an immediate end to the officers' practice of directly intervening in the implementation of orders. Then he set to work with General Doumenc, who explained precisely the tactical and strategic situation of the armies, the lack of large reserve units, tanks and fighter planes. As for armaments. . . When on Friday, May 24, Paul Reynaud asked General Colson, chief of army general staff, "whether it would be useful to call up the last elements of the 1939 and 1940 categories," he replied, "There would be no arms for these young recruits, no uniforms and no blankets to give them. We don't have enough equipment for what is left of Corap's army that we are now re-forming in France. There are not even enough guns available: only five thousand at the most, and these are old-fashioned models. The army depots are full of recuperated and untrained men, but we cannot arm them."

After a two-hour-long talk with General Doumenc, General Weygand deduced the following:

"In ten days of battle in Belgium and on the Meuse, the French army had lost, and I mean exactly that, fifteen divisions. Through the large breach opened in the Allied positions, eight German Panzer divisions, strongly supported from the rear, were advancing on the Channel coast, already reached by their vanguard. To the north of the breach were General Billotte's Army Group I, made up of two French armies (the 1st and 9th under General Blanchard and General Giraud), almost the entire British Expeditionary Force (Lord Gort) and the Belgian army, in all a total of forty-six divisions. It was already surrounded and in danger of being pushed to the coast. To the south of the breach, units taken from the fortified areas of the front and from North Africa were being transported there as quickly as possible, but they were being considerably hampered by the enemy's systematic bombing raids. The units were to form a barrier along the Aisne and the Somme stretching toward the west as far as the coast, and along the still intact Maginot Line."

Having reviewed the situation, General Weygand decided to take the shortest cut. He sent part of General Billotte's Army Group I and General Frère's 7th Army to fill up the forty-kilometer breach between Arras (still held by our troops) and the Somme. This formed a counteroffensive from the north and south to slow down the German advance toward the Channel and to "endanger the enemy's advance troops." Calling Billotte on the telephone on May 20, Weygand said, "We must attack and fight like dogs to finish off the Panzers, who must be at the end of their tether. We must not just dig in on the breach and stay on the defensive; that would be playing their game. We would always be outrun and too late. Attack south."

The implementation of this operation required twenty divisions from the Belgian army. When Pierlot called early on Monday morning, General Weygand replied: "At all costs, you must maintain, or reestablish if necessary, liaison between French and Belgian troops." Sensing from the prime minister's tone that he had "some doubts" about the king's intentions, the new commander in chief decided to go to Belgium the next day to meet King Leopold and Lord Gort, together with General Billotte and General Blanchard. At first General Weygand planned to go by train to Abbeville, then by car to meet General Billotte, but as this was evidently impossible, it was decided that night at GHQ that he should go by plane. At the same time, the commander in chief learned that General Giraud, commander of the 9th Army, had been captured by the enemy, who had now reached Amiens. A message received at 23:05, unconfirmed by the coding section, said that the Germans had captured Laon and reached the Ailette Canal. At 23:30, the message log book read: "A halt in transmission; secondary cable cut." This was the underground cable linking GHQ with Army Group I headquarters, which had been severed near Abbeville by the enemy's vanguard. From that day, messages sent to and from the northern army headquarters had to go via London.

---

That same Monday, May 20, 1940, at 8:30 in the morning, when the entire Belgian army had taken up positions on the front extending from the Dutch port of Terneuzen (situated on the southern bank of the west Schelde) along the canal which links it to Ghent and as far as Audenarde, west of Brussels, the Belgian General Nuyten—who had maintained liaison between GHQ and General Billotte's headquarters—arrived at Baron Kervyn de Lattenhove's château near Saint-André-lez-Bruges, where the king was residing. "Your Majesty," he said, "the French 9th Army has been cut to pieces. There is a rumor that General Giraud may have been killed, as there is no trace of him. There is no news from the 6th Army. The 1st Army is being attacked on the right flank and is being turned around Condé to face south. We have lost communication with the main body of the French troops."

The previous night, when Leopold had learned that General Gamelin had been replaced by General Weygand, the king was also told that the enemy now occupied Cambrai and Saint-Quentin. At ten o'clock in the morning that day, May 20, he was visited as usual by the minister of defense who had come from GHQ. The king asked, "What would be the chances of evacuating our bases to France?" General Denis replied, "The French border is closed to us for forty-eight hours. Besides, all our roads and railways are so blocked that there is no hope of evacuating."

Pierlot was there with General Denis and the ministers of foreign affairs and internal affairs. The king wrote the official report of the painful discussion that took place:

"The king's official report of the meeting held with Messrs Pierlot, Spaak, Denis and Van der Poorten at GHQ on May 20.

"GHQ at Saint-André (Baron van Caloen's château), May 20, from 11:00 to 12:30. Those present: the prime minister (Pierlot) and the ministers of foreign affairs (Spaak), defense (General Denis) and internal affairs (Van der Poorten). Purpose of meeting: the ministers asked to speak with me about my personal attitude if the Belgian army were cut off from the Allied troops and forced to surrender.

"The prime minister once again outlined his ideas expressed in previous meetings, expressing the ministers' distress that they and I should hold such divergent points of view.

"Spaak took up the theme forcefully, 'It is intolerable for us to feel that our king does not share our opinion. I have thought about this day and night and I am unable to find any reason to justify the king's point of view.'

"The four of them complain about my silence, begging me to tell them why I do not agree with them. Long silence. Then I replied:

"Me: The fate of the army? That is not a question, as it is not I who can decide that. Only events will determine its movements and its fate. My personal situation? Actually it is impossible for me to reply. To do that I would need to know the general situation from a practical and military point of view. As long as I am not in possession of those facts, you cannot insist on a reply.

"The ministers are very disturbed by my reply, which says no more than my silence. They beg me to talk, to explain myself.

"Me: I am expecting a visit from General Weygand. This afternoon I shall meet Admiral Keyes who will have seen Marshal Gort. Then I can better appreciate the facts and maybe tomorrow we can talk with all the facts before us.

"The ministers: But we need an immediate answer! Tomorrow will be too late.

"Me: You must not panic. We have not lost all hope yet. I can always leave by plane.

"The ministers: They draw a parallel between King Albert in 1914, who remained at the head of his army.

"Me: There is no possible comparison between us. At that time we still had some national territory left.

"The ministers: Yes, but if you went to France, you could still be head of what remains of your army.

"Me: Obviously, but only in one set of circumstances: if the Allied front is reestablished. In that situation, even if the Belgian army was cut off from the Allied troops, we could always consider going to France, since the French armies would still be fighting. In all our discussions, you have considered only one possibility. Well, there is another possibility: what if the French army has to lay down its arms? In that case, I would not like to be in France.

"The ministers (angrily): Why didn't you tell us that? We had assumed that whether France resisted or not, your mind was made up. We are pleased to see that is not the case. Now, we are beginning to see eye to eye.

"Me: It is you who are arguing from a false premise. You must consider all aspects of a problem and not just one possibility.

"The ministers then understood, and Pierlot resumed the discussion.

" 'We must consider two hypotheses. 1. The Belgian army is

cut off from the Allied forces, but the latter are not defeated and the French front is stabilized. In that case the king would go to France to mobilize new troops to continue the struggle and maintain our institutions. 2. The Belgian army is cut off from the Allied forces and the latter are defeated. In that case, the king would remain with his army.'

"Me: I request that my ministers give me a written note expressing the government's opinion."

——

The king's hypothesis of the French army's defeat once again demonstrated that clear thinking which Spaak called "almost uncanny." Bear in mind that in this meeting, Pierlot, Spaak, Denis and Van der Poorten admitted there was a case when the king should stay with his army. In his memorandum dated the same day, May 20, the prime minister denied it. He wrote in Paragraph III:

"The king stated that: a) if the Belgian army remained in contact with the main body of French troops, he would naturally continue the stuggle; b) if the army were in danger of being trapped, and France and England continued to fight, he agreed he would leave the army to mobilize fresh troops, continue the struggle and maintain the freedom of this country's institutions; c) he also had to consider the hypothesis in which following Germany's success, France and England would make peace, in which case his presence among his army and in his country might still be useful. (The king will see Lord Gort and General Weygand tomorrow to discuss the likelihood of this possibility.)

"Paragraph IV—The prime minister has confirmed there is complete agreement between the king and his government on points a) and b) above. While the government is convinced of France and England's willingness to continue the struggle, it recognizes that the king has acted wisely in wishing to be completely clear about the situation.

"Paragraph V—The prime minister, however, stresses the great danger in the possibility envisaged in IIIc above, of a premature agreement with Germany; the Allies would certainly make Belgium bear all the responsibility for the defeat."

This last point anticipated how Paul Reynaud would react, but was incorrect about Great Britain. From Pierlot's memorandum and the ministers' attitude, I have the impression that contrary to what Leopold thought after his meeting with the minister of defense on May 19, General Denis had not really understood the extreme gravity of the situation . . . which is often the case with generals, as it is with ministers. On the other hand, with his "uncanny" clear thinking, the king was fully aware of the true state of affairs and based his decisions on them. But like General Denis, the government preferred to live in their world of illusions: this was soon proved to be the case.

The king's dilemma was frighteningly simple: either the Belgian army would succeed in retreating to France, whose troops were still able to fight, in which case the king and his soldiers could continue the battle begun on May 10; or, cut off from the French army and with its back to the sea at a time when disaster in France seemed unavoidable, the Belgian army would have to lay down its arms. In that case, Leopold was determined to remain with his army and his nation, in the hope that by remaining on national territory he could defend Belgium's independence and sovereignty until the final victory over Hitler's Third Reich. He had no doubts there would be a final victory for the Allies, but the habit he had inherited from his father of looking at facts realistically told him that it would be several years before the Allies would defeat an enemy who had not encountered a single setback so far.

———

The king wasted ninety minutes that Monday morning, May 20, with his ministers, who, I am sure, tried to persuade their king to desert the sinking ship because they were trying to justify their own behavior in the future. The commander in chief's time would have been better spent in looking at the situation, which was deteriorating hourly.

It is not commonly known that on Monday, May 20, Admiral Ramsey, former chief of general staff for the Home Fleet, who had been recalled from retirement in 1938 to defend the Dover area, received a set of secret instructions, codenamed "Dynamo." These were measures to ensure the immediate evacuation by sea of the British Expeditionary Force, for which the situation in France would evidently soon become untenable. Winston Churchill and General Ironside had at first opposed this plan, but they were finally convinced by General John Dill, deputy chief of Imperial General Staff. The Royal Air Force had already begun to withdraw its bases from a doomed battlefield, and its squadrons of fighter planes were returning to England.

Nevertheless, General Ironside had crossed the channel on Monday, May 20, to talk with Lord Gort at his headquarters in the little parish of Wahagnies in the Pont-à-Marcq area of Lille. His plan was to send the British Expeditionary Force through the passage opened up by the Panzer divisions to join General Frère's 7th Army on the Somme. The Belgian army would take advantage of the maneuver to slip in along the coast behind the British troops. Lord Gort thought the plan too dangerous, and in a meeting with Billotte and Ironside at Lens, suggested a twofold attack on Bapaume and Cambrai. The former was to be led by two British divisions from Arras under General Franklyn and the latter by two French divisions from Bouchain under General Altmayer. The latter plan was adopted.

———

When King Leopold learned from Admiral Keyes that Lord Gort wanted the Belgian army to relieve one of his divisions at Audenarde for a counterattack in which they hoped to gain the upper hand, he immediately gave orders to this effect. Lord Gort was afraid that the Belgian army would be unable to mount a counteroffensive, and the king agreed that this would not be possible in open country as his troops lacked the necessary equipment. When Admiral Keyes explained that the British Expeditionary Force could retreat toward the south, Leopold asked him to communicate to Churchill his own views on this matter. The admiral summarized them in the following telegram:

"On my return to Belgian GHQ I told the King of the proposal to extend the BEF southwards so that part of it could operate in a southerly direction.

"The King pointed out that the Belgian Army existed solely for defence, it had neither tanks nor aircraft and was not trained or equipped for offensive warfare. He also told me that, in the small part of Belgium left, there was only sufficient food for fourteen days, possibly less, owing to the influx of refugees.

"He did not feel that he had any right to expect the British Government to consider jeopardising perhaps the very existence of our ten divisions in order to keep contact with the Belgian Army. He wished to make it clear that he does not want to do anything to interfere with any action which may be considered desirable for the BEF to undertake towards the south, if the circumstances made it necessary. He realises, of course, that such action would finally lead to the capitulation of the Belgian Army.

"The King asked me to try to ascertain the intentions of the British Government, if the German thrust towards the sea succeeds in separating us from the main French forces in the south. It must not be thought that he has lost heart or faith, but he feels he owes it to us to make his position perfectly clear."

In reply to this telegram signed "Roger Keyes, Admiral of the Fleet," Churchill sent a telegram which did not reach the admiral until the next day, May 21.

"Weygand is coming up your way tomorrow to concert action of all forces. Essential to secure our communications southwards and strike at small bodies intruding upon them. Use all your influence to persuade your friends to conform to our movements. Belgian Army should keep hold of our left flank. No question of capitulation for anyone. We greatly admire King's attitude. German thrust towards Lille must not succeed to separate us from main French forces. Have complete confidence in Gort and Weygand, who embody offensive spirit vital to success."

The rhetoric was in character for the man who would say over the BBC, "I can only offer you blood, sweat, toil and tears," showing his determination to resist, without which Hitler would have been victorious in the west. It should hardly detract from this magnificent attitude to point out that the Panzer divisions were forced to halt at the Channel separating England from France and Belgium, a pause that gave Churchill a temporary respite. Moreover, by abandoning its cannons, tanks, munitions and all its equipment, most of the British Expeditionary Force had been able to return to England thanks to what Churchill called in *The Second World War* "the deliverance of Dunkirk." The rescue operation would not have been possible without the help of the Belgian army and a few French divisions who bravely sacrificed themselves. Finally, "no question of capitulation for anyone" (I suppose this means "for whatever reason") is rather ironic when we know that the message for King Leopold was addressed to Admiral Keyes, whereas what Churchill actually intended was this: "On the afternoon of May 20, following orders from London, all interested parties, including representatives from the Merchant Navy, held their first conference at Dover to study the urgent problem of evacuating a large number of troops across the Channel. It was decided that, if necessary, the evacuation would take place from Calais, Boulogne and Dunkirk at a rate of ten thousand men per port per twenty-four hours . . . . These were the plans of Operation Dynamo, which allowed us to save the army ten days later."

When Churchill said "army," he was only referring to the British Expeditionary Force. In other words, when he told Admiral

Keyes, "Use all your influence to persuade your friends to conform to our movements. Belgian army should keep hold of our left flank," Churchill was assigning the Belgian army the task of covering an evacuation operation of which he had not said a word to its chief. Such an attitude in one's partner at an ordinary game of cards would be severely criticized.

———

At about eight o'clock that night, Monday, May 20, 1940, the Spitta Battalion of the 2nd Panzer Division under the command of General Veiel was jubilant. It was the first of the Wermacht battalions to sight the waters of the Channel from the Somme estuary. Beating General Frère's 7th Army to it, the forward elements of the 19th Panzer Division also established strong bridgeheads on the right bank of the river: one at Péronne, a second at Corbie, a third at Amiens and a fourth at Abbeville. This was in spite of the amazing courage and initiative of the French, who were under no orders but determined to do anything to stop the German advance. We have living proof of this in Senior Sergeant Fortunat Thiébaut, who before the war had been troop picket commander of the 541 Republican Guard from Nancy, whose duty was to watch the Franco-Spanish border in the Pyrenees south of Banyuls. Having a commission as section chief and "candidate for a higher grade," he was urgently recalled on August 27, 1939 to join the 32nd Group of Divisional Reconnaissance Infantry at Nancy, which was to be formed at Obernai from some elements of the 3rd Hussars. He was to be deputy to a very young second lieutenant called Frère, who was almost certainly related to General Frère of the 7th Army, who became governor of Lyons and founded the Army Resistance Organization. He died leaving an unforgettable account for his friends of the misery in the Struthof concentration camp in Alsace.

The 32nd Group was first assigned to active cover missions on the Maginot Line, and then from May 10, took part in the Belgian campaign, becoming very experienced at delaying tactics which took it as far as the Franco-Belgian border. Determined to reach Abbeville before the Germans could get to the sea, Captain Miron d'Aussy of the 3rd Hussars assembled all the motorcycle, machine-gun and armored car squadrons that were in reasonable condition and headed toward the Somme on May 21. Fortunat Thiébaut noted sadly, "Despite our great haste through the night, we learned during the morning of May 22 that our efforts had failed, for the Germans had reached the sea before us. . ." Not to worry! Some time later, this valiant little group was in Calais. Thiébaut told me about his brave companions in that 1940 campaign, saying bitterly: "Yes, indeed! Many of them fought very bravely, and it is unthinkable they should be held responsible for a defeat which was largely due to political causes." How right he was!

—

The enemy was not easing up on the front held by the Belgian army since May 19, giving no respite to the men exhausted by long marches. They were attacked at Quatrecht by General Geyr's 9th Corps, and at Zingem—where the Schelde forms a loop—by von Kortzfleisch's 11th Corps. Fierce attacks and counterattacks were made.

That night of Monday, May 20, Colonel Charles de Gaulle summarized the situation thus: "The Dutch army has disappeared, the Belgian army is retreating toward the west, and the British army and French 1st Army are being cut off from France." It was in these circumstances that a meeting was held the next day, which came to be known as the Ypres Conference.

# THE YPRES CONFERENCE

At 8:30 in the morning, Tuesday, May 21, the Belgian listening posts picked up an uncoded radio message from the German army. "We have entered Abbeville which is barely occupied and we are establishing ourselves there." When asked to verify this, British liaison between King Leopold's GHQ and Lord Gort replied that they feared it must be regarded as true.

———

At the same time at Le Bourget, General Weygand was experiencing firsthand the incredible confusion and inefficiency of Vincennes GHQ, where he had been assured the night before that a plane would be at his disposal at Le Bourget the next morning. When he arrived there with Captain Roger Gasser—now his aide-de-camp once more as he had been for eleven years before the war —the general was unable to find anyone who had received instructions on the matter. "We were sent from one end of the airport to the other. Finally we learned that a squadron of fighter planes was to escort my own, but of my plane, no one seemed to know anything. After detailing one plane, then another, the airport commander at last told us we were ready for takeoff. Already one hour had been wasted."

But this was not to be the end of the commander in chief's troubles; now he had to go to the airport at Norrent-Fontes—between Aire-sur-la-Lys and Lillers—where General Billotte was supposed to meet him. As they were flying over the Canche River that flows into the bay of Etaples, the plane was caught in enemy flak, which proved that the enemy had indeed reached the Channel. At 9:30 he arrived at the Norrent-Fontes airport, which to General Weygand's amazement seemed deserted.

"There were very good reasons for this. For two days the place had been abandoned by the squadrons which had occupied it. That is what we found out after wandering through empty hangars that indicated a hurried departure. We met a very dirty little soldier, but with a kindly face, who told us what had happened and asked me what he should do with twenty thousand liters of gasoline which he was saddled with, having received no orders. A telephone would have been most useful to me, but there were none left. And this is how the chief, who had just been given command of all operations with the highest responsibilities, came to be alone in the middle of nowhere, due to the negligence of those who had planned his journey, with no means of reaching the people he had come to meet in Flanders, who were expecting his arrival."

It so happened that the "very dirty little soldier" drove a small van, in which General Weygand and Captain Gasser rode, hoping to find a telephone post, weaving through hordes of Belgian and French refugees, increasing in numbers as the vehicle went east. At last they spotted a car driven by an officer from the transport corps, and the commander in chief was able to call Army Group I general staff. Through the crackling of a bad line he learned that General Billotte had gone to look for him, although no one knew which way he had gone. The safest thing to do was to return to Norrent-Fontes where they were supposed to meet. There they bumped into Lieutenant Colonel Dehesdin, Billotte's deputy chief of staff. He was also unable to say where his commander might be, but General Weygand deduced that he had a chance of finding him in Calais. And then, amidst all that confusion, he came across the true spirit of France.

"While my aide-de-camp was giving orders," wrote General Weygand in *Recalled to Service*, "I went into a little inn next to the airport for an omelette to keep us going until evening. The woman innkeeper was alone apart from a young boy. She had received no news from her husband who had gone to fight in the war. Every few minutes she would go to the door to watch the refugees fleeing from the invasion. She wondered whether she should also leave her house and take flight. While she was preparing our simple meal, I noticed a little picture on one of the walls. It was a popular photograph, often seen in the north, depicting the signing of the armistice at Rethondes in 1918. Inside the carriage on one side of the table were the four German delegates; opposite them sat Marshal Foch with Lord Wester Wemyss and another English admiral on his right, and on his left, his own chief of staff. What a strange coincidence! The moment the woman brought in the steaming omelette, she said to me, "Is that really you there, General?" and she added a few words of hope and confidence that I had often heard since my arrival in France, and which I was anxious to be worthy of."

The inn where General Weygand made a brief stop was in the village of Rély. Captain Gasser himself told me that when the woman learned that her guest was indeed the new commander in chief, she exclaimed, "What you are doing is very fine!"

At 13:00, the general's plane landed at Calais, an airport that had been badly bombed. A telephone call to the town hall soon put Weygand in touch with General Champon, chief of the French military mission to the Belgian army, who came to pick him up by car. The roads were so congested that it took almost two hours to drive the seventy kilometers to the little town of Ypres, where Weygand was to meet King Leopold, General Billotte and Lord Gort at 15:00 at "La Châtellenie" (the Ypres town hall). A spot more evocative of the great battles of World War I or of the heroic deeds performed could not have been chosen.

The king was forty-five minutes late, held up by the same traffic congestion. General Billotte and Lord Gort were also late, but Pierlot, Spaak and General Denis were there when General Weygand arrived. Without waiting for their king, they asked Weygand what his plans were. "Their faces lit up with satisfaction," says Weygand, when he told them that in his opinion, the Belgian army had stayed too long in the east, and that it should hasten its retreat toward the west to join the Allied forces. The ministers exchanged a few significant words, from which General Weygand gained the impression that they disagreed with their king. When the king's arrival was announced, General Weygand went to meet him on the front steps of the town hall. He knew him well from the time he had seen him at Albert's side after the Great War, and he had once had a long conversation with him after his accession, answering the king's many questions about the French army. But it was the first time he had met General Van Overstraeten, the king's aide-de-camp and military adviser, whom he found to be "a man of distinguished appearance, whose turn of phrase was cultured and precise."

Since the conference was strictly on military matters, the ministers were not asked to take part. So talks opened between the king, General Van Overstraeten, General Weygand and General Champon, without waiting any further for General Billotte and Lord Gort. Leopold asked the commander in chief to give his views on the situation.

Without concealing the fact that he thought it extremely serious, General Weygand outlined the plan of action he had just stated, adding that the southerly offensive would be undertaken by General Billotte's armies and the British Expeditionary Force, while the Belgian army would cover this attack to the east. Repeating what he had said earlier to Pierlot, Spaak and Denis, Weygand said he thought that the army had delayed too long on the Terneuzen-Ghent line and should beat a retreat as far as the Yser, which should now be flooded. He thought the Belgian troops were capable of retreating in stages without being too exhausted, and of waging a successful defensive battle on the flooded Yser line.

"Excuse me, General," said General Van Overstraeten, "but I do not agree with you. Several retreats have brought us from Maastricht and Arlon to the Terneuzen Canal, beyond and into the Ghent bridgehead, which stretches along the Schelde to just downstream of Audenarde. The army is getting its bearings again and nearly all its units have assembled. Quatrecht, which was briefly taken by the enemy last night has been recaptured. Similarly, Zingem on the loop of the Schelde has been reoccupied, and our patrols are moving in front of the river. To our right, the Germans have taken Peteghem and have maintained a small bridgehead despite British counterattack. . ."

"I think the Anglo-Belgian positions are too extended and too far to the east," replied General Weygand. "I hope to see the Belgian army back on the Yser, retreating by night in stages, as it seems necessary to break the spearhead of the enemy's offensive. This means assembling all possible troops—including the entire British army—to work on the enemy's flank. It is an urgent matter as the German infantry is close behind its tank units, and as soon as the ordinary infantry divisions are in position, it will be difficult for us to counterattack. My aim is not to penetrate enemy lines, but to contain and limit the breakthrough. Therefore, three French infantry divisions moving from south to north will mount a counterattack tomorrow. It was impossible to make it any stronger as the German air force has cut off all our means of transportation. Another counterattack by two English divisions moving south from Arras has been staged today. Tomorrow they will be joined by Altmayer's corps and what remains of the French infantry divisions, moving west from Cambrai. I would like you to take part in this operation: in exchange, the infantry divisions of the 16th Army would be put under the king's command."

"It has been absolutely essential to stop the retreat," retorted General Van Overstraeten, "because the units were beginning to break down due to the numerous retreats conducted during the night, which are also very bad for discipline. Another retreat would

have a deleterious effect on morale, at a time when the happy outcome of the battles that have just been fought has lifted their
spirits. At this time of year there is no real advantage to night
maneuvers as the nights are short and there is a full moon. This
means that any journey begun at nightfall has to be completed in
daylight, and moreover, troops marching in columns are more
vulnerable to aircraft attack than when in battle position. A retreat
to the Yser would awaken painful memories for the army, which
has no wish to relive those moments. Also abandoning the territory would cause distress to the ever-growing numbers of refugees.
One could say that the fighting spirit decreases in proportion to the
diminishing size of the territory to be defended from the invader.
I can assure you that the army will fight well in its present position,
but I cannot answer for it if it has to undertake another long retreat. So it is worth examining whether an immediate retreat to
the Yser is necessary, given the lack of troops to maintain the present front.''

"But you must choose, and quickly," interrupted General Weygand. "Either you must maintain, at whatever cost, the continuity
of the Allied front—which is what I want to do—or you must
cover the Channel ports and sever the front, which would be
dangerous.''

"Do you not know then that the Germans have captured Abbeville this morning?" asked General Van Overstraeten. "It was
announced uncoded over the radio by the occupying detachment,
and the British believe the information to be true.''

"I had not heard the news," said General Weygand, demonstrating the state of chaos at Vincennes GHQ. This admission
seemed so unbelievable that General Van Overstraeten noted, "I
looked the general straight in the eye. I could not believe he was
not telling the truth. Nor could I believe that such an event could
have had no effect on him.''

King Leopold then gave his opinion that the alternatives stated
by the general of covering or abandoning the Calais straits could
not be decided until they had heard Lord Gort's opinion. They

tried to reach him by telephone, but his staff officers replied that he was absent and would not return until 18:00. Since General Billotte had still not appeared, the conference was suspended, and General Weygand talked with General Van Overstraeten. Since he had only been back two days from the Middle East, General Weygand said he was not fully familiar with the situation. Yet he felt he did not have the right to refuse the position offered him by the government, though he knew the weight of the responsibilities. General Van Overstraeten wrote, "The entire exchange of opinions was very friendly and spoken with military frankness." General Billotte had still not arrived, and Weygand went into the burgomaster's office to talk to Pierlot, Spaak and Denis.

Finally General Billotte arrived, accompanied by General Fagalde, and the conference was immediately resumed. Using a colored sketch as illustration, General Billotte explained the situation of his armies. He concluded:

"We must really face facts after suffering the same experience three times: the combined action of the Panzers and Stukas has penetrated our positions in an incredibly short time. Between Amiens and Cambrai there are three to four thousand enemy tanks, closely followed by mechanized infantry, and other infantry divisions further behind. The French 1st Army is in a very confused state: it is stuck in the Valenciennes region; tired and low, it is unable to attack and barely capable of defending itself. It is relying feebly on Arras, which is held by units of the British line. We are not sure about the British army's plans, but the army is intact and will be capable of a powerful offensive. Another point to consider is what the king thinks is the most desirable situation ultimately for the Belgian army."

After interrupting General Billotte several times to clarify certain points and having criticized the Royal Air Force's strategy, General Weygand said:

"At first I thought it would be advantageous to bring the Bel-

gian army back to the Yser. Quite rightly, General Van Overstraeten objected to this, given the difficulties of night maneuvers at
this time of year, the losses we would suffer from air attacks, as well
as the losses of morale and equipment which a sudden voluntary
withdrawal from almost the entire Belgian territory would cause.
This has led me to consider another solution which seems to be acceptable. It consists of freeing the British divisions for a counterattack at Arras. If the Belgian army will extend its front to relieve
part of the British army, all parties should be happy."

The king accepted this and proposed besides that his army
should relieve the French 16th Army now supporting the left flank
of the Belgian army. Estimating this to be logical, Weygand commented that they still needed to get approval from the British.
Then Admiral Keyes—who accompanied the king to Ypres—left
with General Van Overstraeten to look for Lord Gort. The conference was suspended once more, and the king took the opportunity
to confer with his ministers. The commander in chief of the British Expeditionary Force was still absent, and General Weygand
finally left Ypres without having met him.

———

This account of the Ypres Conference differs from that of General Weygand related in *Recalled to Service* on several counts,
notably the king's reply to the proposal that he should assure
that the Belgian army cover the Allied counterattack. General
Weygand stresses that the king did not immediately agree, "The
king did not commit himself, saying he would think about it. The
next day, I received a telegram from General Champon stating
the king had agreed to my proposal and had given the order for
his army to begin maneuvers toward the west." The truth of the
matter is that this maneuver directly concerned the British Expeditionary Force, and as General Weygand himself had remarked,
the king wanted to discuss the matter with Lord Gort before giving
his approval, which he sent on the night of May 21.

**Above:** King Leopold watching a Stuka attack at Wynendaele Château; **below:** an aerial view of Wynendaele Château.

Hubert Pierlot, the Belgian prime minister.

General Denis, Belgian minister of defense, with Paul Henri Spaak, Belgian minister of foreign affairs.

**right**: Paul Reynaud, who was made
the French premier on March 12, 1940;
**bottom left**: General Georges, commander of the Northeastern Army; **bottom right**: General Gamelin, French commander in chief in the first week of the German invasion.

**Top left:** Field Marshal Gort, commander of the B.E.F.; **top right:** King Leopold with Admiral Keyes; **below:** Winston Churchill with General Ironside.

General Weygand also writes that he told General Billotte he felt some apprehension when he heard "General Van Overstraeten's ideas, the king's hesitation in committing himself and the difference of opinion that seemed to exist between the Belgian king and his ministers at Ypres." These apprehensions surely stemmed from the fact that while waiting for the king General Weygand had talked with Pierlot, Spaak and Denis before the opening of the conference. We shall see later what their opinions were that afternoon of Tuesday, May 21.

*Recalled to Service* was published by Librairie Flammarion in 1950, ten years after the Ypres Conference. There still exists an official document on the Franco-British meeting that took place the next day at Vincennes. It was seized along with the archives at Charité-sur-Loire during an enemy raid and was published in Berlin in 1941 by the minister of foreign affairs for the Reich under classification 56 of the *Auswaertiges Amt*. Here is an extract relating to General Weygand's meeting with King Leopold the previous day:

"General Weygand then outlined the general conclusions he had reached after visiting the front.

"The commander in chief does not think there can be any question of asking the Anglo-Belgian troops still in the north, consisting of over forty divisions, to retreat south simply with the object of joining the main body of French troops. Such a maneuver would be doomed to failure and the troops would certainly be destroyed. On the contrary, the situation requires that, under the cover of the Belgian army on the east, the available British and French troops mount an offensive south around Cambrai and Arras and in the direction of Saint-Quentin, to attack the flank of the German armored divisions now engaged in the Saint-Quentin-Amiens "pocket." At the same time, General Frère's army, now south of the Somme around Beauvais, would rush north to increase the pressure on the enemy's armored elements in the Amiens, Abbeville and Arras areas. The important thing was to keep up a constant pressure and not to allow the German armored divisions to take the initiative; we should keep them on the move, inflict losses and threaten their rearguard. Only under these conditions could the Belgian army's retreat be usefully effected.

"The previous day, General Weygand had unfortunately been unable to discuss the matter with Lord Gort, who could not be reached. But instead, he was able to have a long conversation with the king of Belgium and his general staff. The commander in chief had two separate proposals for the Belgian army, neither of which appeared to appeal to the king. The first suggested by General Weygand himself was that the Belgian army should retreat from the Schelde to the Yser, while covering the French and British troops, which would mount an attack toward Saint-Quentin. In point of fact, the Belgian army, now at the mouth of the Schelde at Audenarde and passing through Ghent, is in an exposed position fraught with great dangers. The support it must give the armies on the western front could just as easily be given from the Yser, helped by flooding (which General Weygand has ordered should be done immediately).

"The second proposal was suggested by General Van Overstraeten, King Leopold's aide-de-camp. According to him, the Belgian army should remain in its present position, and as it becomes necessary, separate from the Allied forces to cover the coast in a huge semicircle, supplies being assured from Ostend and Dunkirk. General Van Overstraeten justified this plan by stressing the troops' exhaustion after continuous marches from Maastricht and the low morale after a long retreat. After a twenty-four-hour rest as soon as the army had arrived at the Schelde, it had rallied again. This was proved when it brilliantly resisted two German attempts to cross the Schelde on May 21. If we were to ask the troops to retreat again and abandon almost the entire national territory, General Van Overstraeten said they would once again be very demoralized.

"General Weygand was strongly against this proposal. He pointed out that the Allied forces were a totality, and that the French and British had come to the aid of the Belgians in Belgium. Now, the Belgians should continue to support the British and French. He added that supplies for the Belgian army as envisaged by General Van Overstraeten would be impossible and the Belgian forces would soon be forced to surrender. The king did not take sides during the discussion. It was not until General Weygand had returned to GHQ that he learned that the Belgian high command had accepted his plan and had decided to retreat to the Yser in two stages, the first one as far as the Lys.

"In those circumstances, continued the general, the Belgian army will act as a cover while the British and French troops attack in the south, supported on their right by the Belgian cavalry, which included a number of mechanized divisions and which the king was thinking of placing at the disposal of French command.

"During General Weygand's statement, Churchill and General Sir John Dill showed their approval, and through their questions and comments demonstrated that their own concept of the battle corresponded closely to the general's, especially with regard to the role played by the Belgian army."

———

I shall return to the meeting that took place at noon on Wednesday, May 22, at Vincennes GHQ, during which General Weygand made his report. I shall leave aside the differences in detail between the report of the Ypres Conference according to my Belgian source, and what General Weygand reported the next day at Vincennes and ten years later in his book *Recalled to Service*, since the plan for the Belgian army was accepted by King Leopold. I shall merely point out that the plan was to assure cover for the French and British troops who were to mount a counterattack toward Saint-Quentin.

I mentioned that the Ypres Conference was adjourned to await Lord Gort's arrival, and that General Weygand left Ypres, where he had planned to stay that night, to fly back to Paris. But he was told by "Admiral North"—the nickname of Admiral Abrial, commander of the Dunkirk fortifications—that the airport at Calais had been bombed again and was now out of action. As it was getting late and he feared he would be held up again by the crowds of refugees on the road, General Weygand ordered his plane and escort to return to Le Bourget, as he had to be in Paris for a conference the next day. Admiral Abrial had offered to put a torpedo boat at his disposal by which he could reach Le Havre during the night. Weygand got into the admiral's car which was to take him to Dunkirk; as the car was starting, he wound down the window to give a piece of advice to General Billotte, feeling certain it would be his last.

The commander in chief was annoyed that he had been unable to discuss matters with the head of the British Expeditionary Force. Knowing Lord Gort very well, he could not understand why he had not been present at a very important conference without giving some reason for his absence. He did not learn the reason until five years later, when the war was over, from Lord Gort himself. Apparently two of the British Expeditionary Force's armies ran into difficulties on the Schelde front, and he had thought it necessary to go there in person in the afternoon of May 21. In view of the situation there, he had decided to bring the troops back to the border.

While General Weygand was at the Dunkirk "Bastion 32" waiting for his 600-ton torpedo boat *Flore*, he was shown the defense plans of the area. He had the dubious honor of witnessing an enemy air attack just as he was about to embark. Flying low, Luftwaffe planes dropped bombs with impunity as there were no British fighter planes in sight. At nightfall, *Flore* got under way, passing through breakwaters ablaze from the incendiary bombs. There were three officers from General Giraud's general staff aboard, and they told General Weygand how the new commander of the 9th Army had been captured by the enemy: having decided that his troops should stay put whatever happened, Giraud had set up his command post near the divisional command post that was destroyed by an armored German attack. The officers also gave details of how such attacks were carried out by the combined action of dive-bombers and tanks. "Thanks to the information they gave me, as soon as I returned I was able to prescribe a mode of defense for our troops which proved to be effective during the early days of the June battles," wrote General Weygand. That is all very well, but how come this information was not forthcoming earlier when Poland was crushed? These methods, already applied in the Spanish Civil War, had been used there with total brutality.

———

After General Weygand's departure, and since Lord Gort was still absent, King Leopold held a meeing with Pierlot, Spaak, and General Denis. From the outset, the ministers were very disturbed. They had heard first from General Weygand that the Belgian army would be asked to retreat to the Yser to cover the planned counterattack. Then they heard after the first adjournment that the Belgian army would stop at the Lys. The ministers had deduced from this that the king had refused to leave Belgium and had intended to act in such a way that the only possible outcome for Belgium would be to lay down its arms and negotiate a separate peace with Germany.

The meeting with the three ministers began at 17:00 and lasted until Lord Gort finally arrived with General Pownall, his chief of staff. The king himself wrote the official report of the meeting which ended at 19:00.

"The ministers were aggressive and unpleasant. First they accused me of hiding my thoughts from them, and then complained that for several days they had been kept at arm's length, kicking their heels at Bruges without knowing what was happening. They tell me I have been neglecting my duties, because for three days the army has been on the Schelde-Terneuzen Canal line and there has been no movement; no initiative has been taken and the army remains inactive.

"Previously at Breendonck I had expressed my fears that we might be separated from the French troops and pushed back to the sea; how come, since I had foreseen such a possibility, I was not doing something when the German army's advance in the south was making a retreat more difficult each day.?

"Me: Ever since the divisions left the Albert Canal, they have constantly been on the move. To manage to hold our present position we had to succeed in our maneuvers and with great speed. If our army does not rest there for two or three days, it will be impossible for it to maintain its cohesiveness.

"Pierlot: I have no wish to interfere in military matters, but I was an infantryman in the 1914 retreat. Also I went to look at the Terneuzen Canal position and I realized that our infantry is still capable of maneuvering there.

"Me: There is another reason. During the discussion I had at Casteau with the French and British military authorities, it was decided that General Weygand would delegate authority to General Georges, and he in turn to General Billotte to assure coordination between the Belgian army and the Allied forces. General Gort and I agreed with this: as from then, we had to conform to General Billotte's orders. We have only received one order from him: retreat to the Schelde.

"The ministers: It is untenable for the Belgian army to remain inactive when we realize that the longer we wait the harder it will be for the Belgian army to retreat toward the Allied armies. There comes a time when, to avoid capture, one does not await orders but acts on one's own initiative.

"Me: You need only look at the map and examine the Allied deployment to see that our right flank is covered by the British army, whose duty is to give us support. I cannot conceivably decide to retreat as it would leave the British army completely in the lurch. That is why I am waiting here at Ypres for Lord Gort, to hear his thoughts.

"What the ministers were saying in plain terms was this: 'You are hiding your policy from us, and it is different from any we would accept. It consists of leading the army into a position where it is cut off from the Allied troops and pushed back to the sea, which would lead to engaging in a separate peace treaty with Germany.'

"The ministers then considered various tactics and strategies which were quite senseless, to try to deploy the army in a different manner from the one that I had accepted."

—

The last paragraph of the king's report written after his meeting with Pierlot, Spaak and General Denis on Tuesday, May 21, does not come as a surprise to me. It seems that since Clemenceau's famous sally, "War is far too serious a matter to be left in the hands of the military," those "chosen by the people" think they are omniscient in the matter. Before 1939, one of our French ministers —who had taken his time about returning to General de Gaulle, to whom he asserted he was on good terms with Roosevelt (the latter had never even heard of his name)—was dispatched to the United States. There he proceeded to demonstrate to the president's military advisers the ineptitudes of their strategy. I doubt whether relations between Roosevelt and de Gaulle, which were already somewhat cool, were improved by this minister. We shall soon see the war strategies of King Leopold's ministers that evening of May 21 at Ypres.

First they complained of being "kept at arm's length, kicking their heels at Bruges without knowing what was happening." Let us remember that together with Van der Poorten they had thanked the king on Sunday, May 19, for keeping them at his side; that after their visit, the king had explained the military situation at length to General Denis; that on May 20 they had had a long meeting—Van der Poorten was also present—with the king at his GHQ at Saint-André-lez-Bruges. What more did they want? During the meeting the king had explained the situation in the clearest possible way!

Pierlot, Spaak and Denis accused him of "hiding his thoughts from them." Could we not say the same about them? The king would have had every right to take offense at his ministers' indiscretion before his arrival at Ypres, discussing military matters with General Weygand, who had come especially from Paris to talk with the king, General Billotte and Lord Gort. It is evident from General Weygand's *Recalled to Service* that he was unfavorably influenced toward the king by the ministers.

The position of the commander in chief of the Belgian army was perfectly clear. How could he have changed the strategy agreed with Lord Gort, when the latter was not even present? That is why he did not immediately accept General Weygand's plans. Note that Pierlot, Spaak and Denis were quite happy to break such an agreement unilaterally—thus endangering the British Expeditionary Force—when they said, "There comes a time when, to avoid capture, one does not await orders but acts on one's own initiative." This offhand manner does not support Spaak's statement at Limoges on May 31 that Pierlot had strongly urged the king, "Under no circumstances should we be cut off from the French and British troops," after which he added, "At that time the king scrupulously—in my opinion, too scrupulously—followed the orders given him by the French high command." It is easy to imagine General Weygand's reaction had Pierlot, Spaak and Denis taken part in the Ypres Conference and tried to put their own "initiatives" across over the head of their commander in chief.

—

The king's meeting with his ministers ended at 19:00 with the arrival of Lord Gort, accompanied by General Pownall. The conference was immediately resumed, led by General Billotte, who outlined General Weygand's plan to the two Britons, adding that Weygand expected much from the Allied counteroffensive, providing it was powerful. "What would the French participation be?" asked Lord Gort. But even before General Billotte could answer, General Pownall interrupted: "Our communication lines have been cut. We have been reduced to diverting our supplies by sea to the Channel ports which have been heavily bombarded. We have battalions in the Arras and Péronne regions and we have a seventy-kilometer front on the Schelde. At Arras we are mounting a counteroffensive with our best troops in a sector which is not our own. We only have supplies for two more days, and our artillery reserves are restless and unmanageable. So we have no wish to engage in a large battle.

"Besides, for some unknown reason, the level of the Schelde is sinking, and our army commanders have just stated we should leave that defense line within twenty-four hours. The Belgian army is unable to relieve us immediately, since we are now under enemy attack at Audenarde."

"The British divisions that have been relieved are not the best," remarked Lord Gort. "As far as we know, out of the entire French army, only one division has remained vaguely intact. . ."

The conference ended pessimistically at 21:30. Every one of the participants felt that the commander in chief's plan was beyond their capabilities.

It was agreed that the Belgian front would first be brought back to the Lys, and the sector held by the Belgian army extended as far as Menin within forty-eight hours to relieve the two British Expeditionary Force divisions on the left flank. "We could also relieve the French 16th Army Corps, which would be more useful at Saint-Omer," suggested the king to General Billotte.

"I don't think it would be of any use in open territory," replied Billotte, "and in fact I would prefer it if Your Majesty were to take command of it."

As they were leaving, they learned that the Luftwaffe had bombed Béthune. General Billotte was heading there and he was apprehensive about having to journey at such a late hour along a road that would be crammed with refugees.

That same night, Leopold informed the French command that he had given orders for the Belgian army's retreat in two stages to the Yser. At the same time he ordered the flooding of the Schelde as requested by General Weygand. Had Lord Gort arrived earlier at the Ypres Conference, everything would have been open to question all over again.

# "THE ARMY REMAINS INACTIVE"

"The army remains inactive." I doubt that the Belgian soldiers who were fighting on the Schelde front would have agreed with the government's opinion—which was even more unforgivable as one of the four ministers who had remained in Belgium at the king's request was a general and the minister of defense. I also doubt whether they had time during the fighting to pay any attention to such a remark. Some Belgian troops had just marched the difficult one hundred and thirty kilometers from Maastricht to Terneuzen, while others had covered an even greater distance from Arlon in the extreme south. At the time the government made the above statement, the Belgian soldiers were repelling the violent attacks of the 9th and 11th armies at Quatrecht and Zingem. That was why the king had told General Weygand at the Ypres Conference that after hard fighting, his men had regained areas taken by the enemy. At Zingem, the artillery had been obliged to shoot this side of the safety limit to turn away the enemy, who were almost close enough for hand to hand combat. The day had been saved by a platoon of the 1st Company of the 3rd Light Infantry Regiment from Le Hainaut. A strong push led by Lieutenant Bourcq succeeded in throwing the enemy back to the other side of the Schelde. By three o'clock in the morning, Lieutenant Wattiez's 6th Company of the 6th Light Infantry, together with some artillery soldiers, had completed their cleaning up operation in the Schelde loop. These operations were even more commendable since the 44th Division of the British Expeditionary

171

Force on the Belgians' right wing was experiencing serious set-backs. This was compensated by a counterattack in the far west on May 21, ordered by Lord Gort. Two British divisions under General Franklyn marched on Bapaume from the Arras region, while two French divisions under General Altmayer marched from Bouchain to Cambrai. Supported by the French 3rd Light Armored Division, the 151st Brigade under the British General Martell made a surprise attack on General Rommel's 7th Panzer Division at three o'clock in the afternoon. The Allied troops were able to gain a victory, which, alas, would be shortlived: the British and French were delighted to see the SS of the Totenkopf Mechanized Division, so proud under their death's head banner, scatter before their very eyes. They captured a complete gun site and brought back about four hundred prisoners.

"The army remains inactive." While Pierlot, Spaak and Denis were saying those words, the 33rd and 34th infantries were caught in the panic caused by soldiers fortifying the positions on the Terneuzen Canal. Having lost their armaments during the retreat, the men were panicked by heavy bombing from planes and mortars. There was a rumor that the enemy had managed to cross the canal, when in fact the twenty inflatable craft launched from the right bank in the hope of establishing a bridgehead had been sunk. Six riflemen from the Belgian 6th Division, sent on reconnaisance to capture prisoners, had crossed the canal on rafts and captured four Sudeten soldiers of the German 309th Infantry Regiment. Also there was a serious lack of staff—many officers had been sent back to France to train recruits—so the 33rd and 34th regiments had been combined during the night, while the 37th was reoccupying the positions left open by those who had fled. On the eve of Wednesday, May 22, the Belgian front was over ninety kilometers long, and General Michiels summarized the situation thus:

"On a front extending from north to south, beginning with the cavalry corps' advance elements at Terneuzen, are the 5th, 2nd, 6th, 7th and 4th army corps. The 1st Army Corps held in reserve only constitutes two incomplete divisions; one small division is guarding the coast. One French division, whose infantry has been reduced to two regiments, is holding the Leopold Canal north of Bruges behind the cavalry corps. We have ordered the bulk of the 16th Army (French) to return and hold the Gravelines Canal at Saint-Omer, to assure the Allied disengagement operation in the south the freedom to maneuver on the west side.

"The Belgian army has once more joined the battle. While German armored divisions have been sighted at Boulogne and Saint-Omer, and the French and British troops are trying to reestablish their line between Cambrai and Péronne, our valiant troops are fighting bravely to give the time and space necessary for this important maneuver. The German battle corps in Belgium will certainly concentrate all their efforts on the Belgian army, while their armored divisions come to their rescue in a mechanized attack. The picture would not be complete without mentioning the complications arising from the proliferation of every kind of evacuation convoy close to the French border, which is more often closed than open. There is also the congestion caused by hundreds of thousands of refugees trying to find a safe zone, as well as the constant bombardment devastating the entire coastal area."

—

When King Leopold returned to his GHQ at Saint-André-lez-Bruges on the night of Tuesday, May 21, he held talks with Admiral Keyes, who wrote the following to the British prime minister:

"He had agreed to take over the line of the Lys as far as Halluin, in order to release British divisions to carry out the offensive contemplated by General Weygand, although this necessitated his placing practically the whole of the Belgian army in the line of about 100 kilometres, opposite which at least eight German divisions had been identified. However, he was tempted to point out that the offensive had been delayed too long and that the only real hope now, that is late hour, was to establish a cover to Dunkirk and the Belgian ports, in order to withdraw the British and French armies which were separated by the German thrust.

"King Leopold pointed out that the well prepared frontier line to be held by the British troops on his flank was unlikely to be seriously attacked, but that to be held by the Belgian troops was weak and would be comparatively lightly held and thus invite attack. He feared that if it were seriously assaulted with strong air support, the Germans would break through, sever the connection between the two armies and overwhelm the Belgian Army. He asked me to send the following reply to the Prime Minister's message, which I had given him at Ypres that afternoon.

"Reference to your telegram, the King feels that you do not appreciate the difficulty of keeping in touch with the left flank of the BEF if it operates to the south as you suggest. He would like above all things to co-operate with the BEF if this were possible; but it is a physical impossibility under the existing geographical conditions.

"His Government are urging him to fly with them to Havre before the army finds it necessary to capitulate. Of course he has no intention of deserting his army. If the British Government understands his motives, he does not care what others may think. I immediately sent you a telegram as requested."

# "THE BRITISH ARE RETREATING"

At 1:15 in the morning, Wednesday, May 22, 1940, the following message was received at Vincennes GHQ: "General Champon informs us that General Billotte met with a very serious accident at 21:00. He is doing what is necessary to convey orders to the 1st Army."

Undoubtedly shaken by this event, the chief of the French military mission did not think of informing King Leopold's GHQ about it until the afternoon of that day. The Belgian liaison officer made this report: "General Billotte is dying. His general staff has received no instructions. The 1st Army is devastated, his general staff exhausted and his eleven divisions reduced to less than three. The Arras counteroffensive is now being carried out by two English divisions and one French. The territory between Arras and the sea is occupied in only a few areas."

General Blanchard heard about his commander's accident during the night and left for Lord Gort's headquarters, now at Prémesques near Armentières, at 7:30 the next morning. There he met General Champon, General de la Laurencie of the 3rd Army Corps and General Janssen of the 12th Division. He informed them of the plan discussed with General Weygand the previous day. As had been decided in a case of emergency, General Blanchard took over command of Billotte's Army Group I and arranged with Lord Gort to send two reserve French divisions to relieve two British divisions, still intact, which would join the attack in the south as planned.

—

That Wednesday, May 22, at five o'clock in the morning, the passengers aboard the *Flore* disembarked at Cherbourg, where transportation awaited them. At around 10:00 A.M. General Weygand arrived at Rue Saint-Dominique to report his meeting with the king the previous day to Paul Reynaud and Marshal Pétain. He was most dismayed to hear of General Billotte's accident, for his condition had now turned critical. Despite intensive care, General Billotte died the following afternoon.

There was only one consolation for Weygand when he returned to Vincennes GHQ, and that was that in accordance with his proposal, King Leopold had decided "to bring his army back to the Yser in two stages." Weygand also was advised he would shortly receive a visit from Winston Churchill and Paul Reynaud.

There was a rumor at GHQ that the enemy had reached Dieppe. In great panic the subdistrict officer at Senlis had ordered the district evacuated; General Doumenc suggested that the officer should be sacked on the spot, but the government refused since the officer claimed he had received written orders from a general, whose name was never revealed.

—

Churchill and Reynaud arrived at Vincennes around 12:00 noon. The British prime minister was accompanied by Sir Ronald Campbell, British ambassador in Paris, General Sir John Dill from Imperial General Staff, General Hastings Lionel Ismay, minister of defense in Britain's War Cabinet and secretary of the Committee of Imperial Defence, and Air Vice Marshal Pierce of the Royal Air Force. Reynaud was accompanied by Captain de Margerie, secretary of the French embassy in London.

General Weygand received his guests in one of the rooms at general staff, where an officer outlined the battle formations and the Allied forces' situation with maps. Churchill informed them that two battalions of Guards—the last two units held in reserve on British territory—had disembarked at Boulogne, and with forty-eight antitank guns, were resisting all German attacks. He added that the British Expeditionary Force had taken measures at Calais and Dunkirk to protect the two ports from any surprise attack like the one at Abbeville.

General Weygand expressed his regret to Churchill at having been unable "to meet Lord Gort in person" the previous day at Ypres, but he added, "that fact did not seem to prevent our Allies from responding."

———

The following resolutions were accepted by all at this "summit" conference:

1. The Belgian army would withdraw to the Yser and remain there, the flood-gates having been opened.

2. The British and French armies would attack in the southwest toward Bapaume and Cambrai as soon as possible, and by the next morning, May 23, at the latest, with approximately eight divisions.

3. As this battle was vital for the two armies and as British communications depended on the relief of Amiens, the Royal Air Force would lend all possible support day and night for as long as the battle lasted.

4. The new group of French armies moving toward Amiens to form a front along the Somme would turn north to maintain contact with the British divisions attacking in the south in the Bapaume direction.

"After this confirmation and that of the king of Belgium," wrote General Weygand in *Recalled to Service*, "I had every right to assume that only a move by the enemy could prevent our success. The assurance I received, that these orders would be sent to Lord Gort, made up for the inconvenience of having missed him the previous day. My mind was put temporarily at ease on that part of my responsibilities for the rest of the day."

———

It was an exhausting day, nevertheless, for this seventy-three-year-old man, after the tiring mishaps of his trip to Ypres and back. At 15:00 he was at Montry with General Doumenc "to prepare the necessary instructions for the chief of staff." Back at Vincennes at 17:00, he met Admiral Darlan, commander in chief of naval forces. At 17:30, he met General Hering, military governor of Paris, and at 18:00 he went to see Paul Reynaud, who accepted his proposal that General Mittelhauser should replace him at Beirut.

General Weygand had no telephone contact with Army Group I headquarters. All communications were made either by coded messages sent through very unsatisfactory radio channels or through the French embassy in London which retransmitted the messages via Lord Gort's headquarters. Besides the loss of time involved in such a procedure and the hazards of the transmissions being retransmitted accurately, Weygand could only operate gropingly in this situation. But there was worse to come.

Reading over the official report of the meeting held at Vincennes on May 22, 1940, between the British and French (it began at noon and ended at 13:15), we notice that Churchill repeated several times "that the reestablishment of communications between the armies in the north and those in the south via Arras was imperative; that General Gort's British Expeditionary Force only had sufficient supplies for four days; that all supplies and material for the British Expeditionary Force were concentrated around Calais along the coast; and that General Gort's main aim was to keep this very vital line of communication open." But there is no mention in it of Churchill's own suggestion of a "precautionary measure," an operation that Admiral Ramsey, commander of the fleet at Dover, had been ordered to prepare two days previously: the withdrawal of the British Expeditionary Force, code-named

Operation Dynamo. It is unfortunate that the British prime minister did not inform General Weygand, by May 22 at the latest, of what would become a reality four days later. Could this voluntary omission explain Lord Gort's absence at the Ypres Conference, at least until General Weygand had to leave for Calais without having met him? The last straw was that after the meeting at Vincennes, Churchill told Paul Reynaud and General Weygand "privately" that "relations between General Billotte and the British commander in chief were not entirely satisfactory, as Lord Gort had not received any instructions for four consecutive days." We know that during the afternoon of Monday, May 20, when Churchill must have been aware of Admiral Ramsey's preparations for the "urgent evacuation of large numbers of troops across the Channel," General Gort, accompanied by General Ironside, who had arrived from England that morning, were at General Blanchard's headquarters at Lens for talks with General Billotte, who had accepted his proposal for a counterattack with two French divisions the following day.

———

At the end of that day, Wednesday, May 22, General Frère informed Vincennes GHQ that German columns from Amiens were moving in force toward the bridgehead at Saint-Pol, while others of similar strength had left Abbeville for Hesdin. They also learned that enemy armored vehicles were moving to Saint-Omer and that Boulogne, which had been heavily bombed, was being attacked by mechanized divisions.

———

At King Leopold's GHQ at Saint-André-lez-Bruges, it had been known since 8:30 that morning that the enemy had attacked Hesdin as well as Saint-Pol. This meant that the starting-point for the counteroffensive proposed by Lord Gort had already been passed by the Germans, and his own headquarters was in danger. The Belgian army on the Schelde front was under attack at

Quatrecht and Zelzate, while on the other side of Ghent, the British were under attack at Audenarde and Tournai.

At ten o'clock that day, the king studied the situation with General Van Overstraeten and General Denis, who was paying his daily visit. "From now on," the king said, "the defense of the Lys seems to me to be most urgent. If we continue the retreat to the Yser, we would run the risk of facilitating the enemy's maneuver to converge on Calais. This move would completely surround the Allied troops around Lille. It would be a disastrous blow for the British and the French, and one from which it would be hard to recover. I have therefore decided to fight on the Lys and its branch canal, starting from Deinze. What do you think?"

"From a military point of view," replied General Denis, "that is the only possible solution."

In the afternoon they heard about General Billotte's serious accident, together with reports from Belgian liaison officers on the state of disorder at Army Group I headquarters. The king was convinced that the counteroffensive decided the previous day at Ypres was doomed to failure, and that he should stand by his decision to establish a bridgehead on the Lys without delay.

—

Having settled on this course of action, King Leopold wrote the following letter to Pierlot:

"My dear Prime Minister,

"I will not conceal the fact that yesterday's meeting at Ypres with you, Mr. Spaak and General Denis was most painful to me. I do not believe I deserve the accusation that the aim of my policy is to lead my country toward a separate peace with Germany.

"In carrying out my official duties as commander in chief of the army, my aim, above all, is to defend this territory while trying to cooperate as far as possible with the Allied armies and to avoid compromising our army. Therefore, the Belgian army's operations are dependent on two factors: collaboration with the

Allied armies, which means that Belgian command must follow the general plans decided by General Weygand; and the fact that the Belgian army is bounded by the sea to the north and by the British Expeditionary Force to the south.

"This situation leaves us no choice; no other means of conduct is possible. I might add that the policy of evacuation, which I have always opposed, also restricts the freedom of movement of our troops.

"These are reasons enough, I think, to refute those remarks made to me. Besides, I cannot allow the ministers—whose field of competence does not lie in military matters—to judge what is possible for the army and to determine, for example, whether the army is capable of carrying out a retreat or not.

"You have also criticized me for withholding information on the military situation from the government, which has a right to take a keen interest because of the political implications. This is quite untrue. At Breendonck I drew your attention to the fact that events were leading toward a situation which could be quite different from the one you had considered certain.

"The only difference of opinion existing between us is that you do not believe there could be any question of my remaining with my army. I replied I could think of no situation which would not justify this attitude.

"Perhaps you will allow me now, Mr. Prime Minister, to tell you what a head of state expects from his government in the present circumstances. As I do my best to keep you informed on military matters, I have every right to expect you, and particularly the minister of foreign affairs, to keep me in contact with political matters which I am unable to follow closely at the moment. I concede, of course, that the ridiculous haste with which all the government administration and a large part of the provincial and community administration rushed to France does put you at a disadvantage. The total collapse of civil authority leads me to only one conclusion, and that is since the opening of hostilities, the government no longer has the means to govern.

"It is even more distasteful for me to have to write this letter, when I know and appreciate the devoted spirit that you and your colleagues display. But the dedication, with which I fulfill my duties in the best interests of this country, will not allow me to let these criticisms pass without comment.

Yours most sincerely,<br>(signed) Leopold."

The retreat to the Lys and its branch canal ordered by the king began on the night of Wednesday, May 22. At dusk the 1st Infantry Division arrived. They had set out at 14:00 in trucks toward the Courtrai sector that had been abandoned by the British 44th Division. The latter had destroyed the bridges, then withdrawn toward Arras and Bapaume according to Lord Gort's plan. The Belgian soldiers marching amidst enormous trucks soon blocked the roads, already congested with refugees who had been turned back at the French border. The inflexible border guards had even been so rude as to call them "dirty Bosch!" Those poor people had left everything behind and were wandering aimlessly, demoralized by the constant air raids and showers of leaflets from enemy planes. There were also those among them who repeatedly whispered, "Why don't we do what the Dutch did? They had the right idea: they stopped fighting! Everyone is free to return to their own homes in Holland!"

No drama is complete without an element of farce. One Belgian army motorcyclist was served with a summons from a policeman, who was quite uninterested in special circumstances. He had been called by an irate woman who had found the messenger's motorcycle parked temporarily in her garage.

Once the French 60th Division had been relieved from the sector they occupied on the Schelde by the Belgians, they too retreated to Dunkirk, where they were to defend the canals. They had seen their Belgian comrades fend off the enemy for two days —if it is any consolation, I am talking about the bad conduct of some of our French combatants—and the men from Sluiskil, Zelzate and other areas were sincerely complimented, "You Belgians fight well!"

———

I have already mentioned Senior Sergeant Fortunat Thiébaut of the 32nd Group of Divisional Reconnaissance Infantry, who, after "a mad race through the night" on his captain's suggestion, was shocked to learn at Abbeville that the enemy had reached the sea before him. In order to refute a common accusation following the defeat of the French campaign of 1940, which describes the soldiers as a bunch of cowards and deserters, when their heroic deeds were often praised by German generals, I should like to quote his account:

"While we were at Saint-Pol-sur-Ternoise, we were ordered by Admiral Abrial, commander of ground and sea forces at Calais, to go there as quickly as possible to organize the defense of the citadel. Our transport and arms were intact and we were even helped by two light tanks and two armored cars, which had been abandoned at the side of the road.

"During the evening of May 22, we arrived at Calais under bursts of automatic gunfire, probably from the German fifth column. We struck back forcefully and captured the citadel. I don't know who was in command there, but we felt very ill at ease. This citadel, built by Vauban, was surrounded by ramparts and inside it were huge buildings used as barracks and depots and various other constructions.

"After evacuating civilians and some unarmed military men, we set about organizing the defenses, placing our tanks and armored cars at the entrances and making gun emplacements on top of the ramparts. My troops were positioned in the northeast corner of the citadel, which had a bastion and recesses. Our orders were to hold it come what may. Unfortunately, we did not have a single heavy gun, not even a high-angle gun. The most powerful weapons were our Hotchkiss machine-guns and our Bren guns.

"A search of the shelters and depots produced an 81 mm. mortar and two 60 mm. but no ammunition. Looking further we were able to find some shells, fuses, charges and detonators. In this way we built up quite an arsenal of usable projectiles which were most efficient against the Germans.

"There was a British 39 mm. cannon on the ramparts we had to defend. The gunners were there too, which was a blessing, until at about 16:00, on May 23, when a British sergeant came and removed the breech, various pins and carried the whole thing away, including the gunners. Having a premonition as to why the sergeant had come, I asked him to leave the cannon with the ammunition, but he did not answer. Meanwhile I learned that four similar cannons placed on gun sites on the ramparts had also been removed. "The British are retreating," I said to myself. We did not see them again throughout the battle, apart from five or six, whom the Germans forced out with the butts of their rifles when they captured the citadel.

"We continued to organize our defenses that Wednesday, May 22. We dug out gun emplacements on the ridge of the ramparts and each gun was placed to fulfill some specific function. Soon the sky filled with German planes, which pounded the French and British defense positions around the city as well as the port installations and a few small boats plying the coast. The next day it was our turn: all day bombs dropped from aircraft and shells battered the citadel."

# A LETTER, A SPEECH AND AN ORDER

In reply to the king's clear and frank letter sent on May 22 from his GHQ at Saint-André-lez-Bruges, Prime Minister Hubert Pierlot's reply was a veritable smokescreen. He drafted his letter the following day, May 23.

"Your Majesty,

"The greatest wish of my colleagues and I is to do all we can to lighten the burden shouldered by our King. We would be most distressed if anything in our attitude could have caused Your Majesty any additional worries. But, if Your Majesty will allow me, I should like to take up the question in his letter of May 22.

"I have never concealed from Your Majesty that I cannot share His opinion on the Constitution, which entrusts the command of the army to the King. That text makes no exception to the general and absolute rule, according to which the Government alone is responsible for the actions of its Head of State. But I do not wish to dwell on this point. It really becomes rather academic as soon as the King admits that his Government should not be kept ignorant of the military situation and 'has a right to take a keen interest because of the political implications.'

"In fact there should be no watertight compartments separating military and political problems. The conduct of this war has a direct bearing on the future of this country. Apart from operational techniques, the sound practice of which should be left for the commander to decide, the Government is answerable for the war. In fact our Constitution states that the ministers, and none other, are responsible.

"As for the manner in which matters have been conducted since the beginning of hostilities, Mr. Spaak and I must have expressed ourselves rather badly if the King understood that we were accusing him of keeping us in the dark. But it is true, nevertheless, that at times we had very scant knowledge with which to understand the situation. In the morning Your Majesty was kind enough to put us in the picture through General Denis, and we are grateful for this.

"Apart from that, after the meetings at Breendonck mentioned by Your Majesty, I must admit I was extremely worried about the decisions I thought I perceived. I had the distinct impression after those two meetings at Breendonck that the army's retreat into a corner with their backs to the sea, cut off from the Allies and forced to surrender, was not just an eventuality forced on us by circumstance, but was actually preferable to the inconvenience of fleeing our own territory. Everything my colleagues and I said was in the light of this conviction. And so we insisted, in the vital interests of this country, that Your Majesty should not join His army, which was on the verge of losing its freedom. It seems that during the meeting at Saint-André we did not completely understand Your Majesty. I apologize for this misunderstanding which was so painful to Your Majesty, and I sincerely regret the displeasure it caused. I must add, for our part, that if our points of view now appear to be the same, we were right to believe that there were different nuances of meaning, which led us to tell Your Majesty what was troubling us.

"These thoughts would not be complete without my mentioning the meeting at Ypres. Given the great importance of the decisions to be taken, I had expressed the wish that my colleagues and I be present at Your Majesty's disposal during the meeting. I was not expecting to take part in the discussion on the military situation, but I would have thought it natural—this is my personal opinion—that the Minister of Defense, General Denis, be included. I would have wished to be present at the end of the meeting to hear

General Weygand sum up his opinions. However faithfully Your Majesty may have given us an account of that meeting, nothing can replace hearing and drawing conclusions from it at first-hand. Moreover, I would have had the opportunity to ask questions, and ask for explanations, instead of leaving Ypres still full of uncertainty because we only received a summary. I make no bones of the fact that this was one of the hardest times of our lives and not just because of the outcome of events, but also because we felt we had not completely fulfilled our duties as statesmen.

"I know that this is not the way things were done in the last war, nor is it practiced by the other countries at war, where the Government—or those ministers best qualified by their positions—while not interfering in the directing of operations, are not kept away from such Councils in which the general conduct of the war is determined.

"We regret we have recently been unable to keep Your Majesty better informed on the external political situation. This does not stem from the Minister of Foreign Affairs' lack of personnel, but from the difficulties of communication. We have no direct contact with Paris and Le Havre; we have not had any couriers; we can only call London on the telephone. We are very grateful to Your Majesty for having allowed us to stay at His side, but it means that government activity will slow down. Despite the inconvenience, we have no regrets about the decision as we feel our place to be on Belgian territory as long as our presence here is possible.

"My colleagues, and particularly the Minister of Internal Affairs, have benefited from their stay in Flanders to speed up supplies, see to the relocation of refugees and answer a host of questions that are very important to the people. I have asked Mr. Van der Poorten, as soon as circumstances permit, to file a report on this matter which should be of interest to Your Majesty.

"As for my colleagues who have left Belgium, I do not think we can criticize them. If there were any grounds for criticism, I would have to take the blame, since they left at my request. I wish to point out that the Government did not leave Brussels until the minute before the enemy attacked. Nor could I have delayed sending them and the administration to Le Havre without risking their being turned back or endangered in the operation zones.

"We have done all we can to avoid the continued flight of the people frightened by memories of 1914 and the example of Poland. The most crowded centers have mostly been cleared, and food supplies are distributed regularly.

"I am embarrassed at the length of this letter. I hope it may persuade Your Majesty that in times such as these, his ministers have no other thought but to serve him, no other motive than their devotion to Your Majesty and their country."

This assurance ended with the ritual form of politeness: "I have the honor of being Your Majesty's most respectful, most loyal and most humble servant," which in these circumstances struck a very strange chord.

---

I have retained the capital letters which were liberally used in this long letter, and I was very tempted to add my own question marks and exclamation marks. To mention only the penultimate paragraph, if the king had not pulled his ministers back by their coattails (they were ready to leave Brussels on May 14) the population in the capital would not have needed to panic by reviving "memories of 1914" and "the example of Poland." But there was worse to come.

Did Pierlot consider it his duty, before the opening of the Ypres Conference, to influence General Weygand unfavorably against the king, something he had already done the previous morning when he made a telephone call to the new commander in chief over the head of the king, the commander of the army? I am inclined to believe that the distinguished Mr. Spaak—who was also not averse to calling himself "a very loyal and humble servant of the king"—put a drop of vitriol into Pierlot's ink which gave a special flavor to his letter. I will extract a few passages.

Referring to the meeting he had had with the king on May 20, together with Spaak, Van der Poorten and General Denis, at which he had voiced strong disapproval of the latter, Pierlot wrote: "I apologize for this misunderstanding which was painful to Your Majesty, and I sincerely regret the displeasure it caused." It was a very fleeting sincerity, as shown five days later by his own words in Paris and reinforced by the Havas dispatch.

Did Pierlot really believe—I am reluctant to say "sincerely"— that the minister of defense should have been with the king in his discussions with General Weygand, General Billotte and Lord Gort on measures which were of the utmost importance and which should be settled as soon as possible? The wisest thing General Denis ever said was on the morning of May 22, after the king explained the military situation with the aid of maps and why he had decided to fight on the Lys. At that time, the minister of defense gave the impression that he understood matters when he said it was the only thing that could be done. But he brilliantly sidestepped that statement in the early hours of May 25, as we shall see.

Pierlot complained he had been unable to hear General Weygand "sum up his opinions." That shows total ignorance of the conditions under which the Ypres Conference was held. General Gamelin had just been replaced by General Weygand, who had left Beirut hastily at dawn on the eighteenth, arriving in Paris the next day after an exhausting journey, followed by another equally tiring trip on the twenty-first. He had to return as quickly as possible to Vincennes GHQ, and was unable to meet Lord Gort, whose presence at the conference was essential. Did Pierlot, Spaak and Denis doubt that their king—who almost certainly was better aware of the military situation than Weygand, who had only just been appointed to supreme command—would not do his best to tell them very precisely what decisions had been taken? If they were not informed daily of the situation by General Denis, whose fault was that?

"I know that this is not the way things were done in the last war," was Pierlot's comment: this totally erroneous allusion was made to contrast Leopold with the lofty person of King Albert, his father. We know very well how the "Roi-Chevalier" put Prime Minister de Brocqueville in his place in a very similar set of circumstances.

"Vanity, vanity, all is vanity. . ." Though I have never met Pierlot, I was inflicted with the presence of King Leopold's ex-minister of foreign affairs in a train from Brussels to Paris. His words, and the very pores of his face, exuded satisfaction with being the important Mr. Spaak himself, and as I looked at him I felt that the passage in Ecclesiastes was still applicable.

———

Spaak had delivered a speech full of self-justification to the Belgian ministers at Limoges town hall on Friday, May 31. It was the day after the Havas dispatch, which accused Leopold of a "premeditated crime." Without denying that it was treason—"the very word burns my mouth and sticks in my throat," he said—Spaak asserted it had not been "premeditated a long time before," and justified his tautology in the following way:

"On the Tuesday following the outbreak of war the prime minister was summoned to GHQ. Although I was not present at that meeting, I can say that our anxieties began from that moment. The prime minister, General Denis and I went to GHQ two days later, on May 16. There was an appalling atmosphere of defeatism. From that time on, the highest authorities in command of the armies were convinced that nothing could be done, that not only the Belgian army but also the Allied armies had lost. This conviction led us to conclude that the war would end in one or two weeks with a general and total surrender.

"The prime minister was alarmed at the king's suggestion in their conversation that the army should retreat. I should say here that it was necessary then for the Belgian army to retreat, not only because it was defeated, but because there was a breach in the south, the French front was broken and it was necessary to avoid being separated and establish a defendable line. From that time, the king—and this is the last time I shall praise him—with a foresight that now seems almost uncanny, predicted what operations would take place. He was certain the German columns would not march on Paris but would make for the sea, and he felt that not only his army but the Anglo-French army, too, would be surrounded.

"The prime minister immediately said that if such an event did take place, there was only one thing to do: retreat from north to south and under no circumstances should we be cut off from the French and British troops, if possible, reserving two or three divisions out of the whole army to continue the struggle on the other side. Alas! from that moment we realized we did not see eye to eye on military matters. Not all the responsibility lies with the Belgian command, far from it. At that time the king scrupulously—in my opinion, too scrupulously—followed the orders given him by the French high command. It is a fact that the latter reacted desperately slowly, that it took several days for it to realize that our army was in very real danger, and it allowed the left flank to trail in northern Belgium when conditions were becoming hourly and daily more difficult to remedy. When the king said he was only following orders from high command, we told him, 'A passive attitude is not enough. If you feel the orders you receive are insufficient, you should initiate others and take the necessary steps to save what you can!' "

—

I have already said this before, but as Clemenceau put it, politicians tend to believe that war is too serious a matter to be left in the hands of the military. There is a parliamentary "bad smell" in the fact that what Spaak had called "the left flank" was the left wing of the French army which, while Spaak was still speaking to his colleagues at Limoges, was protecting the reembarkation of the British Expeditionary Force, the very reason it was allowed "to trail in northern Belgium." Setting himself up as a stategist, the minister of foreign affairs was advising the king to under no circumstances be cut off from the French and British troops, and criticizing him for having "too scrupulously followed the orders given him by the French high command" (which alone had the power of deciding in the last resort). He then said that "with a foresight that now seems almost uncanny," the king realized the enemy's intentions and saw that the French and British armies risked being surrounded. Pierlot's opinion was the same as Spaak's, as we know he wanted to "take the necessary steps" to save what could be saved of the Belgian army. What did that mean—supposing that such a maneuver in a strictly military sense was possible—except that having requested the support guaranteed by Great Britain and France to help repel the enemy from his country, Leopold would then have to dishonor himself and say to the Allies, "I'm sorry, my friends, but I'm pulling out from the disaster that's waiting for you!"

The kernel of the whole affair is that Pierlot and Spaak were both accusing the king of negotiating for a separate peace treaty with Hitler's Germany. Before Spaak spoke to the assembly at Limoges, he had listened unflinchingly while the mayor, called Betoulle, welcomed him and his colleagues with the words, "King Leopold has not only betrayed his Allies, but also his nation . . . It is easy to understand how disgusted we are at the king's crime." In his own way, Spaak really had gall. He ended his speech with a patriotic finale, in which he repeated the entire Belgian government's desire to continue, come what may, the struggle beside the Allies. If you read in the appendix the article in the London *Evening Standard* of September 27, 1940, written by Jaspar, minister of public health, you will see that this stirring, martial spirit deserted him less than three weeks later, when General de Gaulle launched his June 18 appeal to France.

———

While Pierlot was drafting his long letter to the king on May 23, news that the enemy had mounted a strong attack on Boulogne arrived at the king's GHQ at Saint-André-lez-Bruges. The king immediately ordered a detachment of one French infantry division to the Gravelines to Saint-Omer canal, supported by part of the 16th Corps, to stop the German armored vehicles from crossing the canal.

One hour later, a brief message was received at Vincennes GHQ: "Mechanized column entered Béthune tonight." The king did not receive this information; he had only been told that "Blanchard's army was awaiting orders" at Béthune. When he learned that this was not so, that Lord Gort wanted the Belgian army to relieve his troops on the French front from Menin to Maulde with a view to forming a defensive front on the La Bassée Canal, Leopold replied, "Since morning, we have already sent, of our own accord, one infantry division from the French 16th Corps to the Gravelines-Saint Omer waterway. We shall place one more division on the Menin-Comines front on the Lys on the morning of the twenty-fifth. We cannot do any better."

The king's "almost uncanny foresight" accurately predicted that the British Expeditionary Force and the French 1st Army would be forced to fight with their backs to the sea in order to cover the Calais straits. Events were hurtling forward so fast that it was now impossible to consider the Lys front as one stage in the retreat to the Yser. The Belgian army would have to wage a decisive battle on the Lys.

———

When General Weygand was informed early in the morning of Thursday, May 23, that enemy armored troops were moving up north from the Somme, he upheld his order to attack and concluded his message to General Doumenc as follows:

"We must exploit the enemy's present position immediately. Make sure that the maneuver is understood by all, and that they fight with initiative, determination and unfailing steadfastness."

At 11:50 he broadcast his first "General order to the French armies":

"The Government has entrusted me with the position of Chief of Staff for Defense and Commander in Chief over all operations. I count on every one of you to carry out your duties in every situation with determination. No failure, from whichever quarter, will be tolerated. Resist strongly. Return every blow by an even bigger one and remember, only he who strikes the hardest can gain victory.

(signed) Weygand."

This stirring appeal was not heard by all: less than twenty-four hours later, Vincennes GHQ was informed that between forty to fifty officers from the 1st Sector (Lille) had "retreated" to London. General Doumenc immediately replied, "As Lille was in danger, these officers must be considered as traitors and deserters. Relieve them of their command." Barely ten minutes later, the government announced, according to the well-known formula used by politicians to avoid responsibility in any situation, "An inquiry will be held."

# THE BATTLE ON THE LYS

The Belgian rearguard, which stayed to cover the canal from Ghent to Terneuzen, saw the first enemy shells bombard Zelzate at 9:30 in the morning of May 23, followed by an air raid in the afternoon. The area soon became a blazing furnace. Retaliating with the only three guns remaining, the 3rd Battery of the 18th Artillery fired almost two thousand rounds before nightfall.

At 14:00 the German 256th Division attempted to cross the canal, but their assault was repelled by the 2nd Guides and the 2nd Bicycle Riflemen. On the other hand, the 37th Regiment in the south was overpowered by the Wehrmacht's 208th Division. Taken prisoner with his company, Lieutenant Genin managed to escape and return to Belgian lines with valuable information. Major Gerling of the 32nd Regiment led his men in a counter-attack and was killed, whilst the 37th continued to fight bravely. Sent to reinforce the 11th Division, the 14th Regiment advanced under German cannon fire and bomb explosions. Its lst Battalion led by Major Goormachtigh reached the canal and thrust back the German 309th Infantry. The 2nd Battalion led by Major Eppe pushed the German 338th Infantry back to the other side of the canal and reached Terdonk to save commanding Captain Boits's company from the enemy's grasp. Some elements of the German 309th Infantry had penetrated the breach and were threatening the 2nd Guides' flank. They were pushed back three times by Captain Waucquez of the 18th Artillery, who had transformed his gunners into foot soldiers for the occasion. After ten o'clock at night, with the help of the 2nd Lancers' Bren gun carriers, the guides and riflemen retreated with the 13th Division.

Things were not going too well at the Ghent bridgehead, where the municipal council was opposed to defending the city. Thanks to them, the rumor that Ghent was an open city spread to soldiers of the 16th and 18th Divisions, and some had even allowed their arms to be confiscated by the police. When Colonel Van Loocke, commander of the 41st Regiment, heard about this he tried to restore order but was shot by a German submachine-gun, as was his adjutant Lieutenant Lafosse. To prevent the enemy from infiltrating the city the engineers blew up the bridges on the Ghent to Bruges canal.

On Friday morning, May 24, the Belgians occupied their new positions. Due to the battles fought in the last two weeks and the costly retreats, the twenty-two divisions had now been reduced to an actual count of fifteen.

Just like the Lys, the Lys branch canal was only a ditch some twenty meters wide, and to maintain the water level, the Balgerhoeke Bridge, which was too close to the locks, had to be destroyed. The wooded banks gave good cover to the enemy who took advantage of the meanders of the Lys River (which was no more than fifty centimeters deep), bordered by thick undergrowth and built up areas on the right bank. The Belgian large caliber artillery was reduced to four gun sites on tracks with a poor supply of shells left over from deliveries made in 1918 by the defeated German Imperial Army. The bulk of the Belgian troops were massed on the canal, opposite General von Küchler's 18th Army. Whereas a division in a defensive position usually covers a six-kilometer front at the most, it was spread over eleven kilometers on the Lys, for it seemed unlikely that von Reichenau's VIth Army would join in the attack as it was fighting General Prioux's 1st Army.

Numbers were not the only problem. There was also the physical condition of the men, who had suffered severe hardships since the beginning of the campaign. Their morale was very low, undermined by a series of retreats that led to the gradual abandonment of national territory. Then there were the refugees milling on the roads, desperately seeking some place of shelter. Moreover, the Allied troops had vanished, and the absence of the British fighter planes left the ground troops open to the Luftwaffe's dive-bomber attacks. . . . The men had just begun to dig trenches on the left bank of the Lys when they were caught in enemy fire from the Germans' forward units. Woe betide the wounded! The army only had two hundred ambulances—some of them ordinary delivery trucks that had been requisitioned—and when Torhout Station was bombed, the evacuation of the wounded (by trucks) was only possible thanks to a railway battalion. One of the Red Cross trains sent to France returned with one medical student aboard, representing the entire staff of the health services.

———

On Thursday, May 23, a Panzer group of five armored divisions arrived from the Ardennes at General von Kleist's orders and reached the Channel coast, as Boulogne was occupied by General Veiel's 2nd Panzer Division. This thrust forward created a corridor, bounded on the south by the Somme, behind which stood General Frère's 7th Army. He had been unable to implement General Weygand's counteroffensive to the north, and had a difficult time trying to "seal" the strong bridgeheads set up by the Germans on the river's left bank.

To the north, the corridor was bounded by what the British Expeditionary Force called the "Canal Line," bordered by the waterways and canals linking Lens, Douai, Béthune, Aire-sur-la-Lys and Saint-Omer, ending at Gravelines between Calais and Dunkirk, where General Schaal's 10th and General Kirchner's 1st Divisions were now pushing toward. While General von Kleist's Panzer divisions were waiting to charge in the same direction, at 12:31 on May 24, a telephone call was received from Hitler, who was then visiting General von Rundstedt's headquarters at Charleville. He ordered them to halt in front of the Canal Line held by Lord Gort. Why?

The reason for this decision, which upset German battle plans and helped implement the "Dunkirk miracle"—the evacuation of nine British divisions and ten thousand or so Frenchmen—is still a matter of controversy. I tend to agree with Fabribeckers's theory in his remarkable book *La Campagne de l'Armée Belge en 1940* (*The Belgian Army's Campaign in 1940*). I have taken the liberty of adding my own notes and comments to the following quotation:

"The reason for this order is still unknown, but almost certainly it was due to one or all of the following.

1. To bring Britain round to signing a peace treaty by sparing its army. (Hitler had a real admiration for England and had reserved a very special role for it in his "New Europe." He was to offer England very favorable peace terms in July 1940.)

2. To raise the prestige of Marshal Göring and his Luftwaffe above that of the generals and their armies. (Göring was a member of the Nationalist Socialist party, and in fact one of its first members. This was not the case with many of the Wehrmacht generals of whom Hitler was wary. He was jealous of their success, rather like Stalin who saw the Red Army generals as rivals—a worry that was spared Mussolini. Hitler went further than the Kremlin dictator by urging "Reichsführer" SS Heinrich Himmler to create the Waffen-SS, a "party" army, to offset the regular army.)

3. To avoid using the Panzers in this marshy canal region where Corporal Hitler of the Bavarian 16th Infantry had seen British tanks bogged down during the Poelkapelle offensive in October 1917.

4. Fear following the Arras counteroffensive.

5. Preparation for the second phase of the battle in France. After destroying Army Group I in Flanders, the Panzer divisions would be needed for a rapid attack across the Somme, behind which the French and British could reinforce their troops by drawing recruits from the colonies as they had done in 1914."

I believe all of these hypotheses contain an element of truth.

Hitler was wrong in supposing the British Expeditionary Force would fight behind the Somme, but it is not unlikely for the former corporal of the German Imperial Army to want to take revenge on France for the defeat in 1918. The three extraordinary photographs of him taken on Friday, June 21, six weeks after the offensive began in the west, when he has just been informed of the French army's surrender, are good proof of that. In the first, he is clasping his hand to his heart as though overcome with joy; in the second, he is beating time with a rolled up paper like the conductor of an orchestra; in the third, he is dancing a triumphant jig. Hitler wanted to humiliate France before tearing it apart in the way prescribed by his astrologer Alfred Rosenberg, the Nazi theorist. He had planned to place three "colonization" centers for "Westland" (the new Lotharingia) at Amiens, Laon and Dijon. In his eyes, crossing the Somme was a major objective. I heard from Madame Brucamps that he went in person to Yzeux to harangue his troops before launching the assault which he hoped would crush France once and for all. "The Germans already looked victorious," she said, "and yet they seemed afraid to cross the Somme."

———

Two remarkable works have shed new light on the German messages that were decoded by the Enigma machine during World War II. The first, written by Gustave Bertrand and published by Librairie Plon in 1972, is called *Enigma, ou la Plus Grande Enigme de la Guerre* (*Enigma, or the Greatest Enigma of the War*). It did not receive the praise it deserved, perhaps because the author was a member of the special services of national defense, whose activities are little known for political reasons. There are many people who, after France was liberated, made a career of lending a new significance to the word "Resistance," one that is not connected with the fight against the enemy but against Marshal Pétain. Two years later, a second book entitled *The Ultra Secret*, written by an officer in the British Secret Service, F. W.

Winterbotham, was published by Weidenfeld and Nicolson. It also deals with the Enigma machine, but unfortunately. makes no mention of the important part played by the French special services of national defense in its discovery and use. But it was not enough just to decode the enemy's orders; it is obvious that France's weakened condition prevented it from reacting as well as the British and American general staffs.

I will, therefore, use Winterbotham's book (I have previously quoted from it with reference to the eve of May 10, 1940) to illustrate a point which played a most important role in the war in the west. I would go as far as to say it actually sowed the seeds for the collapse of Hitler's formidable power, due to an error in judgment made by the master of the Third Reich that Friday, May 24, 1940. If Hitler had released his Panzer divisions to annihilate the British Expeditionary Force, his offers of peace would certainly have been accepted by the British government. This would have enabled him to use all his ground and air troops to attack the U.S.S.R. in June. Besides, if Great Britain had signed a peace treaty with Germany, how could the United States have come to the aid of Europe, presupposing that they felt inclined to enter the conflict under those conditions?

ULTRA was the code name given by the British Secret Service to their means of decoding almost all the radio messages sent to every rank in the German command, including Hitler himself. Based on actual facts, Winterbotham's gripping tale throws light on the decisions made by the Anglo-Americans, since they were able to read the enemy's most secret messages like an open book. "Very often, we were able to read the enemy's messages a few minutes after their transmission, and they would be duly relayed to the interested parties," who, except for General Montgomery, certainly took advantage of them.

On Thursday, May 23, 1940, the British knew from ULTRA that General von Brauchitsch (named two years previously as commander of the ground troops) had ordered General von Bock (commander of Army Group B who after crushing Holland in four days prepared to do the same to Belgium) and General von Rundstedt (commander of Army Group A who had formulated the plan that crushed the French army in the Ardennes) to "continue their encircling maneuver in force" in order to annihilate the French Army Group I, the British Expeditionary Force and King Leopold's army. To put this into effect von Rundstedt had to rush immediately to Ostend while von Bock supported him by moving north.

During the same day, May 23, ULTRA revealed that von Brauchitsch had asked General von Kluge (commander of the 4th Army that was part of Army Group A) to take his orders from von Bock and march north. At first London thought this was only a tactical order, whereas von Brauchitsch—to whom von Rundstedt had never acknowledged receiving the order—suspected the leader of Army Group A of having ignored his orders.

Von Brauchitsch was right. Deciding it would be wiser to regroup his armies, von Rundstedt had spoken to Hitler, who was visiting his headquarters that day, and was delighted when Hitler cancelled von Brauchitsch's order. This suddenly immobilized all the Panzer divisions, which were told to remain in position until further orders. Winterbotham had once spoken to Hitler before the war, and he points out that such a step was rather out of character:

"It seems to me there was some other reason for his decision, and I at once understood what this little man hoped to achieve. Since 1934, when I had first met him, he had expressed his earnest wish to remain at peace with Great Britain. I was sure he was afraid to have England as an enemy, and that now he had almost finished France off, he wanted to establish peace in the west before pursuing the great mission so dear to his heart—if indeed he had a heart!—which was the destruction of Communist Russia. I felt that day he was deliberately allowing the BEF to return to England, for as far as we know, he never gave further orders to his armored divisions to resume their advance toward the

British Expeditionary Force. I felt he thought that war against England was no longer a military matter but now rested in the political arena. I was also certain he had no intention of putting the BEF behind barbed wires, as that would have been a constant source of anxiety to him, when his wish was to conclude a peace treaty with Great Britain. . . . We know now that after ordering the Panzers to cease their encircling movement, he told his general staff in France (according to a German general's eye-witness account) exactly what he had confided to me in 1934: that England's great civilization which had benefited the world should be allowed to survive, and all he hoped was that Britain would recognize Germany's position in Europe. His aim was to make peace with Great Britain on an honorable basis. His offers were rejected because he had completely misunderstood the British mentality."

The order Hitler sent from Charleville was not appreciated by German general staff. According to General von Rundstedt, his Army Group A was caught between the devil and the deep blue sea, while General von Bock's Army Group B was ordered to send its tanks and mechanized divisions toward the Valenciennes Salient. Von Bock decided to attack Courtrai anyway, just south of the Belgian front on the Lys.

—

That Friday, May 24, less than five hours before Hitler abruptly changed battle plans, Vincennes GHQ received the following message from Army Group I at 8:55: "The British abandoned Arras at dawn, without any order to this effect from the French. There is a large gap in the line. We fear some of the British units that have left may be used elsewhere." At 16:00 a message was received from the 2nd Bureau, which proved they were working well since only a mere three and a half hours had elapsed since Hitler's decision. "We presume that Germany intends to surround Tourcoing and Lille by a maneuver from west to east and one from Courtrai." This also showed that the Führer's orders had been promptly carried out, and that compared to the French transmission network, the enemy's communication system worked excellently.

General von Reichenau's VIth Army intended to push toward Ypres to cut off the Belgian army from the British Expeditionary Force. The courage of the 8th Infantry and the 2nd Ardennes Division put paid to that plan. The following day, von Reichenau's army had to contend with counterattacks from the 12th Infantry Division on the Lys branch canal and the 1st Ardennes Division on the Lys. But King Leopold watched anxiously as his resources dwindled with the fighting. He hoped, in vain, that the British Expeditionary Force would attack the German flank that was pressing toward Ypres. But the British Expeditionary Force had only one objective, and that was to carry out Operation Dynamo.

—

"Lord Gort assured me later," says Winterbotham, "that it was Brauchitsch's first message sent on May 23 that influenced him in his decision to retreat to the sea as quickly as possible. He knew that if the BEF were destroyed or captured, nothing could protect Britain from a Nazi invasion as long as the Wehrmacht could cross the Channel. A soldier at heart, Gort was determined to save his men and through them his country from the danger that threatened the entire Western world. The same went for Churchill, for whom Brauchitsch's messages on May 23 acted as the signal to hasten Operation Dynamo and assemble all boats capable of making the voyage from Dunkirk. Thanks to ULTRA, we knew that Brauchitsch was not bluffing, and the fact that others were convinced of the danger hovering over us made ULTRA an important new factor in the conduct of the war.

"Whatever Weygand's real motives were at this juncture, when he declared to the British that the reconstituted French 7th Army was going to launch an attack in the north to free us from the grip of the Panzers, while asking the BEF to launch an attack toward the south, we can at least presume that Weygand was completely unaware of the true situation. Some people have claimed he was looking for a pretext to make the British responsible for France's defeat, given all the evidence that Gort could not risk mounting a similar attack from the north at such a late time. There is no doubt that had he done so, the British Expeditionary Force would have been wiped out.

"Rundstedt, a wily, experienced old fox, who had brought the BEF and the Belgian army to exactly where he wanted, had only to deal with one French army which was in a state of total disintegration. He knew he could finish them off where and when he wanted. . . . Lord Gort found he had the respite he needed and was determined to lead the BEF to the beaches of Dunkirk. Without wishing to detract from the merit of that epic evacuation, I am certain that if Hitler had left his Panzers and air force alone, which were both intoxicated by their successive victories, the little boats that left for England would have had very few passengers aboard."

———

General Weygand, completely ignorant of Operation Dynamo, was most surprised at the message recorded at 8:55 that May 24 at Vincennes GHQ, which came from General Blanchard, the successor of General Billotte as head of Army Group I. The British withdrawal to the Haute Deule Canal, effected without prior warning during the night of May 23 to 24, seemed to him "to have immediate impact on the offensive of Army Group I."

"This withdrawal extended the gap between the Allied armies from forty to over sixty kilometers. It reduced the width of the front leading the attack by three-quarters, and as a result reduced the chances of penetrating the enemy. The depth of the rearguard behind the 1st Army south of the Scarpe River was reduced by half. Besides, this action had considerable repercussions on morale, as it gave the impression that the British Expeditionary Force had renounced all participation in the offensive."

General Weygand continues:

"A commander can only decide an action, leaving aside the question of temperament for a moment, in the light of what he knows. On May 21, General Billotte told me nothing that might have made me change my plan. On May 22, King Leopold agreed to it, and the prime minister (i.e., Churchill, who claimed it was his plan) and the chief of British general staff had fully concurred with my views at Vincennes. But Lord Gort had a different opinion and said so in London on May 19 (the day before Churchill suggested that as a 'precautionary measure' the admiralty should take steps to assure the repatriation of Lord Gort's British Expeditionary Force). Such considerations make me regret even more that we were unable to meet at Ypres on May 21. The commander of the British Expeditionary Force would certainly have let me know that the difficulties he envisaged might prevent the realization of my plan. If he ever mentioned it to General Billotte, the secret is buried with them. Since he was unable to meet me that day, and especially after the accident that befell Billotte on the night of May 21, should not Lord Gort have come to see me, or at least sent his chief of staff, in view of the seriousness of the situation?"

Considering the information he had, we can understand why Lord Gort was embarrassed to meet Weygand face to face or through an intermediary. At 16:30 on Friday, May 24, a message received at Vincennes GHQ confirmed the one received thirty minutes previously: "There are four Panzer divisions in the Arras, Saint-Omer, Boulogne, Hesdin and Saint-Pol areas (Boulogne is in flames) and four more in the Cambrai region."

The same message continued: "It is imperative that someone important be sent to raise the morale of Army Group I and especially the 1st Army: the men are exhausted after eight days of continuous fighting."

That message clearly indicates the distress of the French soldiers. But where could the "someone important" be found? Surely not among the politicians, those puppets who despite everything were still so full of their own self-importance. The new commander in chief? Weygand was totally absorbed in planning the battles that he had only the bare outlines of, and he could not possibly leave Vincennes GHQ. Who then? Someone like de Gaulle?

At first it was decided that de Gaulle's 4th Armored Division would cross the Somme and lead the attack to the north, then it was to be used to cut back the German bridgehead at Amiens on the left bank of the river. Finally the 4th Armored Division was to be placed at the disposal of General Altmayer, who had left the reserves to take command of the 10th Army, to attack the German bridgehead at Abbeville. Colonel de Gaulle could not be in all places at once. Besides, he was relatively unknown and only appreciated by the men directly under his command.

---

On Friday, May 24, the battle had flared up on the Belgian front from Menin in the south as far as Eeklo in the far north near the Dutch border. King Leopold's army was faced with nine German divisions, which were later reinforced by the 3rd Panzer Division. The attack was particularly fierce on the Menin-Deinze line, and the king saw that the enemy intended to push through his right flank and cut it off from the British Expeditionary Force. To his great sorrow, as was reported to Lord Gort, he did not have the means to extend the front as far as Comines. He received confirmation from his liaison with the BEF that the latter had withdrawn from Arras and was moving north because two Panzer divisions and a German mechanized division had reached the zone between Boulogne, Saint-Omer and Saint-Pol-sur-Ternoise. This meant that the Belgian lines in the rear were in serious danger. So the king ordered the installation of an antitank barrier on the Ypres-Furnes-Les Moeres line. At 22:30 a call from the chief of general staff announced that the 1st and 3rd infantry divisions were turning back in disorder as some officers had panicked. The commander of the 4th Army asked the king for instructions.

The reply was as dry as the occasion deserved: "Formal and general order: stay where you are. Tell the commander of the 4th Army that he leaves on pain of death." The warning produced immediate results: ten minutes later, the chief of general staff telephoned, "I gave the categorical order to stay in position. So be it."

———

During that difficult day of Friday, May 24, King Leopold was not visited by any of his ministers, and I hardly suppose he was sorry, as this was not the time for idle chatter. An hour and a quarter after he sent the order to the commander of the 4th Army, the king received a call from Pierlot, who said that the British minister of foreign affairs, Lord Halifax, had telegrammed Admiral Keyes, asking him to make arrangements for the Belgian king's departure for England. It was not until 00:25 that night that the king was able to meet Lord Keyes, who denied any knowledge of the telegram.

The admiral of the fleet had acted according to his conscience. Responding to the Belgian minister of finance, Gutt, who was then in London, Lord Halifax had indeed telegraphed Sir Roger Keyes begging him to prevent the king from being captured if there was any imminent danger of that happening. But estimating that for the good of all the king's duty was to encourage the army by his presence, the admiral decided to postpone relaying that message. Returning to the matter at one o'clock in the morning of Saturday, May 25, Pierlot called Van den Heuvel, the king's aide-de-camp, to ask him what the king had decided. Major Van den Heuvel replied that the king was still directing his troops, then added what he had been ordered to say, "Of course, the king wishes the Belgian ministers to be free to act as they think best." They did not need to be told twice.

# THE MORNING OF MAY 25

It was not yet dawn on Saturday, May 25, 1940, when Major Defraiteur and Captain Ducq of the Operations Section of general
staff were visited by four important people at the Saint-André-lez-
Bruges GHQ. The visitors were no less than Pierlot, Spaak, Van
der Poorten and Denis, who wished to know the situation at the
front and the maneuvers that had been carried out the previous
day. They also asked to see the information map which showed the
location of the units engaged in battle with the enemy. They
exclaimed vociferously to the two officers that the army could not
resist for more than two days, and maybe even twenty-four hours.
Major Defraiteur—who later became minister of defense in
Belgium—reported the visit in a signed statement dated May
29, 1940, in response to the speeches broadcast over French radio
by Reynaud and Pierlot the day before. He concludes in this way:
"On the morning of the twenty-fifth the ministers stated that the
Belgian army was incapable of resisting more than a day or two."
This statement of a qualified witness shows how untrue was the
claim made by Pierlot and Denis on the evening of May 27 in
Paris, that they were "in a daze."

When the four ministers had given their opinions, Major Defraiteur asked them if they wished to speak to General Michiels,
but they declined: Pierlot and his colleagues wished to see the king
without delay. While the officer got in touch with Wynendaele
Château to ask whether the king was there and if he was willing
to receive a visit so early, the ministers asked Captain Ducq about

the condition of the roads to France, fearing the bridges may have been blown. Two hundred and fifty kilometers away at Vincennes GHQ a message dated the previous day from Army Group I was received: "The Belgians have been attacked in the Courtrai region. The enemy has gained a hold on the left bank of the Lys."

———

It was 5:10 in the morning when the king received the four ministers at his residence, Wynendaele Château. As was his custom, he made an objective resumé of the meeting—which was the last one—as soon as it was over. A meticulous man, Leopold was aware that errors are caused by a lapse of memory and that an *a posteriori* interpretation of the facts can be misleading. Spaak gave a totally different version of that meeting at Limoges on May 31. To examine it properly, I shall reproduce the king's report in its entirety, begging my readers' forebearance.

*1. The King's Report, May 25, 1940.*

"The ministers were received at their request by the king at 5:10.

"The meeting lasted until 6:20. It was the last meeting the king had with his ministers after the almost daily visits since the start of hostilities. The meeting took place at Wynendaele Château in the large drawing room on the first floor. The atmosphere was painful, tense and dramatic. The king and his ministers remained standing. Pierlot spoke on behalf of his colleagues and expressed their unanimous opinion thus:

"The democratic countries will not be defeated. So Belgium's fate must be linked to that of the Allies. The latter's military situation has deteriorated, but it is not desperate. The Belgian army must beat a retreat, withdraw from Belgium and take refuge, if necessary, as far as the Somme. We should ignore military factors or moral considerations that stand in our way. (Pierlot seemed to dismiss the fact that the Germans had already reached the Somme.)

"If the Belgian army should be unable to escape, we must save a few divisions, or a few regiments, or even a few soldiers. But above all, we must save the head of state so that Belgium can continue the struggle side by side with the Allies, a struggle they will pursue until victory is attained, even if it means retreating behind the Loire.

"In the long run, Germany will be defeated. Time is on the side of the Allies, who have infinite arms resources. The king cannot surrender with his army. If the king returns to Belgium to rule under German authority, he will be under their thumb like another President Hacha of Czechoslovakia. The Belgian people will turn their backs on him—at least the French-speaking Belgians will—and it will divide our country.

"If on the other hand the king goes to France, his voice, and that of his government, will be heard. He will live in freedom and the Belgian institutions will continue to function outside the country. By leaving his army and his country, the king is not deserting them.

"But if he were to consider negotiating a separate peace treaty with Germany, that would be unforgivably shameful and disloyal to the Allies, since Belgium is tied to them by an indissoluble moral pact and a sense of obligation and gratitude.

"Finally, if the king were to disregard his government's views and decide to remain in Belgium despite everything, I am certain that those members of his government already at Poitiers would refuse to resign; they would consider it unconstitutional for the king to be opposed to his government. By doing this the king would create two Belgiums with two governments, of which only the one in France would be legitimate, recognized by the democratic powers. It would mean the end of this country and its institutions.

"Surrender has become an inevitability. In this case, the four ministers who remained with the king at his request—for which we are grateful—feel obliged to leave Belgium, as they cannot allow themselves to be taken prisoner by the Germans. They are therefore making a final attempt to beg the king to leave with them.' "

———

I shall interrupt King Leopold's report, written in the minutes following that early morning meeting, to raise a few points which seem a matter of common sense to me. For instance "The Belgian army must beat a retreat, withdraw from Belgium and take refuge, if necessary, as far as the Somme." As the king remarked, Pierlot, speaking on behalf of his colleagues, appeared to ignore the fact that the Germans had already reached the Somme. One must admit that it does seem very surprising, at least for General Denis, since he visited GHQ daily and must have been informed of it by May 21 at the latest. No doubt out of charity the king does not point out the fact that his ministers—who felt that "military factors" could be ignored, although the powerful German Panzer divisions would have prevented the Belgian army from retreating to the river—were disposing of the "moral considerations" which might have opposed such an action. What did they mean by this, except that such a retreat would have left the British Expeditionary Force high and dry, not to mention the repercussions for the French armies? In that case, Pierlot must have been joking when he felt obliged to remind the king that Belgium was linked to the Allies "by an indissoluble moral pact and a sense of obligation and gratitude."

We cannot but smile at "If the Belgian army should be unable to escape, we must save a few divisions, or a few regiments, or even a few soldiers." "The Allies, who have infinite arms resources," was a statement valid when the United States entered the war eighteen months later, but this was unforeseen in May 1940. We should also note in passing that the king was not going to "return" to Belgium, since he had no intention of leaving it. Nor did he have any intention of ruling "under German authority," since he had said he would stay with his army, which means he would be treated as a prisoner of war. It was precisely to save some of his soldiers that he made his only approach to the invader in the autumn of 1940. "The Belgian people will turn their backs on him": although Pierlot and Spaak enjoyed making prophesies, this one was no more true than the many others. In August 1940, Van de Meulebroeck, the Brussels burgomaster, worthy heir to the brave Adolphe Max, who had become famous in that very role during World War I, wrote the king a letter bearing his signature and that of 2,441 colleagues. The letter was written just after the campaign in Belgium and dated June 14, 1940:

"Your Majesty,

"Once again Belgium is the victim of a tragic and undeserved fate against which the army, under Your Majesty's orders, has fought bravely to its ultimate abilities. Through the voices of the servants of the community who remained in Belgium, we wish to assert to the world Belgium's moral unity and its undying loyalty to the king and the monarchy, which has made this country great. In paying homage to Your Majesty in these tragic times, we express our fervent and eternal loyalty, and we are sure we speak for the entire population, which still believes its destiny as a free and independent nation."

"The servants of the community who remained in Belgium": there were others, like Spaak and his colleagues, who had preferred to have the French border between them and the invader, leaving behind the electorate who had voted for them. Nevertheless, in the view of the minority who had emigrated and claimed to be patriotic, Spaak and his associates followed the Jacobite tradition of 1792, where a patriot was "a person who believed in new ideas." Spaak himself said at Limoges on May 31, "We shall settle our accounts."

Leopold replied to his ministers' entreaties, that tragic dawn of May 25, 1940, in the following way:

"Although he has never lived through such anguish, now his

mind is made up: he has decided to stay with his army and amongst his people and to share their fate. In this way he will fulfill his role as head of state and commander in chief of the army. He is obeying the dictates of his conscience. To leave at such a time would be plain desertion. The king will serve the best interests of his nation by remaining in Belgium. Contrary to the fears of his ministers, he does not feel that his attitude will lead to the division of the country, for by remaining among his people he will increase the chances of maintaining Belgium's independence and the continuity of the monarchy. If he leaves he will never return. Moreover, he will be more of a prisoner abroad than his ministers imagine, for his actions and decisions will be controlled by the power harboring him.

"The king leaves the ministers free to make their decisions according to their consciences. And as constitutional sovereign he gives them advice and not orders. 'My duty is to remain; it is up to you to find where your duty lies.' "

—

Having said this, Leopold read them a letter he was going to send that day to George VI:

"Belgium has fulfilled the pledge she made in 1937 to maintain her neutrality and to resist with all the forces at her disposal the moment her independence in threatened. Her means of resistance are now on the point of being totally destroyed.

"On the morning of May 10th, when my country was traitorously attacked without warning, the Belgian Army immediately established a good line of defense in cooperation with its Allies. But retreats were forced day by day on the Allied armies in Belgium because of the development of military events outside the country. The Belgian Army withdrew in good order to the position it holds today.

"It is impossible to retreat farther.

"Since the entire army is now involved in action, it is an impossibility to create a new reserve.

"Because of that, the aid which we can give to the Allies will come to an end if our army is encircled.

"In spite of all the contrary advice which I have received, I feel that my duty compels me to share the fate of my army and to stay with my people; to act otherwise would be a desertion.

"I am convinced that I can better aid my people by remaining with them than by trying to act from outside the country, especially against the rigors of a foreign occupation, the threat of forced labor or of deportation and food shortages.

"In remaining in my country I fully realize that my position will be very difficult but my main thought will be to prevent my compatriots from being obliged to associate themselves in action against the countries which have aided Belgium in her struggle.

"If I felt myself incapable of so doing, and only then, I would abandon the mission which I have assigned myself."

———

I should like to comment particularly on three points in this unequivocal letter:

1. "In spite of all the contrary advice which I have received" formally confirms that the king had been constantly urged by his ministers to abandon his army and leave Belgium.

2. "To prevent my compatriots from being obliged to associate themselves in action against the countries which have aided Belgium in her struggle" refutes the allegation that the king was hoping to make a separate peace treaty with Germany.

3. To protect his people from "the rigors of a foreign occupation, the threat of forced labor or of deportation" again reveals the king's clear thinking which Spaak called "almost uncanny" at the Limoges meeting on May 31. Like northern France, Belgium had suffered the hardships of a German occupation during the Great War, and King Albert must surely have spoken about it to his son. Leopold hoped that his presence in Belgium, even as a prisoner of war, would act as a protective shield between the temporary victor and his people. Even if that hope had never

come true—which was not the case—it would still be impossible to deny that here was a very noble man, whose mission was one of self-sacrifice.

———

When the king had finished reading, Spaak asked for permission to sit down, saying that the nervous tension they felt prevented them from "talking freely." So saying, he fell into an armchair. The king also sat down, so did Pierlot, General Denis and Van der Poorten. "I see again," said Spaak, "that once Your Majesty has reached a decision, there is nothing more to be done. I want to say that, as minister of foreign affairs, I refuse to sign any treaty with the enemy." Then looking at everyone in turn he asked, "Do you realize it's all over for Belgium?" He leant back in his chair, his arms hanging limply at his sides, and murmured incoherently and repeatedly, "Do you realize it's all over for Belgium?"

After a while he changed his tune, "I wonder if it would not be better if the four of us resigned. . . . Out of loyalty to Your Majesty I don't want to abandon him, but I don't want to be minister during an occupation. Let us four all resign. . . . Our colleagues won't, but never mind. . . . I don't know what to do."

"My dear colleague," interrupted Pierlot, "I advise you to think the matter over tonight before deciding to resign."

Perhaps to comfort Spaak, General Denis said, "Let us not forget that there are hundreds of thousands of Belgians in France capable of taking up arms, who are eager to fight!" Coming from the Belgian minister of defense, and a general to boot, that statement surprised the king. He quickly pointed out that in order to train men and send them to battle, one needed officers. Apart from a few Belgian officers on duty in France, all available officers were engaged in the battle that was hourly becoming more intense. Let us not forget that the previous day, Friday, May 24, when Paul Reynaud suggested calling up the last units in the 1939 and 1940 categories, General Colson had replied that they only had "5,000 guns at the outside, and outdated models at that."

Then Pierlot asked: "If we leave, does Your Majesty intend to set up a new government?"

"Since I am not a dictator," replied the king, "I would obviously need to name one or more ministers to continue the fight against the enemy so that my decisions may be countersigned."

His listeners—I shall give them the benefit of the doubt—seemed to think that the king wanted to use one or more ministers to negotiate a peace treaty with Germany after the surrender, which seemed inevitable. The May 30 Havas dispatch echoed that feeling, saying that according to an important Belgian politician, "That was just one more deception before the final crime." Who could this man be? That night of May 24 to 25, there were only four ministers at Wynendaele Château: Pierlot, Spaak, Van der Poorten and General Denis. Noting Van der Poorten's letter of September 25, 1940, I think he was not involved, and I think the same goes for General Denis. That leaves Pierlot and Spaak: and since an excellent way of seeming important is to proclaim something far and wide, I would settle for Spaak.

The four visitors left early in the morning at 6:20. A few hours later, when the king's mind was on other worries, he received a letter from the prime minister.

"Your Majesty,

"Following the audience the king granted us this morning, my colleagues and I believe it is our duty to join the other members of our government.

Your Majesty's most respectful and loyal servant,

(signed) Hubert Pierlot."

If he was still "most respectful and loyal," the "most obedient servant" so often repeated before, had disappeared—and for good reason! Aside from respect, we shall soon see what was left of his loyalty.

2. *Speech made by Spaak at Limoges, May 31, 1940.*

We have already seen during the Belgian army's difficult retreat from the Ghent to Terneuzen canal to the Lys River that tragedy is imperfect without an element of farce. Spaak added an element of the grotesque, which Hugo said was "the richest resource that nature can offer art," before his assembled colleagues at Limoges on May 31, 1940. If we consider grotesqueness in parliamentary eloquence, Spaak certainly surpassed himself. I have already referred several times to this speech, couched in heroic-sentimental terms, but I ask the reader to have patience and read it in its entirety, to understand how he told the story of his last meeting with the king early on Saturday, May 25, in the presence of Pierlot, Denis and Van der Poorten:

"We have just lived through ten most painful and anguished days, horrified by the disastrous policies and decisions that were being made, over which my colleagues and I have exhausted all emotion and indignation during our last few days in Belgium.

"As the prime minister has asked me to do, I simply wish to tell you the whole story, briefly, clearly and objectively. I shall give you an objective account without seeking to lessen the responsibilities, and, I might add, without needlessly blaming those responsible. That is not our aim. When I say 'our,' that is not quite how I should put it, but there is no need to paint an even blacker picture than reality itself.

"When people say this treachery—the very word burns my mouth and sticks in my throat—had been premeditated a long time before, I must say that is not true. Every one of us, from the highest to the lowest, entered this war honestly, with a will to do our duty. Pierlot, General Denis, Van der Poorten and I, we know that this tragedy was born, developed and finalized in a two-week period and I shall tell you how.

"We began to be worried immediately after the first few days of the war. Would you blame us for not having mentioned it immediately? There are some ideas so horrifying, some policies so senseless, that before believing that the highest authorities in the land could have become so profoundly mistaken and had lost not only all political sense, but, I am forced to say it, moral sense as well, that before even envisaging such a possibility when one begins to have doubts and hesitations, it seems better to put such thoughts aside and not believe them. It is only very slowly that the facts become known, that certain words are spoken, and then one has to face reality and one is forced to act.

"On the Tuesday following the outbreak of war, the prime minister was summoned to GHQ. Although I was not present at that meeting, I can say that our anxieties began from that moment. The prime minister, General Denis and I went to GHQ two days later, on May 16. There was an appalling atmosphere of defeatism. From that time on, the high authorities in command of the armies were convinced that nothing could be done, that not only the Belgian army but also the Allied armies had lost. This conviction led us to conclude that the war would end in one or two weeks with a general and total surrender. But I have jumped ahead in this story, as things were not stated this way during the earlier meeting; that happened toward the end.

"The prime minister was alarmed at the king's suggestion in their conversation that the army should retreat. I should say here that it was necessary then for the Belgian army to retreat, not because it was defeated, but because there was a breach in the south, the French front was broken and it was necessary to avoid being cut off and establish a defendable line. From that time, the king—and this is the last time I shall praise him—with a foresight that now seems almost uncanny, predicted what military operations would take place. He was certain the German columns would not march on Paris but would make for the sea, and he felt that not only his army but the Anglo-French army, too, would be surrounded.

"The prime minister immediately said that if such an event did take place, there was only one thing to do: retreat from north to south and under no circumstances should we be cut off from the French and British troops, if possible reserving two or three divisions out of the whole army to continue the struggle on the other side. Alas! from that moment we realized we did not see eye to eye on military matters. Not all the responsibility lies with the Belgian command, far from it. At that time, the king scrupulously—in my opinion, too scrupulously—followed the orders given him by the French high command. It is a fact that the latter reacted desperately slowly, that it took several days for it to realize that our army was in very real danger, and it allowed the left flank to trail in northern Belgium when conditions were becoming hourly and daily more difficult to remedy. When the king said he was only following orders from high command, we told him, 'A passive attitude is not enough. If you feel the orders you receive are insufficient, you should initiate others and take the necessary steps to save what you can!' That is roughly what was said on the Tuesday and Thursday. We already saw that the king had an idea in mind which appalled us. In the case where the Belgian army might be forced to surrender—a possibility which must be faced in wartime —we never hesitated to tell the king that he could not remain with his army. The king as head of his army should fight to the last moment, but he has a duty—as well as the means available in modern transport—to try at the last moment to escape in order to continue the struggle. From that Thursday, May 16, we began to worry about this question. I have a very clear recollection of this, and I want to tell you how, little by little, we began to feel anxious. The king did not say that day, 'I have no intention of following you, nor of abandoning the army.' Instead he asked us, 'What did Queen Wilhelmina do?' We replied that the queen of Holland was in London and she had just stated she intended to continue the struggle. Then to our surprise, the king asked, 'Do you think she did the right thing?' We said there was no possible doubt about it and it was the only action she could have taken in those circumstances. The conversation was not resumed that day. You will understand the state we were in when we returned to Brussels, wondering if he would do such a disastrous thing."

I hope the late Belgian minister of foreign affairs, who has been decorated with many other titles since May 1940, will allow me to interrupt him for a moment. How come he did not see that the difference between King Leopold and Queen Wilhelmina was that she was not a commander of her army and, therefore, had no feelings of military solidarity with her soliders? Besides, I believe I am correct in saying that it was against her will and her deepest conviction that she left her country. Let us now return to the distinguished Mr. Spaak.

"Events moved quickly. We left Brussels on Thursday, May 16, for Ostend. On the Friday we held a cabinet meeting at which the other ministers intuitively sensed our concern and asked us about the army's retreat. I have no need to tell you that the fourteen ministers decided unanimously that under no circumstances should the Belgian army be cut off and that if, unfortunately, a part of the army, or worse, the entire army were taken prisoner, the king should leave. We were so anxious that when we left the cabinet meeting, Pierlot wrote the following letter dated May 17 to the king. I shall read all of it to you, as rereading it on the train this morning, we were struck by how much this letter predicted what, alas, came to pass. (Spaak then read the letter which I reproduced earlier.)

"I think this letter is a precious historical document, as it shows that we never for a moment failed to do our duty or to give advice. If there was some comfort during those terrible days, it lay in the fact that the fourteen men governing the country have remained completely and absolutely unanimous in their opinions, whether Flemish or Walloon.

"That letter was sent Friday night. On the Saturday, since the situation at Ostend had become particularly difficult and the administrative work impossible, we decided to send the administrative departments to France, together with a certain number of ministers. That day the three of us went back to GHQ and on the basis of that letter we resumed our discussions—as we continued to do daily up to the last moment. I shall not go through all our disappointments, from the hopeful days to the time when we felt that it was all over. All I can say is that all of us, the prime minister—the Luxembourger—the Flemish from Lierre, the general and the minister from Brussels, in our own ways used all possible arguments. We even resorted to insults, and before you accuse me of dishonor, desertion and treachery, I must say we addressed those words to the man who was going to commit them. We did all we could. I do not believe there is another argument we could have used, and we were quite unanimous.

"The king said something which gave us a glimmer of hope, 'I know how difficult are the decisions I must take and the responsibilities I must carry, so I request some ministers to remain with me at GHQ.' He asked the prime minister, the minister of defense, Van der Poorten—minister of internal affairs—and myself to remain. I said that we felt some hope that day, May 18. We returned to our colleagues at La Panne and said, 'The decision has been made. We will join the king and continue the mission you have entrusted to us. We still hope to succeed.'

"On Sunday, May 19, Monday, May 20, Tuesday, May 21, Wednesday, May 22, Thursday, May 23 and Friday, May 24, we visited the king. I won't repeat what we said each time: it was always the same. But suddenly—I have to admit it, as it is written in a document which will be published (Spaak here refers to a memorandum written by Pierlot after the May 25 meeting, which I shall quote later)—we thought we had won our case. During the discussion, the king said, 'We are agreed on two points. If my army is not cut off from the British and French troops, I shall continue the battle. If the Belgian army is cut off and I am certain that the British and French will continue the battle, I shall follow you to fight at your side. But there is one thing you have not considered —and he said this rather eagerly—a possibility you do not wish to contemplate, which is that if the war is over, I must remain in my country.'

"We replied—and I only mention this one point—'Your Majesty, even if you are right—and you are wrong all along the line—

don't you understand that you cannot make peace to save Belgium unless you are free? As a prisoner, you cannot do that.' That day's statement was so clear that we wrote a report of the conversation and sent it to the king. That took place on Tuesday, May 21, but in the conversations that followed on Wednesday and Thursday, we felt the king was again hesitant.

"I promised to tell you everything. We felt that little by little the king was returning to his original idea—misguided but honorable—that the head of an army, who is also king, must remain with his troops and suffer their fate, even to the point of being taken prisoner. I say this idea is misguided because the king is not just a general.

"We were forced to understand, nevertheless, that as a military man, he might have some scruples of conscience. We had to fight against that idea. Our surprise and horror grew, however, when we realized that not only was the commander going to stay with his troops, but the king would also accept a role under occupation. That was the final blow. We said everything we could, but it was like trying to move a mountain because our words no longer had any weight or effect with him. I am trying to explain the course of events, and I may make a mistake as I have to apply a bit of psychology, but what we felt was that some of the king's ideas were basically false.

"Firstly, that the Belgian army could only fight on Belgian territory; secondly, that the Allies troops had lost, the war was over, peace was about to be made and as a result (here I must say what I feel) one should change one's colors and try to reach some degree of agreement with the would-be conqueror. I tell you in all sincerity that the king believed—or still believes—that he could help the Belgian people, that he could prevent deportations and the economic ruin of the country. Those ideas are quite false, quite erroneous. I will explain why, and as I said before, I wish neither to accuse nor to justify. We felt the reasons the king was putting forward were crazy, stupid, and even worse, criminal, because the king was showing a complete lack of moral sense which horrified us. This is what he said: the king claimed that despite the appeal we made to the French and British, we had no obligation to them. We said, 'Your Majesty, you could have acted differently if the country had allowed you to. Like the king of Denmark, you could have made some semblance of isolationist defense, made some pretense, but as soon as you agreed to ask for help, and thousands of French and British soldiers came to die in defending Belgium, you are bound to them. If you abandon their cause now, you are a dishonorable traitor.' There is one Belgian in a thousand or even ten thousand who would think the opposite, and our misfortune is that that Belgian is our king, supported by one or two people around him. You understand that if we had proof of treason, we would tell you. We have certain responsibilities, and when we know the full facts, as I hope to return to a victorious Belgium, we shall settle our accounts with those whom we have cause to reproach. At the moment we only have conjectures. We felt the atmosphere at GHQ was so defeatist that it must have weighed on the mind of the king.

"Now we come to the last day, Friday, May 24. The troops had again retreated, not of their own accord, but under German pressure. On Friday night we learned that the Germans were at Balgerhoek, which is level with Maldeghem, just six kilometers from Bruges where we were based. Do I need to tell you that we had decided to stay until the last moment because we understood the symbolic importance of the ministers' presence on Belgian soil? We were prepared to risk leaving by whatever means available. We were pushed into a corner, under siege, but we did not think of leaving, judging that our duty was to remain up to the last second, and particularly in order to persuade the king.

"When we heard that the Germans were six kilometers from Bruges, we telephoned GHQ, which never kept us informed. It was 10:30 at night. The chief of general staff told us calmly, 'News is bad. The front between Courtrai and Menin has been broken. We are doing our best to seal up the breach, but a regiment of German tanks is poised for action.'

"The Germans were just a few kilometers away from us to the north and south. We wanted to do our duty but—I have no hesitation in saying this and I hope people will feel we did the right thing—we did not wish to become prisoners. This was because we felt that if things turned out as badly as we imagined, and if the ministers were there to sanction it, even tacitly, then it was not a military action, but a political one. To tell you how far we went, the prime minister told the king the next day, May 25, 'Your Majesty, if I were single I might remain at your side out of personal loyalty, but I do not wish to bequeath to my children a name that has been dishonored by the king's policy.'

"We decided to leave. For GHQ that was the least of their worries. Naturally we stayed in Bruges without one soldier to protect us, not one cannon, no information, nothing. However, during the night we telephoned Gutt in England, asking him to arrange a means of departure. There were only four of us, but we also had a group of fifteen to twenty loyal supporters who wished to come with us. Dunkirk had been bombed, Ostend was out of the question, and so was Nieuport. But all went well, and we had the easiest journey of all the Belgians.

"There is no need to tell you that every now and then, General Denis, Van der Poorten and I would look sadly at each other, saying that in a few hours we would be prisoners. We telephoned the king and told him, 'Your Majesty, you know the military situation. It is imperative you take a decision now.' I shall pass over the details. The king did not reply that night. We made the heartbreaking attempt once more at four o'clock in the morning, together with our staff, to find the king. He was not at GHQ but in a château near Torhout. That is where we last saw him. I do not want to be dramatic, but when I say the meeting was tragic, I am using the appropriate word.

"We waited for the king, and he received us standing up. He was unkempt, haggard, his eyes full of tears and his jaw tightly set. He was more or less standing to attention in front of us. The prime minister said, 'Your Majesty, my colleagues and supporters are leaving. I shall stay by the king until the last moment, until the army has ceased to fight. But I will stay on one condition: that the king promises to try to leave with me.' Then the king said: 'I have made my decision; I shall remain with my army and my nation.' The conversation continued and I must tell you some of the details as they prove we could not possibly stay. We said, 'Your Majesty, you have sealed your fate. What instructions do you give us?' And then—don't laugh—although I know what the king replied was stupid, it shows what a state he was in, 'Stay with me. You must help me govern the country.' We replied, 'Do you believe Hitler would entrust Belgium to Spaak, Denis and Van der Poorten, even if we were to accept?' The king had evidently not considered the consequences of his actions—and that is the tragedy and will be his punishment—and he thought for a while. 'No, obviously not,' he said, 'but you could stay as my personal counselors.' We replied, 'Doesn't the king realize that a government will be formed in France, composed of our colleagues, and if not by them, by others (you see we had thought of everything)? What would the king's position be with regard to that government? The king replied: 'If that happens, the government would be against me.' We asked, 'Does the king intend to rule in Brussels?' He replied, 'Yes, but I intend to have ministers, I am not a dictator.'

"Then, gentlemen, we realized it was useless to continue the discussion as the king was in a state of physical and moral debility due to the atmosphere he lived in.

"If I may say one more thing in his favor, he was not a man cut out to lead the war. I would not say he was a coward. Despite our sadness, I have no interest in attacking him too much. I would simply say he was not a general. We all felt during the war that he had only one aim: not to have his men killed or his towns destroyed. In certain ways I can sympathize with that attitude. But when one is fighting against the Germans in the present circumstances and one does not allow men to die or towns to be destroyed, one cannot win the war or save the country. We told the king,

'We are leaving. We cannot stay with you here,' and we gave him to understand that we would fight against him."

———

The warning the ministers gave the king early in the morning on Saturday, May 25, that they would "fight against him" was quite superfluous, since it only confirmed the state of affairs existing over the last ten days. The main basis of Spaak's curious indictment was this: if the king had decided to stay with his army and his people, then he obviously intended to negotiate a separate peace treaty with the enemy; if the king tried his best to keep his four ministers there, it was to make the negotiations constitutional, and this was a betrayal in which the ministers refused to take part. It is surprising that no one in Spaak's audience at Limoges gave the counterargument that springs naturally to mind, "If you had stayed with the king, you could have officially refused to acknowledge his dealings with the enemy, thereby invalidating them automatically."

Out of all this oratorical gibberish I have just inflicted on my reader, perhaps he or she will realize one important truth. Spaak, who was "the king's most respectful, loyal and obedient servant" (at least that is what he claimed in his letters to the king), was now the king's most virulent opponent, but this behavior was quite normal. He who perjures himself is inevitably guilty of betrayal. In this case the betrayal lay with the man who was denouncing it before his colleagues, who were not attending to their duties. Meanwhile, he took the precaution (to protect himself) of claiming that the betrayal had not been "premeditated for some time." Ten years later, this determined champion of democracy—which I believe is defined as the will of the majority—rejected the results of a plebiscite on the monarchy on March 19, 1950. Some 57.68 percent were in favor of Leopold resuming his duties as king. When he returned to Brussels on July 22, the king was met by such a wave of violent demonstrations and strikes (actively supported by Spaak's raised right fist) that because of his concern for national unity, he abdicated in favor of his son, Crown Prince Baudouin. That was a gesture befitting a man who, according to Spaak, the budding strategist, could not allow his men to be killed or his towns destroyed. Spaak deduced, from this laudable concern to save his people and their possessions as far as possible, that King Leopold was "not a general."

---

It is tempting to answer this nonsense, more worthy of a mountebank than a minister of foreign affairs, with the brief but eloquent "No comment," were it not a question of honor, which cannot be answered by silence. Besides, Spaak's most serious allegations must be countered.

According to the orator at Limoges, the first "anxiety" felt by the ministers was after Pierlot's first interview with the king at the start of hostilities. That was on Wednesday, May 15—not Tuesday, May 14, as Spaak claimed—when the king asked General Denis to bring the prime minister, whom he had just heard was about to leave Brussels, which he considered too dangerous, for Ostend. The king explained that such a move would seriously affect the morale of people living in Brussels who were already very worried, and furthermore, the king wished to remain in close contact with his ministers. "The Germans have breached the French front at Sedan," he said, "and their armored divisions are pressing toward the Channel. There is a possibility that our army and the British Expeditionary Force may be cut off from the main body of French troops." This dismayed Pierlot, who asked the king to order the Belgian army to retreat toward France. "It all depends on how the situation develops," replied the king, supported by General Denis, who had visited him daily since May 10. So the minister of defense was obliged to remind his prime minister that the general conduct of operations depended on the decisions of the overall commander in chief, who happened to be French and was called General Gamelin.

During that same meeting, the king asked Pierlot to intercede once again with the French and British governments and obtain a written statement assuring Belgium of its independence when peace was signed and its sovereignty over the Congo. Did Pierlot and his ministers deduce from this that King Leopold intended to negotiate a separate peace treaty with Germany? Did Spaak draw the conclusion that the king, like the "highest authorities in the land" (one would have thought the government was next in line) had come to be "so profoundly mistaken and had lost not only all political sense, but, I am forced to say it, moral sense as well?" For a minister of foreign affairs he had a very short memory: the Munich Agreements, which proved to be shortlived promises to Czechoslovakia by France and England, had only been signed eighteen months previously.

Spaak claims that when he went to the king's GHQ with Pierlot and General Denis on Thursday, May 16, he felt "an appalling atmosphere of defeatism" (and it was he who had packed his bags to go to Ostend the previous day!). The king received the ministers at 14:00, having learned in the morning from General Billotte that the serious news from the Meuse front around Sedan had forced the head of Army Group I to abandon the plan of maintaining its positions on the Antwerp-Namur line and to retreat "at least as far as the Escaut (Schelde)." That is perhaps when the king saw "with almost uncanny foresight" the possibility of surrender. Spaak called defeatist what was simply realistic, and as a politician he preferred the world of make-believe to facing hard facts. Besides, the king said quite unequivocally that such a possibility depended on maintaining contact with the Allied forces, which in turn depended on how successful the French army was in dealing with the flow of German forces pouring through the breach in the Ardennes.

"One day, I intend to write a complete account of these events, choosing each word carefully, something I am unable to do now in this improvised style," said Spaak to his audience. The account never saw the light of day, no doubt because it would have been impossible for its author to hide the fact that from the very beginning he was panicked by the thought of being captured by the Germans (*they* would have been surprised to learn the importance they attached to his capture). His improvised speech at Limoges contains a number of unfortunate statements. "We were forced to understand, nevertheless, that as a military man, he (the king) might have some scruples of conscience," or "We waited for the king, and he received us standing up. He was unkempt, haggard, his eyes full of tears. . . He was more or less standing to attention in front of us." The son of the "Roi-Chevalier" standing to attention in front of a man like Spaak? That seems highly unlikely. And how could we believe—knowing how firmly he always set an example—that a man who was "unkempt, haggard," could have written such a clear and dignified letter to George VI, read it to his ministers, then giving a very clear summary of the situation, at the end of which Spaak excused himself by saying that everyone was suffering from "nervous tension" and collapsed in a chair, his arms dangling limply while he muttered incoherently! Having had the misfortune of watching Spaak, so full of himself, during the journey from Brussels to Paris, I felt that he could never forgive King Leopold for having seen him that morning of May 25, 1940, collapsed in an armchair at Wynendaele Château and muttering to himself. Undoubtedly the harsh criticisms levelled at the king came from political opportunism, which he could display so brilliantly, but I would not be surprised if a good part stemmed from remorse at having betrayed a loyal friend. When he was trying to convince the king to leave his army—and his nation—to its fate, Spaak was urging the king to go back on his promise. When the king refused, he called it "a collapse of moral sense," which shows the strange concept he had of honor. When he claimed he had replied using terrible words of "dishonor, desertion and treachery" to the son of Albert I, he must have been lying, as he would have been thrown out for such insolence. Spaak states that he received a call on Friday, May 24, at 22:30 from General Michiels, who "calmly" told him that the news was bad, but the Belgian army was doing its best to seal up the breach between

Courtrai and Menin even though a German tank regiment was threatening it. Spaak does not realize that the calmness of the chief of general staff, compared to his own nervousness, contradicts his own statement that there was "an atmosphere of defeatism" at GHQ. Finally Spaak says of the king: "I have no *interest* in attacking him *too much.*" Here he shows his true colors, proving once again that the "interests" of a man of politics do not necessarily coincide with those of the nation.

While he was reciting his "improvisation" at the Limoges town hall, there was some laughter at the back of the hall. One of the ministers shouted severely, "We are not in the Chamber here!" I think that sums it up.

At the Breendonck GHQ and at those at Denis-Westrem and Saint-André-lez-Bruges, Spaak always thought he was "in the Chamber," as he did at Limoges, where he used political ploys. Eighteen days later at Bordeaux he got his come-uppance when he had to face facts that he could not deny. But as Destouches said in *Le Glorieux* (*Man of Glory*), inventing his own proverb, "If you chase truth away, it comes back on the double." And World War II was so rich in all kinds of catastrophes that Spaak could crawl away and then return with all his bluster, as a man who has well and truly "arrived." Once again using a term which is not my own, I would add, "Yes, but in what a state!"

# "THE HARDEST ROAD"

Nowhere can I find any remark made by Pierlot against the Limoges speech of his minister of foreign affairs. As far as I know, after Spaak's words at the beginning of the meeting: "Every one of us, from the highest to the lowest, entered this war honestly, with a will to do our duty," Pierlot only commented with General Denis that this was the case and nobody could possibly doubt it. But following his final audience with the king early on Saturday morning, May 25, Pierlot carefully wrote a report, which differs significantly from the version Spaak gave at the Limoges meeting. Although he suppressed certain details noted by the king, his report generally agrees with that of the king:

"Toward the end of that night (May 24 to 25) Pierlot once again asked Major Van den Heuvel over the telephone whether he could speak to the king. He was told that the king had gone south without leaving word when he would return, but since the king had taken provisions with him he might be absent for some time. The king would probably go back to his GHQ unless he returned to his new residence. Major Van den Heuvel was rather evasive about the location of this new residence, saying he was not sure whether he was authorized to reveal it.

"By searching through the telephone directory we were able to establish, by the postal code, that his residence was Wynendaele Château northwest of Torhout. Without further ado, the ministers left Bruges with their associates and personnel for one last audience with the king and to be able to reach a decision about their departure. It was four o'clock in the morning. All was quiet on the front. Between Bruges and Torhout, the cavalry corps, although thoroughly exhausted, was moving in excellent order.

"When the ministers arrived at Wynendaele, they left the little convoy of cars on the road and entered. They were received by Major Van den Heuvel. The king had just returned and was resting after his tiring night. The ministers declared they would wait until he had risen, but after some hesitation, Major Van den Heuvel awoke the king, who appeared immediately. Pierlot said:

" 'We have already told Your Majesty several times that should part or all of the Belgian army be forced to lay down its arms, Your Majesty should do everything in his power to avoid being captured by the enemy. We gave our reasons. Surrender, however serious, is only a military action, but it would become a political act if Your Majesty were to sign it or if Your Majesty were still head of the army when surrender takes place. Besides, if the army has to surrender, Your Majesty's role as head of the army would cease, and Your Majesty could carry out his functions as head of state alongside the Allied governments, both on a political and a military level, by making use of all Belgian military potential in France. That is Your Majesty's duty, and the entire government is convinced of this. Moreover, we have strong apprehensions about Your Majesty's return to occupied Belgium, especially if he has to continue his royal functions under enemy control; we would certainly support him, even if Your Majesty decides to stand down.

" 'As for the ministers, their presence alongside Your Majesty at the time of surrender would lend further political overtones, which must be avoided at all costs. If the Belgian army surrenders, the four ministers will no longer be in their place of operations but where they can continue to function: alongside their colleagues and the Allied governments.

" 'Having reconsidered one last time, and given the present decisive turn of events, it is necessary to organize the departure of my colleagues and their associates—a total of about twenty people—whose journey to the coast and embarkation could soon become impossible. That is why, unless Your Majesty has any formal objection, three ministers and their personnel will leave today for Dunkirk where ships await them. As for the prime minister, following Your Majesty's suggestion at a previous meeting, he will remain until Your Majesty has arranged his own departure. Your Majesty shall choose the time so that he can reconcile the duties he deems necessary as head of the army with those as head of state. If Your Majesty wishes, he need only leave when all resistance has ceased. But the prime minister would ask Your Majesty to show his firm intention of leaving rather than being taken prisoner. Unless I receive that assurance, I shall leave with my colleagues for the reasons already stated.'

"After a moment of silence, the king replied with some effort:

" 'I have decided to stay. Over and above the more concrete considerations from a logical or political point of view, there are certain questions of feelings which cannot be ignored. To leave one's army is to desert. Whatever the fate of my troops, I must share it. Furthermore, to tell you more exactly what I think and to show you how I arrived at this decision, I shall read you a letter which I am sending to the king of England.'

"The king then read a letter in which he explained to the British king the motives behind his decision, adding that whatever happened, he would never consent to anything against the interests of the Allies. Commenting on the last part of the letter, the king added that he was thinking particularly of the case when the occupying power might use Belgian industry to manufacture armaments. 'If I were ever forced into that position, I would withdraw.' Replying to a minister's question, the king said he meant he would abdicate.

"Like the meeting the previous day, we were all standing up. After the king had said this he gave indication that the meeting was over. But Spaak intervened, saying, 'Your Majesty, the king cannot be separated like this from the government. We wish to speak to Your Majesty one last time, to tell him what we think. After that, Your Majesty may do as he pleases, but he cannot refuse us one final word. Could we not sit down to continue this discussion and say exactly how we feel?' This was spoken out of respect and, if one may put it that way, sorrowful cordiality. We felt a strong desire not to break the threads, however tenuous, which still bound the ministers to the head of state. The king eventually sat down and signaled the ministers to do the same. Spaak resumed:

" 'The ministers unanimously feel that Your Majesty is making a serious mistake. If he falls into enemy hands his cause will be severed from that of the Allies. He will renounce the continuation of the struggle with them, contrary to the moral obligations he has toward them after having called on them for help. However serious the surrender of the army may be, it would be a greater disaster if Your Majesty were taken captive and the political fact of the nation's existence compromised in any way. Your Majesty will find troops in France with which to raise a new army. He can continue the struggle, not only with military but also with economic means of our nation which is still well-endowed abroad, with resources from its colony. He can do what both the king of Norway and the queen of Holland did, he can remain true to a cause which binds our country. If Your Majesty stays, what can he hope to do? Contrary to what Your Majesty said, he will not share the fate of his troops. He will not be incarcerated in a German fortress, but in his own palace. Anything he tries to do will compromise him and will compromise our independence, since Your Majesty will be acting under enemy orders. Everyone's conscience will be deeply troubled. I ask Your Majesty to inform us what role he thinks he can play, a role he has repeatedly referred to, and how he will continue to fulfill that role in Belgium.'

"The king replied: 'I don't know. I don't know what I will be able to do, but I hope I can continue at least to uphold the economic existence of this country, to facilitate food supplies and spare my people from worse sufferings such as deportation . . . . If I do not remain in Belgium, I am certain I shall never return. The Allied cause is lost. Very shortly, maybe in a few days, France too will have to give up the fight, as it cannot hope to succeed with so few troops. No doubt England will continue to fight, not on the Continent, but at sea and in the colonies. This war might last a long time. It will not be possible for Belgium to intervene, and so Belgium's role is over. During a protracted war, Belgium may only have limited independence, but this will allow our nation to exist until a time following unforseeable events, when circumstances become more favorable for our country. There is no question now of trying to continue the war alongside our Allies. The decision I am making is a terribly painful one. Of course, life would be easier for me in France, if I went there to live with my children until this torment is over, but I believe that when one has two roads to choose from, the path of duty is always the hardest. That is the one I have chosen.' "

—

I shall interrupt Pierlot's undated account of his last audience with the king. We should give Pierlot credit—contrary to Spaak—for his dignity of tone, without quibbling over his account that "all was quiet on the front," when he himself told *Paris-Soir* on June 1, 1940, "We could hear the violent sound of cannon fire all along the road, which continued throughout our meeting with the king." That is a minor detail. Nor is it surprising that Pierlot presents the minister of foreign affairs as a man in complete control, to the point of showing "respect and sorrowful cordiality" toward his king, since Pierlot was to be associated with Spaak as soon as he turned his back on the king. On the other hand, it is surprising that this honorable man—brave veteran of the Great War and exemplary citizen in peacetime—after his account of the audience at Wynendaele Château, could have let the May 30 Havas dispatch pass without public protest, or say at Limoges on June 1, "That is the truth!" after Spaak's "improvisation," without refusing to associate himself with Spaak's base accusations against a sovereign to whom he had so often claimed to be a "most respectful, loyal and obedient servant." Once again this is an oft repeated example of how far apart military and civilian courage is from moral courage.

From the first part of this report, I can draw the basic conclusion that all Pierlot's reasoning was based on the conviction that France would not abandon the struggle, whatever the setbacks suffered up to that date, Saturday, May 25. Unless the prime minister was displaying a total lack of understanding, we can only assume that the minister of defense, General Denis, who visited the king's GHQ daily, had been unable to make himself understood by the head of the government. But in that final audience at Wynendaele Château, the king left no doubt in the minds of his minister when he said, in Pierlot's own account: "Very shortly, maybe in a few days, France too will have to give up the fight, as it cannot hope to succeed with so few troops," once again demonstrating his "almost uncanny foresight." When the king said, "The Allied cause is lost," he was not being defeatist but only defining the situation at that time. He foresaw that England would continue the war "not on the Continent, but at sea and in the colonies," which one must admit is not far off the mark. He then added, "This war might last a long time" and referred to "unforeseeable events" that might benefit Belgium, meaning that those "events" could only affect the invader. But on Saturday, May 25, 1940, who could have predicted (surely not the Kremlin, which did everything to avoid the possibility) that Hitler would attack the U.S.S.R thirteen months later, or that the U.S.A., entrenched in its isolationist policy, would be thrown into the conflict by Japan's attack on Pearl Harbor in December 1941? Only de Gaulle, and that was three weeks later, on June 18, prophesied, "This war has become a world war," which seemed absurd to the staid political world.

This error of judgment led Pierlot to tell the king that his duty was to go to France with his government to make use of "all Belgian military potential in France" (events that followed soon after put paid to that). He alleged that if the king were to remain in

Belgium under occupation, the invader would take advantage of some of the attributes of royalty. The king stayed in Belgium and that did not happen. Furthermore, he assured his ministers that "whatever happened, he would never consent to anything against the interests of the Allies." According to Pierlot's words, Spaak used a mixture of "respect and sorrowful cordiality"—far from the terrible words of "dishonor, desertion and treachery" the latter claimed to have said to the king in his speech at Limoges —to say that the king's presence in occupied Belgium would compromise "the political fact of the nation's existence." It was quite the opposite, in fact, as shown by the 2,441 burgomasters' letter to the king which I have already quoted. The minister of foreign affairs said the king "will find troops in France with which to raise a new army." This was just a figment of his imagination. Spaak continued, the king "will not be incarcerated in a German fortress, but in his own palace." I can only say how much I benefited from it in the Resistance, as I had the honor of having some brave Belgian soldiers in my group who found the presence of their king in Belgium a source of encouragement, and I never saw that any of their "consciences were deeply troubled."

———

If Pierlot lacked courage in Paris and Limoges, he was fundamentally an honest man. At Vichy on July 21, 1940, Belgium's national day, he addressed his exiled compatriots thus: "We earnestly wish that foremost in the minds of all Belgians is the hope for national unity around the king, and that all those who deep in their hearts believe they have done their duty will wish for this too." This speech was coupled with a statement made on behalf of the Belgian ministers in France, which said if Pierlot said on May 28, during those tragic circumstances, that the king had just begun separate negotiations with the enemy, events now clearly prove that only a military action had been accomplished. Several times, Pierlot and his colleagues had protested against the unfounded accusations of treachery made against the king. It is a pity that those protests had so little effect at the time but, none-theless, it is good that they were made a little late, due no doubt to the turn of events. Let us continue with Pierlot's report on the meeting at Wynendaele.

———

"It seemed evident that the king's mind was made up. Nothing could sway his determination. So the ministers asked, 'In Your Majesty's opinion, what should we do?' The king replied, 'Frank-ly, I will tell you clearly that you should follow the promptings of your own conscience. If you believe you should leave, I will not oppose it.' Then Spaak said, 'We cannot be satisfied with that answer. We ask for instructions, but first we want to know what Your Majesty thinks his role will be in Belgium. For instance, will Your Majesty have a government?'

"The king thought for a while before replying, as though he had never considered the question. Then he said, 'Obviously, since I do not wish to be a dictator.' Spaak continued, 'And that government cannot be the present one.' Answer: 'Probably not. It's certain that the occupation forces would not agree to that.'

"Pierlot added, 'Your Majesty knows that we, too, would not agree to that. We are concerned about leaving Your Majesty in these tragic circumstances. If I was single, perhaps I would feel the same way and I would remain with Your Majesty out of per-sonal loyalty. But I do not wish to bequeath a name to my children which might have certain connotations.

"'But if Your Majesty institutes a new government in Brussels, what will be the position of the present government, not only for the ministers here now, but those in France? Does Your Majesty think they should resign?' The king replied, 'That seems a logical solution to the situation.' Pursuing his line Spaak said, 'We must think of the reaction of the Belgian people, who are in a free country, when either the present government or any other that may be instituted decides to continue the war alongside the Allies, while—if I have understood correctly—Your Majesty will have made peace or will have considered the war between Belgium and Germany over. I am sure we must consider this possibility and that it will in fact happen.'

"Pierlot asked, 'If the present government adopts the position outlined by Spaak and continues the war in France, will that government still be Your Majesty's government?' 'No,' replied the king, 'it will be against me.' The king's replies were clear, but always after a moment's thought, as though the possibilities raised by the ministers had not been envisaged or carefully thought over."

---

Had it been otherwise it would have been surprising. Over and above his functions as head of state, Leopold had assumed, with precision and urgency, those that were constitutionally his responsibility as head of the army. And after two weeks of difficult fighting, he had just embarked on a battle whose outcome affected the existence of the Belgian army. When Pierlot and the ministers of defense, foreign affairs and internal affairs arrived at Wynendaele, the king had just returned from a tour of the front lines to encourage his soldiers in the hope that the breach between Menin and Courtrai could be sealed. In his interview with *Paris-Soir*, Pierlot said the king received his visitors "immediately, wearing his general's uniform."

It was 5:10 in the morning and the king had probably just written the letter to George VI that he read to his ministers. So it was to an exhausted man, gnawed by the fate of his soldiers and his country, that they were speaking. We can imagine that of these four politicians, between General Denis's two visits to GHQ, at least three of them had plenty of time to think over the future possibilities from a political angle. They were as far away from the worries of a soldier trying to stop the advance of the German armored divisions as they were from the hundreds of thousands of men, women and children wandering on the roads in search for food and shelter, under constant strafing from the Luftwaffe. The dialogue noted by Pierlot shows, if it is even necessary, that the king was speaking on behalf of those on a more fundamental plane of existence.

———

"During the same interview," Pierlot goes on, "the ministers were painfully aware of having to leave the king in such a predicament and often wondered whether they should not remain with their sovereign, ready to resign their official posts. The king seemed to stress this point of view. 'It would be in Belgium's interests to have as many people as possible with moral authority who could maintain cohesion and unity in this country. Besides, even if the ministers resigned and no longer participated in governing, they could continue to cooperate with me by giving me advice or counsel.' But the ministers soon saw the moral impossibility of this hybrid proposal, 'Our place will no longer be beside Your Majesty, and even if we resign, our presence will lend—as we have already stressed—a political nature to events, which we wish to avoid, or at least, we do not wish to act thus. Our place is with our colleagues, with whom we will work once the government has been completely reconstituted.'

"The ministers were thrown back to a consideration they had already brought up in a previous audience, 'Whatever Your Majesty's intentions, his conduct will be interpreted in Belgium and abroad—especially in the Allied countries—as a betrayal of the cause to which the king and Belgium were morally bound from the time they called for support from France and Great Britain. Far from being a rallying point, the figure of the king will be a contradiction among his compatriots. The institution of the monarchy, which has been the most efficient symbol of our national unity, will be compromised, perhaps irreparably.'

———

"A contradiction"; I am surprised that a Christian like Pierlot did not realize he was paying the greatest compliment that any man could hope for to the king, for that is how Christ himself defined his role. As for the compromise which his decision would inflict "perhaps, irreparably" on the monarchy in Belgium, no one in good faith living in 1976, as I write this book, could deny that the monarchy in Belgium remains, as elsewhere, the strongest cohesive element in national unity, perhaps because as Charles Maurras used to say, "Royalty means having someone to love."

———

" 'Finally,' said Pierlot, 'when the news is spread to France where there are two million Belgian refugees, what will be the reaction to our compatriots?' 'On that score,' replied the king, 'there are six million other Belgians in Belgium. Those who went away are not as important as those who stayed behind.'

"Each of the four ministers there personally took part in the exchange, so that the impression was that they were completely unanimous. But all their entreaties were in vain. Before the end of the audience, Pierlot raised another worrying point: 'In the terms and in the spirit of the Constitution, the ministers are answerable for all the king's actions, whether they have formally assumed responsibility for them by a countersignature or whether these are public actions carried out by the head of state in the course of duty. From the time the Belgian state was founded in its present form, all governments have considered it their main duty to protect the throne. We have never failed in this duty. In the present case, we have to say that our attitude will be different. Your Majesty has adopted a line of conduct contrary to the unanimous opinion of the government, which has never ceased to express its reservations. It would be too unfair to ask us to bear a responsibility in which we have had no part. This is a problem of the utmost seriousness, on which the existence of the institutions of our country depends. We consider that Your Majesty's actions will compromise everything. We have already said this: we do not want history to consider us the cause of this catastrophe. So we will be obliged, if Your Majesty persists in his point of view, not only to stop protecting him but also to publicly dissociate ourselves from him. We know that such an action is contrary to normal constitutional practice. It is unprecedented and breaks the traditions of our public rights. But we do not think that any other attitude apart from the one I have just outlined is possible.'

"The king replied: 'I understand your situation. You hold convictions, which I know are sincere, and they must dictate your actions.' The audience was drawing to a close. The king stood up. Before leaving, the prime minister asked one more question. Referring to something the king had said a few moments ago, whose meaning was not quite clear to the ministers, Pierlot asked what the king meant when he announced he would prolong the resistance as long as possible, and while there was some hope of it being useful.

" 'Does the king consider that, barring some unforeseeable event that might change the situation, the Belgian army's surrender might still be avoided, or is it certain?' His reply was, 'It is not certain; it is inevitable.'

" 'For how long could it be delayed?' asked the prime minister. Reply: 'Twenty-four hours at the most.' The king left after dismissing the ministers and shaking their hands as usual, but with a marked feeling of apprehension and coldness. The inevitable had happened. The ministers left Wynendaele Château at 6:00 A.M., still deeply moved by the dramatic scene in which they had taken part."

—

Let us remember this phrase from Pierlot's account: whether "the Belgian army's surrender might still be avoided, or is it certain?" and the king's reply, "It is not certain; it is inevitable." Then Pierlot asked again, "For how long could it be delayed?" and the king's reply, "Twenty-four hours at the most." The reader will find this reply similar to General Weygand's words to Captain Roger Gasser as he left Paul Reynaud's office, two days later, on Monday, May 27, 1940.

That Saturday, May 25, the king—whom Spaak described at the Limoges town hall six days later as appearing "unkempt, haggard, his eyes full of tears and his jaw tightly set," and added "he was more or less standing to attention before us"—launched the following order of the day to his army:

"Soldiers! The great battle we were awaiting has begun. It will be hard. We will conduct it with all our strength and with all our energy. It is taking place on the very territory where in 1914 we victoriously gained sway over the enemy.

"Soldiers! Belgium expects you to do honor to its flag. Officers and soldiers! Whatever happens, my fate will be your fate. I ask of each man his determination, discipline and trust. Our cause is just and true, and providence will guide us.

"Long live Belgium!"

"My fate will be your fate," said the king to his army, and thus countered the propaganda leaflets dropped by the Luftwaffe on Belgium. These showed a map in which the northern group of Allies was pushed back to the sea, its front and sides surrounded by German troops. The propaganda read in Walloon and Flemish: "Comrades! This is the situation! War is over for you. Your leaders are about to leave by plane!" There then followed a commentary in which the king was accused of abandoning his army to its fate, which urged the soldiers to throw down their arms to end the fighting which no longer held any meaning for them.

Such propaganda could have had a very damaging effect on those troops stationed at the breach for the past two weeks, already bitter at having had to abandon national terrain after a series of retreats for reasons unknown to them, which added to their state of extreme exhaustion. It was to lessen their confusion that their supreme commander had drafted this order of the day.

———

Five minutes after the king had received his early morning visitors in the reception hall at Wynendaele Château, his GHQ received news that the 1st and 3rd infantry divisions—who were holding the left bank of the Lys from Menin through Courtrai as far as Ooigem—had "disintegrated" under heavy enemy attack. While the king was undergoing a different form of attack from Pierlot and Spaak, his general staff prescribed measures to counter that situation. At 10:15, the king was informed by the British Colonel Davy, Lord Gort's liaison officer, that four divisions of the British Expeditionary Force would hold the waterway from Gravelines to Douai, passing through Saint-Omer and Béthune; four others would remain in the Menin position at Maulde; and the two last would be in reserve, south of Lille.

The king's predictions were coming true: the British command had adopted the solution of a bridgehead with its back to the sea. As those troops had not undergone too many trials, the bridgehead had some chance of maintaining its position as long as the French army could fill the pocket in the Valenciennes area as soon as possible. General Dill, who came to visit him at midday, had given Lord Gort a formal order from Imperial General Staff to take up the offensive in the Péronne region with two infantry divisions. The king remarked to General Dill that the enemy's advance seemed to be concentrated along the Ypres-Dixmude axis. Battle was raging, supported by the valiant Belgian army. A counterattack allowed them to bring back two hundred prisoners in the sector of the 5th Army Corps. But General Delvoie arrived with an order from General Blanchard confirming the orders from British Imperial General Staff: a counteroffensive would be launched on Monday, May 27, at Péronne by two divisions of the Expeditionary Force and three French divisions. General Blanchard came in person to confirm this to the king at 19:10, very pessimistic about the outcome of the operation. King Leopold made no comment, having decided after the Ypres Conference that this could not take place. Before seeking some rest at about 10 o'clock that night, Saturday, May 25, after his exhausting day, General Michiels informed him that the Belgian army was "holding well, everywhere."

# HEROIC TO THE LAST

Would the trust and determination of the Belgian soldiers in the front line have wavered on the morning of Saturday, May 25, if they had known that the remaining members of the government had left Belgian territory? I doubt it. Everything leads me to believe that the swarms of refugees on the roads would have been indifferent too. Of the many Belgian friends I made who had fought fiercely during the heroic Eighteen-Day Campaign and who also distinguished themselves in the valiant Resistance, not one of them ever doubted that the king would not remain at the head of their army.

That morning of Saturday, May 25, Admiral Keyes sent the following message to Churchill:

"The King was told last night by his Ministers that Lord Halifax was telegraphing to me to persuade His Majesty to withdraw with his Government. I have now received your message of 24 May.

"For the last eleven days the Ministers have been urging the King to fly with them. The four who by his orders have remained here spent some hours last night urging him to go with them at once; thus deserting his Army at a moment when it is fighting a stern battle to cover the left flank of the BEF. Deprived of the King's leadership, the capitulation of the Belgian Army would inevitably be hastened and the BEF endangered."

"King Leopold has written to the King to explain his motives for remaining with his Army and people if our armies become encircled and the capitulation of the Belgian Army inevitable. Dill

247

takes letter and a special Order of the Day from the King to his Army.

"I trust that H.M. Government will not be unduly impressed by the arguments of the Belgian Ministers who, apparently, have had no thought but the continuation of a political regime, whose incapacity and lack of authority have been only too apparent during the last fortnight. Their example has been followed by nearly all the local authorities and the result has been absolute confusion. Moreover they urged the British and French Ambassadors to precede them, in order to justify their own flight—a course which did not add to the prestige of the two countries."

— —

On the morning of May 25, General Michiels, chief of general staff noted: "The 10th and 9th divisions have sealed the breach made by the enemy yesterday when they forced their way through the 1st and 3rd divisions on the Lys front. The attackers have been identified as consisting of four divisions. The Belgian artillery under orders from high command is doing a magnificent job, continuously bombarding the enemy's zones of attack as far as it can fire." This is a "calm" statement, as Spaak had said when he was leaving for France, as though calmness was a sign of defeatism. It reminds me of the time General de Gaulle invited me to accompany him on a stroll around Colombey-les-deux-Eglises. At Bar-sur-Aube, he pointed to a middle-class house fronted by a courtyard facing the road. "During the first few days of September 1914, General Joffre directed the Battle of the Marne from this very house. The owners offered him their own room facing a little garden on the other side, but he declined, saying he preferred a smaller room with a window on the courtyard. On the eve of the decisive battle, the soldiers and dispatch riders passing to and fro could see their commander in chief leaning at the window peacefully smoking his pipe. Occasionally, he gave them a friendly gesture as if to say that all would go well. His calm attitude helped every one of them to win that battle."

During the night of May 24 to 25, while King Leopold's ministers were trying to persuade him to flee with them to France, General Weygand had a surprise, which he described as "pleasant, but shortlived."

"General Blanchard informed me that he was keeping to the agreed plan and launching his attack on the twenty-sixth despite the British retreat. I expressed my approval. But a few hours later an officer from his general staff arrived to report to myself and the prime minister on the exact situation of the troops he commanded. Commander Fauvelle arrived just when the daily meeting of the ministry of war was about to begin, so I asked him to make his report to the prime minister and Marshal Pétain as well as myself. He considered the situation of Army Group I critical. He had a sketch-map showing the positions of the troops under his command and demonstrated that Group I had no more than three divisions still capable of fighting, and that apart from some boxed ammunition, there was only one cannon unit behind them. Also the British seemed more concerned with their reembarkation, while the Belgian soldiers' attitude was open to doubt. It was obvious that in such a situation it would be easier to create a vast bridgehead covering the French ports than to carry out an offensive in the south. But that meant abandoning the most essential part of my plan in the face of enemy pressure."

———

This is the first time General Weygand refers to the British Expeditionary Force's reembarkation, without specifying in his book how he was informed of it. We do not know why Commander Fauvelle felt "the Belgian soldiers' attitude was open to doubt," unless the French military mission attached to King Leopold's GHQ—which, therefore, had contact with General Denis on his daily visits—had influenced General Blanchard by reporting statements such as those General Weygand had heard from Pierlot and his ministers at Ypres on May 21. A note written at 10:30 on May 25 at Vincennes GHQ supports this: "General Weygand says he is counting on the Belgian army to conduct a vigorous attack. The situation is fairly good. Morale excellent. We are counting on General Champon to keep up the morale of the Belgian troops."

———

I do not know what means General Champon had at his disposal to "keep up the morale" of King Leopold's soldiers. Had he mentioned to General Blanchard the "appalling defeatism" which Spaak said had pervaded Belgian GHQ since May 16? It was certainly contradicted by the king's order of the day on Saturday, May 25, after measures had been taken to allow his army to retreat in order to the Lys front. Apart from inevitable failures, the Belgian army was always able to demonstrate its resolve to fight to the end, and sometimes even beyond.

———

The same went for the defenders of the Calais fort—amongst other examples—and particularly for our friend Fortunat Thiébaut, who, with his comrades of the 32nd G.D.R.I., was also determined to fight to the bitter end in the bastion they had occupied since May 22. During the whole of Thursday, May 23, they had been bombarded by artillery and from the air and this had been stepped up at dawn on Friday.

"Shelling was more frequent and on target, the shells were whistling overhead. To the south we could see intense activity on the ground, where the Germans were deploying their artillery batteries. The small knots of French resistance, who were still trying to slow down the Germans' progress in the southern outskirts of town, were being attacked by air force and artillery, and were gradually falling silent. Some British fighter planes tried to intervene, but they were soon forced out.

"All day the fort was heavily bombed by the artillery and the air force. In the evening, the foot-soldiers, covered by tanks, cannons and armored vehicles of every description moved toward the town and the fort. We are using our machine-guns and mortars, and we are holding off all the German infantry.

"On May 25, the German infantry, who had taken advantage of the dark to edge toward the fort to gain a hold, were vigorously pushed back. At about eight o'clock, the French flag which usually flies from the belfry in the town was replaced by the Nazi flag. We were very disheartened but could do nothing about it.

"The air force and artillery were attacking the fort in full force. Everything was burning, exploding, crackling. The air was very hot. The smoke and gas from the blazing fires made it difficult to breathe, and some of us wore gas-masks.

"At about ten o'clock a German officer came to the main entrance of the fort and asked the soldiers to surrender. He was insistent, adding that if we refused the fort would be bombarded even more. We refused point-blank. Soon after, a series of planes flew past and dropped bombs on the fort while the artillery pounded at us continuously. The remaining buildings were ripped apart, pulverized and burned. The tanks and cannons launched an attack on the southern ramparts of the fort, trying to open up a breach. We were losing more and more men when the planes passed, despite the protection of the ramparts—Vauban had built them strong! Nightfall brought an end to the armored vehicle and plane attacks, but the German infantry once again used the dark to try to infiltrate the ramparts. . . ."

——

Most of the Belgian soldiers were fighting just as doggedly on the Lys front. In repelling an attack by the 192nd German Infantry Regiment, commanding Captain Lochs of the 7th Company of the 15th Regiment and Lieutenant Mutsaerts were killed by a burst of machine-gun fire. The enemy used this moment of indecision to come up behind the 7th Regiment in the north and the 11th in the south. Caught unawares at his command post, Ordies, commander of the 3rd Battalion of the 11th Regiment, killed one German, chased off the others and ran toward the position held by his soldiers. He found they had been taken prisoner, was himself disarmed, but succeeded in escaping back to his command post, where he fended off the enemy with a rifle. He was recaptured, escaped again by hiding in a rye-field, but this time he emerged right in front of a motorcycle column of German ground troops, who got the better of him. He had already been taken prisoner in Liège on August 6, 1914: with the many years spent behind barbed wire during the Great War, he was a prisoner for a total of nine years.

———

At 19:00 on Saturday, May 25, the French War Council held a meeting. Just like the account General Weygand gave three days earlier of the Ypres Conference, this account (no doubt seized at La-Charité-sur-Loire) was found in the Nazi archives of the *Austwaertiges Amt* after the surrender of the Reich. It states that the following members were present: Lebrun, president of the republic; Paul Reynaud, prime minister; Marshal Pétain, deputy prime minister; Campinchi, naval minister; Laurent-Eynac, air force minister; Rollin, colonial minister; General Weygand, commander in chief of the Allied armies; Admiral Darlan, General Vuillemin, General Buhrer (head of the colonial troops) and Paul Baudoin, secretary of the council. In his book *Recalled to Service*, General Weygand also mentions the British General Spears, "who was acting as Winston Churchill's spokesman and trusted official," of whom Paul Reynaud inquired "whether he had known about the British reembarkation." General Spears's reply was that "such a plan must have been discussed as an answer to a worsening situation, but he did not believe it would be put into action without a direct order from the British government." Given that he was talking about Operation Dynamo, which was to begin the next day, Sunday, May 26, one cannot help feeling that this "trusted official" was carrying discretion a little too far on this occasion. Here is the report on that meeting:

"The meeting opened at 1900.

"The prime minister stated the meeting had been called to hear General Weygand's report on the military situation and to examine the various possibilities that might arise. General Weygand took the floor. He said he would present the military situation in two parts: the first dealing with the north, and the second with the front from the Somme to Switzerland.

"The Northern Region: General Weygand briefly described the operations in which the two French armies in Belgium were presently engaged; how after the front was breached in the Maastricht area, the first units beat a retreat; how the 9th Army (General Corap's), consisting of nine divisions, then gave way on the Namur-Sedan line. The remnants of this army retreated in disorder. The disintegration of Corap's army opened up a wide breach in the French positions, through which the German army immediately moved toward the coast. The roads were open and their armored vehicles encountered little resistance. They succeeded in separating Army Group I—formerly under General Billotte and from three days before under General Blanchard—from the rest of the French army. Army Group I consists of the Belgian army (20 divisions), the British army (8 divisions), the French 1st Army (8 divisions) and the cavalry corps, making a total of 38 divisions.

"Since he took command (on Monday morning), General Weygand had been trying in vain to free those armies. Today the situation had become more serious. That group of armies faces the enemy on the the east, west and south, and the territory they are occupying is so narrow that they are unable to deploy their forces satisfactorily. General Blanchard, commander of Army Group I, is preparing an attack, which should take place on the night of 26 to 27 and continue on the morning of May 27 toward Bapaume. 'I do not know what will happen,' said General Weygand. 'My last telegram to General Blanchard this afternoon leaves him free to operate, and I asked him, above all else, to honor the flags in his safekeeping. So it is my duty to consider the worst possibility, that is to say, what would happen if we no longer had the troops that constitute the Northern armies. I have discussed this possibility with the prime minister.'

"Paul Reynaud, prime minister, interrupted the general to tell him of a telegram he had received that afternoon from Churchill, the British prime minister. The telegram confirmed the retreat of two British divisions from the Arras region, which jeopardized the plan decided the previous Wednesday by General Weygand with full approval of the British and French prime ministers. Churchill acknowledged in this telegram that the French Northern armies was practically surrounded and that all its communications had been cut, apart from Dunkirk and Ostend.

"General Weygand continued his report, this time dealing with the second point about the rest of the front. He believed there were three possible fronts: one covering Paris and abandoning the Maginot Line; the other retaining the Maginot Line, but necessitating a methodical withdrawal which had become an impossibility due to the disproportion of Germans compared to French there.

"General Weygand then gave his conclusions: 'We must hold our present position on the Somme-Aisne line and defend it to the very end. There are a number of weak points, notably the Crozat Canal and the Ailette. We might be split wide open. In that case, each small unit will have to form a core of resistance and hold out to the last to save the honor of the country.'

"General Weygand went on to say that France had committed a grave error by entering the war when it had neither the necessary material nor a viable military plan.

"The prime minister thanked General Weygand for his excellent account on the conduct of operations and the general conduct of the war. The conduct of operations had been approved by the French and British governments the previous Wednesday. As for the general conduct of the war, the prime minister agreed with General Weygand that if we were to lose the Northern armies (and that would be a hard blow to morale, total strength and materials), we would have to save France's honor by engaging in a fight to the last man. 'Having said that,' the prime minister went on, 'it is by no means certain that our adversary will grant us immediate armistice, and isn't it imperative for the government to avoid capture if the enemy takes Paris?'

"The prime minister also asked General Weygand what advice he would give the government on matters concerning the retreat. Tours is much too close. The Massif Central would become a prison. It seemed that Bordeaux or that region would offer the best solution.

"The president of the republic, Lebrun, interrupted to ask General Weygand what he thought the government's position would be if the French armies were dispersed and destroyed, according to the possibility outlined by the general. What freedom would the French government have if they received peace offers? Would it not have greater room for maneuver before the French armies were destroyed? 'We have signed agreements which prevent us from negotiating a separate peace treaty,' continued the president. 'If Germany were to offer us relatively advantageous conditions, we should in any case examine them closely and consider them with a clear conscience.'

"General Weygand understood the concerns of the president of the republic perfectly. He realized that the cessation of hostilities was a question to be decided among the Allies. He also realized that one could not consider the extreme possibility he suggested earlier, meaning a futile battle to save French honor, without considering the consequences for England. The prime minister stated that if offers of peace were made, France would have to say to England, 'Here are the offers we have received. What do you think of them?'

"General Weygand thought that given the present serious situation, it would be wise to examine these problems with the British government at the earliest opportunity. England was in great danger of losing all its present army, which would have formed the nucleus of its future army. It would understand our concern.

"Marshal Pétain wondered whether the obligations between France and England were entirely reciprocal. Each nation had obligations to the other in proportion to the aid given. In actual fact, England had only contributed ten divisions, whereas there were eighty French divisions engaged in the battle. The comparison should not only be based on the military effort of the two countries but also on the degree of suffering expected.

"General Weygand said that England should expect an invasion by Germany. He thought it would be useful for the French and British governments to hold talks very soon to discuss their views on the immediate future.

"The prime minister stated that on the night of May 16 to 17, Winston Churchill had indicated that were France to succumb, England would continue the struggle with a more powerful air force to try to starve out Germany. Churchill had already shown he was in favor of an all-out struggle until the time the United States should actively intervene. Paul Reynaud had asked Mr. Bullitt in what positive way President Roosevelt hoped to aid France. He had asked the question over a week ago, but had not yet received a definite answer."

———

In *Recalled to Service,* General Weygand only refers to the May 25 conference without going into it in detail, but he points out that Churchill's "trusted official," acting as spokesman for the British prime minister, "also mentioned the growing misunderstanding between Lord Gort and General Blanchard." He added that General Spears "spoke in such impolite terms about General Vuillemin," that he had to ask him to be "a little more discreet."

———

I wonder how the Belgian ministers, who were at Wynendaele Château fourteen hours previously, urging the king to retreat "behind the Loire" if necessary, would have reacted if the French War Council had met one day earlier. In that case they would have read the official report, showing that Lebrun was clinging to the hope of negotiating a separate peace treaty with Germany, a suggestion which was only feebly turned aside by Paul Reynaud. I also wonder what General Spears's reaction was at that committee when he heard General Weygand say that England was in danger of losing its entire Expeditionary Force, when the "misunderstandings" between General Blanchard and Lord Gort stemmed from the fact that the latter, without being able to say anything, had already acted on London's orders to evacuate the British Expeditionary Force. That was why, from the evening of May 23, without any warning to the new commander of Army Group I or to Vincennes GHQ, Gort ordered General Franklyn, commander of the British 5th and 50th infantry divisions to abandon Arras. While Churchill's "trusted official" was taking part in the French War Council, Lord Gort was beginning the maneuver which completely separated the British Expeditionary Force from the French—and the Belgian—army, and was bringing his troops to Dunkirk.

———

That Saturday, May 25, 1940, according to Admiral Keyes, who was at Saint-André-lez-Bruges GHQ, King Leopold showed the British General Dill on the map "the weak point on the Belgian right flank, the weakness of their defense line generally, and the impossibility of holding it and also keeping contact with the British army."

The following report comes from the preface written by the admiral of the British fleet to the book *Prisonnier de Laeken* (*Prisoner at Laeken*) by Cammaerts. Lord Keyes writes:

"General Dill promised to ask Lord Gort to do what he could to help contact being maintained. As the British Army was about to attack to the southward, the King felt that he could best help by keeping touch as long as possible with its left flank. He had already withdrawn his mechanized cavalry division from the left flank on the coast to reinforce the right flank, and he now gave orders for the 15th Division (infantry with no artillery nor machine guns) from the Yser further to reinforce that flank. This exhausted all his reserves. In the king's great effort to help the BEF, (the Belgian army) was strung out from Halluin to the sea on a front of 90 kilometres, and was threatened by German attacks at several points."

More than anything, that answers Spaak's base imputations. Our British friends were the only ones left and I am infinitely grateful to them, for without Great Britain's determination, Hitler would have won the war in Europe and no doubt well beyond Europe. There is no doubt that the British were right to recall their Expeditionary Force, described by General Weygand as the "nucleus of their future army." Even if it had guarded the Channel from the French side, it could not have prevented our disaster in June 1940. It, too, would have been crushed without reprieve, which would certainly have led England to accept Hitler's offers of peace. But all the same. . .

There can be no doubt that when General Dill was talking to King Leopold, he knew that the British Expeditionary Force was preparing to initiate the next day what Admiral Ramsey had been preparing at Dover since Monday, May 20. The fact that he nonetheless promised the king to support the Belgian army— which was being used to cover Lord Gort's left flank—by ordering General Alan Brooke's 2nd Corps to attack the German VIth Army's flank shows singular self-control.

As he left Saint-André-lez-Bruges GHQ, General Dill went to Lord Gort's headquarters, where General Blanchard, new commander of Army Group I (General Prioux was to take over what was left of the 1st Army), had already arrived. Blanchard had come to ask the head of the British Expeditionary Force to abandon the retreat to Dunkirk, and Dill asked for twenty-four hours to think it over after he had conferred with Lord Gort. Unless there had been a counterorder from London, the reembarkation was to begin before the twenty-four hours' delay was up. As soon as the head of Army Group I left, Gort and Dill got in touch with the secretary of state for war, Anthony Eden, whose reply was: "I have had information all of which goes to show that the French offensive from Somme cannot be made in sufficient strength to hold any prospect of functioning with your Allies in the north. Should this prove to be the case you will be faced with a situation in which the situation of the BEF will predominate."

Lord Gort softened that abrupt reply by telling General Blanchard that to his great regret the British Expeditionary Force would be unable to take part in the maneuver requested by General Weygand, which meant it would have to dissociate itself totally from the movements of the French army. At the same time, Blanchard received a grim message from General Weygand. The latter had already referred to it in the War Council which convened at 19:00 under the chairmanship of Lebrun: "You must remain sole judge of the decisions to try to save what can be saved, and above all, to honor the flags in your safekeeping." At the end of the meeting Paul Reynaud decided to go to London the next day, Sunday, May 26, to meet Churchill and sound out the British government's views on the eventual negotiation of peace between France and Germany.

—

I would like to add one telling phrase, one which I failed to place at its correct date of Tuesday, May 21. We know this thanks to Sir Roger Keyes, to whom Lord Gort said as he was leaving Ypres, where he had arrived so late that General Weygand had to leave for Dunkirk without waiting any longer, "I do hope the Belgians don't think us awful dirty dogs!" The admiral of the fleet's reply was that he did not know. Although Leopold did not know of the decisions made in London and the meeting held at Dover the previous day under Admiral Ramsay, the king's main concern was to do all he could to help the British Expeditionary Force to avoid being surrounded. Had he been informed, he would certainly have approved of the measures taken for the reembarkation of the British Expeditionary Force to England. He knew, like General Weygand, that it constituted the indispensible nucleus of the army which Great Britain had to form to gain final victory. .

# OPERATION DYNAMO

On Sunday, May 26, General Weygand presided over a meeting held from 8:00 A.M. at Montry and attended by General Doumenc, chief of staff of the French armies, General Georges, commander in chief of operations in the Northeast, General Roton, General Georges's chief of staff, and General Besson, commander of Army Group III. At the end of the meeting, he signed his second general order to the French armies, timed at 9:30 at Vincennes GHQ.

"1. The battle that will decide the fate of our country shall be fought without any thought of retreat from the position we now occupy. All ranks from commander in chief to heads of units must be prepared to fight to the death. If the leaders set the example, the troops will hold fast, and they have every right to enforce obedience if necessary.

"2. In order to ensure we stop the enemy, we must maintain constant aggression; if the enemy attacks in one sector, we must respond forcefully and rapidly.

"If the enemy forms a bridgehead on our front and uses it to attack with tanks and armored vehicles, be it the smallest of bridgeheads, we must push the enemy back to its lines with our artillery and air force and by counterattacking. Infiltration must be met by infiltration.

"If a unit discovers it is no longer linked on one of its sides because the next unit has been routed, on no account should it retreat. It must try to reestablish contact, and if it cannot, it

261

should group tightly together to form a resistance core. The same applies whether it is a division, a regiment, a battalion or a company.

"3. All the rearguards to the main line, starting from the front and as far back as possible, must be organized into resistance blocks, particularly along the main roads which the Germans have always used. Make sure you destroy what is necessary.

"4. The military police should see that the rear of each zone is blocked off.

"5. Division generals must contact their colonels daily, colonels their heads of battalions, heads of battalions their companies, and captains and lieutenants must contact their units and their men.

"Action, solidarity, resolution."

I could not have put it better myself. All that was needed was the means and the morale to carry it out. As it happened the means were lacking, but morale made up for it. Adequate means are in vain if morale is lacking, but some considered this to be of secondary importance: witness the reply given by a British general to a Belgian request, according to two messages recorded on Sunday, May 26, at Vincennes GHQ.

"2350. The situation on the Belgian front remains essentially unchanged, although the line is tenuously held in the far south. Belgian GHQ is expecting an attack on Ypres tomorrow. It intercepted a message to the German 18th Division ordering it to take Gheluwelt tonight and to continue the operation tomorrow. The Belgians request protection from British fighter planes to counter German propaganda literature telling Belgians not to count on the British for help.

"2358. The British General Barratt has replied that he will make a decision tomorrow, but that his intervention, if it takes place, will be very weak, as it is merely to satisfy a question of morale."

That Sunday, May 26, at 10:15 A.M. General Blanchard signaled

Vincennes GHQ: "Army Group I in difficulties."

On Sunday at 5:00 P.M., Admiral Keyes told the king that Lord Gort feared the left flank of the British Expeditionary Force might be exposed. In the preface to the book I mentioned earlier, he wrote:

"Lord Gort asked me to urge King Leopold to withdraw the Belgian Army towards the Yser. I gave this message to the King, who said they would do their best, but the only way of averting an imminent and complete disaster was for an immediate British counter-attack between the Lys and the Schelde. I telegraphed this to Lord Gort and found that similar appeals had been conveyed by the British Mission from the Belgian GHQ by telegram and despatch rider since an early hour that morning.

"The king told me later in the day, May 26, that he had discussed the matter with his General Staff, who considered that a withdrawal to the Yser was a physical impossibility under the pressure the enemy were exerting. A withdrawal over roads thronged with refugees, without adequate fighter cover, would be costly and would only end in disaster; moreover, it would mean the abandonment of all their ammunition, stores and food.

"On the other hand, his GHQ declared that a British counter-attack on the vulnerable flank of the enemy must be undertaken if a disaster was to be averted, and that the opportunity might only last a few more hours. An officer from the British Mission was sent to GHQ that evening to explain the Belgian views.

"But the British Army was in no better condition to deliver the counter-attack for which the GHQ pleaded, than the Belgian Army was to disengage and withdraw to the Yser as demanded by Lord Gort. Although King Leopold did not know at that time, and no message to this effect ever reached him, Lord Gort had already received orders to withdraw to the coast and was preparing to do so."

Apart from the intervention by the British officer mentioned by Admiral Keyes, Lord Gort was also presented with a letter by the chief of the Belgian mission attached to his GHQ dictated by the king at ten o'clock that morning in reply to his request for the Belgian army's immediate retreat to the Yser:

"Today, May 26, the Belgian army was violently attacked on the Menin-Nevele front, and the battle has so far stretched over the entire Eeklo region. Lack of Belgian reserves prevents us from extending further to the right, the limit designated yesterday.

"We regret to have to say that we have no troops left to block the Ypres area. As for the retreat to the Yser, it is quite out of the question, as it would destroy our combat units quicker than any battle, and without inflicting any losses on the enemy. The Yser-Yperlée region has yet to be flooded. The waters in the ditches along the east side of the river are swollen. All the preliminary work for flooding has now been completed. The order to flood the east bank of the Yser as far as Yperlée was given at 9:00 A.M. on May 26. It should be noted that the flooding will be fairly slow as we are in a low-tide season. There will be no flooding north of the Passchendaele Canal until further notice."

Lord Gort replied one hour later by letting the king know through Colonel Davy his regret that he could not at the present moment satisfy the request for a counterattack around Courtrai to relieve the Belgian right wing as his own left wing was in no condition to achieve this. He added, however, that two new divisions arriving in the Comines-Zillebecke sector could, eventually, be assigned to that task.

———

At midday on May 26, the battle reached a peak, particularly in the Vynkt and Oostrosebeke sectors. In order to strengthen the Belgian 7th Corps who were hard put, the king ordered the 16th Infantry Division to march to Tielt. As the situation was so serious, he dictated a message which General Michiels signed and brought to General Champon for transmission to Weygand:

"To the chief of the French mission attached to the Belgian army.

"Subject: situation of the Belgian army.

"For the past three days the Belgian army has been engaged in a full-scale battle on a ninety-kilometer front extending from Menin to north of Deinze, without any help whatsoever, apart from some intervention by the British air force.

"We are defending the territory foot by foot, causing considerable losses to the enemy. We have no more reserves and the attack—whose probability has been announced several times by Belgian command—will cause the unavoidable separation of British and Belgian troops around Ypres. That will seriously endanger the Belgian army, the British army and the ports on the Calais straits.

"Belgian command informed the Ypres Conference of my intention of defending the Lys line and the Deinze Canal up to the coast to the bitter end. During that same conference, it also agreed to increase that burden by relieving two British divisions and determining not to retreat to the Yser because of the disorganization the army would suffer.

"Belgian command is convinced it has rendered all the help the Belgian army is capable of giving the Allied armies by inflicting severe losses on the attacking German troops and by giving a precious moment of respite that will benefit the Allied armies' operations. Apart from that, we received no instructions whatsoever from Allied command, apart from General Billotte's approval given during the Ypres Conference.

"Belgian command begs you to convey to the commander in chief of the Allied armies that the Belgian army's situation is serious and that its commander in chief will continue to fight until all its means are exhausted. The line of resistance it is now maintaining at all costs is, according to the latest news, at Zonnebeke, Rolleghemkapelle, Isegem, Tielt, Nevele, the Lys Canal as far as the coast with advance units toward Philippine and Breskens. The enemy is now attacking the front from Eeklo to Menin. We have almost reached the end of our resistance."

———

At 18:30 that Sunday, May 26, General Blanchard arrived at the king's GHQ to announce that French and British troops were both retreating to a new front from Gravelines to Menin via Estaires. He knew nothing of Lord Gort's real purposes, and had tried to locate him in vain. "Two British divisions are moving toward Zillebeke," he said, "and Imperial General Staff will decide how to put them to use. As far as I am concerned the best I can do is to direct a light mechanized division of fifteen tanks toward Ypres." At this, said Admiral Keyes, the king ordered the rest of the French 60th Division to be transported by truck to a position behind the Yser, where the banks were flooded and the bridges mined to keep it out of the hands of the enemy, which now had at least eight divisions, some armored, supported by enormous numbers of bombers, to launch a decisive attack.

———

How hard they fought that Sunday, May 25, on the Lys front! If morale was all that was required, the enemy's attack would have been checked. But there was too great a disparity of means. In the morning a rumor in the ranks of the 12th Division said that 2,000 pilots of the Royal Australian Air Force were coming to the rescue, while at the same time it was said that large numbers of British reinforcements had landed at Zeebrugge. Alas! That was wishful thinking. After intensive artillery preparation and under cover of aerial bombardment, the German 208th Infantry had succeeded in crossing the Lys branch canal between Ronsele and Oostwinkel, overpowering the 6th Company of the 23rd Regiment and forcing the 2nd Regiment on its left to retreat. In a counterattack, the 3rd Battalion of the 22nd Regiment commanded by Major Belleter regained the position, and when night came, the pocket was completely sealed off to the west. Further north, in the sector occupied by the 18th Division, the enemy was attacking the lines of the 5th Company of the 7th Light Infantry. After defending himself with grenades, a sergeant was seriously wounded. His commander, Captain Delatte, immediately launched a counterattack. Wounded by a bullet in the right arm, he continued to urge his men forward. A second bullet caught him in the thigh but he still continued to give orders. A third bullet caught him right in the heart and he was killed instantly. The Germans continued to advance, pushing prisoners in front of them. Commanding Captain de Grunne tried to check this and walked toward the enemy, leaning on a stick in his left hand, while his right hand gripped a pistol. He too was killed. The breach widened and a wave of Germans advanced on Maldegem, always using their prisoners as protective cover. But when the prisoners realized this, they allowed the 1st Rifles of the 12th Division to open fire with their machine-guns and the Germans were put to flight. At Calais, on the other hand, it was all over.

———

Fortunat Thiébaut writes: "From dawn, the bombing had resumed. The shelling was now concentrated on the southern ramparts of the fort, and eventually it opened up wide breaches through which the German infantry surged. Having gained that part of the ramparts, the German soldiers advanced slowly but inexorably toward the other ramparts. Aerial bombing and artillery fire gave way to machine-gun fire and grenade explosions. Our possiblities of resistance dwindled as the Germans advanced.

"At about 1400, we were ordered to cease-fire and lay down our arms. The Germans had reached the gates of our last entrenchments, which they threatened to blow up with machine-guns and grenades. All that remained of the fort were odd remnants of blackened walls. The ramparts were almost completely gutted and the ground, pitted all over, was littered with bodies and debris.

"The survivors were stripped of their watches, rings and valuables and then assembled into the bomb craters to be photographed for Nazi propaganda. A few moments later, they set off on foot for the prisoner-of-war camps in Germany. That marked the end of the defense of Calais, where for several days a handful of French soldiers had stood up against enemy troops far superior in numbers and with the benefit of the most modern and powerful arms of that era."

---

At 15:00 on Sunday, May 26, 1940, Operation Dynamo—readied since Monday 20 by Vice Admiral Ramsay at Churchill's orders—got under way. The admiral had requisitioned any vessel capable of transporting men by sea, from the smallest steamers that sailed from Newhaven, Southampton, Dover and Folkestone for the Continent, to those he had brought from the Irish Sea, not to mention coasters or trawlers operating in the Channel or the North Sea, as well as motorized yachts and landing-craft. The British people had responded magnificently to his appeal, and private boats normally moored on the Thames River plied to and fro between the British coast and Dunkirk, Malo-les-Bains, Zuydcoote or La Panne under enemy fire. Begun on May 26, Operation Dynamo continued until June 4, evacuating a total of 338,226 officers and soldiers, among whom were more than 113,000 French. What Churchill called the "miracle of Dunkirk" could never have been so successful had it not been for the dedication of the Belgian army, which held out against the enemy and covered the operation, and other similar instances of heroism displayed by the 12th, 32nd and 68th French divisions. General Janssen, commander of the 12th M.I.D., died in that resistance which protected the reembarkation. General Fagalde, Vice Admiral Abrial and Rear-Admiral Platon all conducted themselves in ways which cannot be praised enough. A quarter of the low-tonnage vessels used in Operation Dynamo were sunk, as were thirteen French and British antitorpedo and torpedo boats. The Royal Air Force lost one hundred and six planes, but it downed a large number of the Luftwaffe's aircraft. The British army could now be re-formed.

# THE EVE OF THE LAST DAY

On Sunday morning, May 26, Hitler summoned General von Brauchitsch, commander in chief of the Wehrmacht ground forces, to reprimand the VIth and XVIIIth armies for their slow progress. Hitler had abruptly changed his decision made two days before: ordering the Panzer divisions not to pass beyond the Lens-Gravelines line through Béthune, Aire-sur-la-Lys and Saint-Omer. He now ordered von Brauchitsch to launch an immediate attack toward Cassel and Dunkirk. The effects of that order were immediately felt on the Lys.

During the night of May 26 to 27, the Belgian lines between Ingelmunster and Tielt, bordered in the south by the Roulers Canal, gave way under the pressure of the 30th and 255th divisions of the VIth Army. Taking advantage of this, von Reichenau launched General von Kortzfleisch's XIth Corps toward Torhout, and General von Schwedler's IVth Corps toward Mount Kemmel. It was 5:00 A.M. when the German 30th Division pounced on the position held by the Belgian 7th Corps, concentrating on the angle between the Roulers Canal and the Courtrai-Tielt railway line. At 7:30 the 2nd Battalion of the 42nd Regiment launched a counterattack, but heavy bombing prevented it from achieving more than just holding a position from which to slow down the enemy's advance.

With all their reserves exhausted, the Belgian army could not hold on any longer because they often had no telephone communication lines, the relief recruits had been issued with rifles

269

from World War I, half the sappers had joined the infantry, and the fortress units which had retreated from Antwerp, Namur and Liège were being used as laborers. "Our front is fraying away," said General Van Overstraeten, "like an old rope that is about to snap." Indeed, the rope was fraying away hour by hour, but the strands were holding on despite strong enemy pressure. At 10:30, von Reichenau ordered von Kortzfleisch to attack Dixmude. In the early afternoon, the riflemen of the 3rd Group of the 3rd Artillery Regiment fought until they ran out of cartridges and the 2nd Division of the Ardennes Light Infantry battled to protect the road to Bruges. At 15:00 the 6th Battery of the 3rd Artillery Regiment was about to be overrun near Ardooie, so they blew up all their installations when they ran out of ammunition. The enemy met with fierce resistance in the village, where they were held at bay until nightfall, but the breach was almost seven kilometers wide and the road to Bruges lay wide open. King Leopold's GHQ was already preparing to leave for Middelkerke, between Ostend and Nieuport. At 17:25 the order was given to the troops in battle to retreat to the Roulers-Koolskamp line if they could, and if not, to continue fighting where they were. Five minutes later, the 6th Division was in such grave danger that it was ordered to burn the flags.

There were many instances of outstanding bravery all along the front, which was now in flames, the officers often losing their lives as they set an example to their men. By a tragic coincidence, Ysebrandt de Lendonck—who was so short that he was nicknamed "Poussière" (speck of dust)—commander of what was left of the 3rd Lancers—was killed just where his horse had been shot beneath him during the last offensive in 1918. When night came, the breach had been sealed again by the valiant Belgian army. The German 18th Division paid homage to their bravery in their historic account *Unser weg zum meer* (*Our Road to the Sea*):

"The Belgians, who were covering the British army's cowardly retreat with extraordinary courage, barely supported by a few

English batteries, put up a stubborn resistance to the pursuit we had begun on May 25." In his book *La Campagne de l'Armée belge en 1940* (*The Belgian Army's Campaign in 1940*), Chevalier de Fabribeckers pointedly remarks that the accusation of cowardice made against the British soldiers is unjust. They were merely obeying orders from London when they retreated to Dunkirk. In a letter Hitler wrote to Mussolini on May 25, he gave a generally fairer account: "By and large, the Belgian soldiers fought bravely. Their experience of war is much greater than that of the Dutch. At first their tenacity was astonishing, but it has visibly decreased now that their main function consists of covering the British retreat. The British soldiers had all the characteristics reminiscent of the World War I: brave and tenacious in defense, unskillful in attack and very poorly commanded. Their arms and equipment are first class, but their general organization is bad."

"Very poorly commanded," "general organization is bad"— these are harsh criticisms. Hitler did not take into consideration that Lord Gort was theoretically dependent on the commander of the French Army Group I since the German breach in the Ardennes, and obliged to follow orders from London, where the evacuation of the British Expeditionary Force had been planned since May 20. This put him in an awkward position—to say the least—particularly after General Billotte's death, since there was no way for him to respond to the Belgian army's requests. Some time later, after Rommel's defeat at El Alamein, thus putting an end to his dream of marching through the Middle East, perhaps as far as India, he experienced the vigor of British command and the excellence of its logistics. The same went for the Japanese in Singapore soon after, when the young Lord Mountbatten— placed in command of the Allied forces in Southeast Asia when all seemed lost—accepted the unconditional surrender of 700,000 men who had long considered themselves invincible.

And what did Hitler have to say about the French soldiers in that letter to his henchman Mussolini? "There are some very bad units fighting next to some excellent units. All in all, the difference between the regular divisions and the reserves is extraordinary. Many active divisions fought desperately; the reserves are far less able to sustain the shock that war has on the morale of the troops."

He added this remark, for what it is worth: "For the French—as for the Dutch and the Belgians—there is the added fact that they realize they are fighting in vain toward objectives that are not related to their true interests. Their morale is very low for they see that the British, wherever they are, are only concerned with their own units, and are leaving the more dangerous sectors to their Allies."

There may be some truth in that remark, but it was nonetheless true that General Fagalde's men, and those of General Janssen and Admiral Abrial, fought to the very last to protect the British Expeditionary Force's reembarkation; they did so because they felt, like the Belgian army, that the cause against Nazism was a common one, and that cause would be lost if the British were forced to sign a peace treaty with Hitler.

—

Reynaud left for London at 10:00 A.M. on Sunday, May 26, as had been decided at the War Council meeting. During lunch with Churchill and Lord Halifax, he discussed the possibility that France might have to enter into negotiations with Germany, but the British remained evasive. He returned to Paris that night after a short visit that had yielded no positive results, and he was unaware that a telegram was sent to Lord Gort as soon as he left: "Prime Minister had conversation M. Reynaud this afternoon. It is clear that it will not be possible for French to deliver attack on the south in sufficient strength to enable them to effect junction with Northern Armies. In these circumstances no course open to you but to fall back upon coast . . . . M. Reynaud communicating General Weygand and latter will no doubt issue orders in this sense forthwith."

The statement that General Weygand would issue orders "in this sense" was completely hypothetical, but Churchill's telegram to Lord Gort had been preceded by a telegram from Eden: ". . . In such conditions only course open to you may be to fight your way back to West where all beaches and ports east of Gravelines will be used for embarkation. Navy will provide the fleet of ships and small boats and R.A.F. would give full support. As withdrawal may have to begin very early preliminary plans should be urgently prepared." A similar order sent by the British Admiralty to Vice Admiral Ramsay at 18:17 to begin Operation Dynamo did not reach him until almost four hours after he had himself decided to mount the operation without awaiting orders. At 22:30 he met the first contingents of troops which had crossed the Channel, and by midnight he could proudly say that 27,936 officers and soldiers of the British Expeditionary Force had already returned home. On Monday, May 27, the British General Adam took charge of the reembarkation operations at Dunkirk, which was to include, if at all possible, a certain number of French. No provision had been made for the Belgians: apart from the fact that their situation was considered "too critical," their front—which was further from Dunkirk than the French defense lines—served to slow the enemy down and increase the chances of success for the reembarkation. King Leopold had still not been informed that Operation Dynamo—its very existence was unknown to him—had been put into action the previous day. That fact lends a somewhat bitter irony to the following messages recorded at Vincennes GHQ that Monday, May 27:

1045. Belgian GHQ requests the British to mount a counterattack to help them. The British have the means readily available.

1050. The British consider it a futile operation.

1100. General Champon is insistent: such a counterattack stands a good chance of having important results.

1105. General Weygand is personally approaching Lord Gort.

1110. Lord Gort will refer it to London.

1115. General Weygand asks Lord Gort to act immediately. Lord Gort is adamant. He will await London's decision.

1145. Lord Gort requests orders from London.

1350. The Belgian chief of general staff indicates the Germans are mounting a strong attack on the entire front and that a general retreat is in progress.

1730. London considers it unnecessary to mount the counterattack requested this morning at 1045 (by telephone from Lord Gort). Never mind. It would be too late anyway as the enemy has advanced five kilometers. But it's a pity.

Poor Lord Gort! He knew exactly what he should do, but he had to keep his mouth shut. One whole hour elapsed between the time Belgian GHQ made their request and the time he unhurriedly asked London the question to which he already knew the answer. And this was despite two intercessions from General Weygand who, like King Leopold, was also quite unaware of the real reasons behind this lack of urgency. London took its time, as we can see from its message "unnecessary to mount the counterattack" requested more than seven hours previously by Belgian high command. Then it had the gall (I can find no nicer way of putting it) to add "Never mind. It would be too late anyway." As for "But it's a pity," at the end of the message, only the friendship I have toward the British people prevents me from commenting, particularly as at 9:20 A.M. that Monday, May 27, when Lord Gort returned to his command post, he immediately asked King Leopold's army, which was already engaged in a hopeless battle, to cover his left wing with an "immediate retreat" to the Yser. The king certainly showed perfect self-control when he dictated the following message to Colonel Haily of the British mission and Colonel Hautecoeur of the French mission attached to his GHQ:

"It had been decided, at the king's request at the Ypres Conference, that the Belgian army would defend the position it then occupied, that is to say, the Lys-Deinze line to the sea, and that it would relieve two British divisions on its right, thus extending its front as far as Halluin adjoining the position manned by the British. We replied, to a subsequent request from British GHQ to extend our front in order to relieve a third British division, that a Belgian division would be brought on the morning of May 25 to the area northwest of Menin, with a view to taking up position on the Lys from Menin to Comines.

"Meanwhile, the German attack, having forced a passage to the Lys on both sides of Courtrai on May 24, compelled us to use that division which was supposed to go northwest of Menin. We expressed our regrets that evening to the liaison officer at British GHQ that we were unable to extend our front. At the same time, we drew his attention to the probability and danger of a German attack and a rupture of the front in the Courtrai and Ypres regions.

"On the morning of the twenty-fifth during General Dill's visit, we reiterated our apprehensions, indeed, our near-certainty, that the attempt to breach the front would take place. Besides that, we notified the British liaison officer (Colonel Davy) at about 1600, that because we were using all our reserves, the furthest possible limit the Belgian front could be extended to the right was along the Gheluwe-Zonnebeke line.

"Yesterday, May 26, we nevertheless extended our right wing as far as the Lys between Menin and Wervik, until the German attack—which overwhelmed our 2nd C.D.—took Gheluwe at 0930. Our right wing then regrouped on the Zonnebeke-Dadizele front, which it held until nightfall. We have also kept one detachment at Ypres up to the present time.

"Both British command and General Blanchard requested that the Yser line up to Ypres be held by Belgian positions. That was achieved four days ago. Moreover, we believe that general cover for the British left flank has been efficiently effected by the positioning of the Belgian army and by the battle in which it has been fighting for the last four days about fifty kilometers beyond the Yser."

Lord Gort had not yet received that message when one of his aides-de-camp arrived at Belgian GHQ at 11:00 A.M. to speak to the king. "Since the British Expeditionary Force is holding a ninety-mile front between Gravelines and Ypres (he was exaggerating, a glance at the map showed that this is no more than sixty kilometers), I regret to have to inform you that we are quite incapable of mounting the counterattack for your benefit. The best we can do is to block the Comines-Ypres line with two divisions. Lord Gort requests that your army should on no account retreat north, but that it should reinforce the Yser front."

At this renewed request, the king replied that the retreat to the Yser had begun, as best as could be expected under fire. He repeated that he considered the Ypres-Passchendaele sector to be the most dangerous point, but said he had no more men left to send there.

—

"Any hope of direct cooperation from the British or French is out of the question, although the Allies have been informed that we have no more troops and that our ability to resist is almost finished; that is how it was at the beginning of May 27," wrote General Michiels, chief of the Belgian general staff. "Our very last reserves—three weak regiments—are engaged in battle. Liaison with the British is being maintained, but to our cost, and the enemy intends to break down this resistance which is causing it considerable loss of time and men. Our men are holding the entire front; they are fighting in position, only relinquishing their hold an inch at a time and inflicting heavy losses on the enemy. The artillery are using all their ammunition and firing as far as possible, blowing up any emplacements that fall into enemy hands. Despite their valor, large breaches have appeared since noon: in the north toward Maldegem, in the center near Ursel and to the right between Tielt and Roulers. The enemy is gradually pouring through the breaches to reach the command posts. Around Tielt, about six or seven kilometers of the front is undefended. The enemy needs only to push through this gap to reach Bruges. Many losses: there are many wounded in the medical centers and the hospitals are filled to overflowing. Numerous artillery emplacements are without ammunition, particularly 150 mm. howitzers. The army has reached the limit of organized resistance. The circle of fire is decreasing. Thousands of civilian refugees are milling around in a small area, all within range of artillery and air force fire. Our last means of resistance have succumbed under vastly superior technical means, without either hope, or renewed aid or any solution other than that of total destruction."

At 12:30 on Monday, May 27,1940, Admiral Keyes addressed the following message to Lord Gort at King Leopold's request:

"From King Leopold to Lord Gort. He wishes you to know that his Army is greatly disheartened. It has been incessantly engaged for four days and subjected to intense air bombardment, which the R.A.F. have been unable to prevent. The knowledge that the Allied Armies in this sector have been encircled, and that the Germans have great superiority in the air, had led his troops to believe that the position is almost hopeless. He fears a moment is rapidly approaching when he can no longer rely upon his troops to fight or to be of any further use to the B.E.F. He wishes you to realise that he will be obliged to surrender before a debacle.

"The King fully appreciates that the B.E.F has done everything in its power to help Belgium, and he asks you to believe that he has done everything in his power to avert this catastrophe."

At 13:15, the king received a telephone call from the chief of general staff: "The front has been breached where the 7th and 5th Army Corps are. The situation is critical. Similarly, the attack on the 6th Army Corps has increased in violence."

At 14:00, the king was in conference with General Michiels and General Nuyten, who both felt that the army had already done all it could, and that the only way to prevent the final horrific massacre after such a debacle was to cease fighting immediately.

Half an hour later the king informed General Van Overstraeten of this meeting and the latter thought it best to wait until the end of the day to reach a decision. At the king's request he left to discuss the matter with General Michiels.

That Monday, May 27, at 3:00 A.M., Admiral Keyes received a telegram from Churchill, referring implicitly to the bond of friendship which united the hero of Zeebrugge and the son of the "Roi-Chevalier." The prime minister said:

"Impart following to your friend: Presume he knows that British and French are fighting their way to the coast between and including Gravelines and Ostend, and that we propose to give fullest support from Navy and Air Force during hazardous embarkation. What can we do for him? Certainly we cannot serve Belgium's cause by being hemmed in and starved out!"

At the same time, another telegram, this time to Lord Gort, left London:

"Now is the time to let the Belgians know. It is desirable that you contact the king personally. Keyes will see to it. We are asking them to make a sacrifice."

Admiral Keyes had informed King Leopold. He knew what the answer to "What can we do for him?" would be, for the king was determined to share the fate of his army to the very end. Knowing that the British Expeditionary Force would try to reach England, the rest went without saying: his soldiers must keep the enemy where it was as best they could. On the morning of Saturday, May 25, at Wynendaele Château, as Pierlot was leaving he had asked the king how long the surrender could be delayed and the king had replied, "Twenty-four hours at the most." That delay was already twice as long, thanks to the army's heroic resistance. Now it was a question of stopping the bloodshed, preventing disorder, and putting an end to the suffering of the people and the crowds of refugees trapped between the lines of fire and the French border. Spaak, the budding strategist, decided that the king's concern showed "he was not a general."

———

At 7:00 A.M. on Monday, May 27, a meeting chaired by Admiral Abrial was held at Cassel. It was attended by the British General Adam, who was to direct reembarkation operations, representing Lord Gort; General Fagalde, commander of the troops covering Boulogne, Calais and Dunkirk; General Prioux, new leader of the French 1st army; and General Koeltz, aide to the commander in chief's staff. No Belgians had been invited. At the same time, a meeting was held at Dover under Admiral Ramsay and attended by the French Admiral Odend'hal—chief of the French naval mission in London—Admiral Leclerc and the British Admiral Somerville. The two meetings had the same objective: to coordinate the evacuation which was to include some French troops. However General Koeltz's mission was different. At Cassel he read an order from General Weygand, who was planning to regroup the 1st Army north of the Lys and to extend the bridgehead to recapture Calais, which had been held until Sunday, May 26, "by the extraordinary courage of the men in the fort and the various bastions." In his book *Recalled to Service*, General Weygand supported this; "Frigate Captain de Lambertye, commander of the seafront, was one of the last victims," together with Frigate Captain Ducuing, whose orders were to defend the strategic Cape Gris-Nez position and who was killed at his command post after heroic resistance. Boulogne, which had already been evacuated by the British troops on the twenty-third on orders from London, also saw a desperate battle, so desperate that on Saturday, May 25, General Lanquetot and his men were even commended by the enemy and received battle honors. On May 27, a message from General Weygand was sent to General Blanchard, telling him to: "Resist to the last, behind lines covering Dunkirk and other Channel ports. Each day of battle gives one more day of respite for the French army to prepare the battlefield on the Somme and Aisne. No price is too high. It must be paid." At midday, General Weygand met Paul Reynaud at the daily meeting at the ministry of war: "The prime minister reported on the news in London. People were pessimistic, he said, which no doubt accounted for General Gort's decision to retreat." Gort, unknown to those at Rue Saint-Dominique, had in the meantime received very precise instructions from Eden: "Wish to stress that your only duty from now on is to evacuate most of your troops to England." That was certainly General Adam's main preoccupation, since he had paid little attention to the reading of General Weygand's order at the Cassel meeting. Besides, the meeting came to an abrupt end as enemy shells began to rain down. The enemy had spilled through the breach on the Lys front and were pressing toward Bergues, obviously to occupy Dunkirk.

———

It was almost 15:00 when General Koeltz and General Champon arrived at Belgian GHQ. They both talked to General Michiels, chief of general staff, who gave them a resumé of the situation. He reminded them that Belgian command has asked the British twenty-fours hours previously to make a counterattack on the enemy's flank and rear between the Lys and the Schelde, and added he had just been told that according to Lord Gort, the British Expeditionary Force was incapable of carrying out such an operation. The Belgian army was fighting heroically, he said, but had no more reserves; its last means of resistance had been crushed, overwhelmed by tremendous enemy pressure. It would soon be totally destroyed as it had already suffered considerable losses, and the medical centers were overflowing with the wounded. The situation was hopeless.

General Michiels's account was confirmed by General Van Overstraeten, who arrived for the meeting, during which he compared the Belgian army's will to resist to a worn out rope that is about to snap.

Since the king had not decided about the proposal of a cease-fire made less than an hour before by General Michiels and General Nuyten, the Belgian officers did not mention it. At the parliamentary inquiry held on April 17, 1951, General Koeltz said this about the meeting with General Van Overstraeten: "I understood, as did General Champon, that the Belgian army, which was being attacked from the front and threatened on the right flank, would have to retreat west."

If we accept that General Koeltz had not been informed by General Champon—which would be surprising—of the message the king had asked General Michiels to send the day before to General Weygand at the French military mission (giving the Belgian army's situation and stating unequivocally: "We have almost reached the end of our resistance"), then how could Koeltz imagine that the already exhausted troops could "retreat west" in mid-battle, without it resulting in complete disaster? (He could see on the map the wide breaches at Maldegem and Ursel and between Tielt and Roulers where, in General Weygand's favorite word, the front was "split" along a seven-kilometer stretch.) Through working with his colleague from the British military mission, General Champon must have known that in reply to Lord Gort's repeated requests to bring the Belgian troops to the Yser, the king had said that such a movement "would destroy our combat units quicker than any battle, and without inflicting any losses on the enemy." On Sunday, May 26, at the latest, the chief of the French military mission would have informed General Weygand that a cessation of battle on the front where the remaining Belgian army continued to fight, only giving ground inch by inch, would soon be unavoidable. If they were surprised in Paris, that was not because of King Leopold. We have proof enough to the contrary.

When Professor Jacques Prienne, the Belgian academic, was in Geneva, he was visited by France's former military attaché to Bucharest. This Colonel Thierry was a famous veteran of World War I, and he had this to say:

"In 1939, I rejoined the service. First I was chief of general staff under General Giraud, then I was assigned to organize the radio telephone station, a service attached to the premier's office.

"My services heard King Leopold's telephone communications to General Blanchard, commander of the Northern armies, announcing the desperate situation the Belgian army was in and its imminent surrender.

"Those messages, transcribed or recorded, were immediately relayed to the prime minister and the minister of war. Paul Reynaud knew, therefore, when he made his speech on May 28, that it was untrue that the king had surrendered without warning the Allies.

"These documents I kept and locked safely away. In October 1940, the Vichy government wanted me to hand them over, and when I refused, I was sentenced to death by the Germans. I left France secretly on November 11, 1942.

"I consider it my duty to tell you this, and I authorize you to make it publicly known."

---

It was nearly 16:00 that afternoon of Monday, May 27, when King Leopold's general staff passed him this brief report:

"The commander in chief considers that:

"1. From a national point of view, the army has fulfilled its duty; it has used every means of resistance; its units are incapable of fighting tomorrow; a retreat to the Yser is out of the question: it would disorganize the units more than a battle and would add to the congestion of the Allied armies that are already dangerously confined in the region between the Yser on the one hand, and Calais and Cassel, which are being attacked by the Germans.

"2. From an international point of view, if we sent a representative to enquire about conditions for a cessation of hostilities, it would benefit the Allies by gaining them the night of May 27 to 28, and part of the morning of the twenty-eighth. Such a delay is better than any gained by continuing the battle, at the cost of a catastrophic disorganization of the army."

—

It is obvious from this message that in the afternoon of Monday, May 27, 1940, Belgian GHQ still did not know that Calais had fallen the previous day. I cannot believe that neither the chief of the French military mission nor General Koeltz had been informed, but I can find no trace of them having told General Van Overstraeten or General Michiels. Similarly it seems that General Koeltz preferred to say nothing about the conference at Cassel presided over by Abrial, nor about the discussions that same morning on the evacuation of the British Expeditionary Force together with a certain number of French troops. Why the silence, unless it was because the Belgians were to be kept out of the operation?

—

The hour for the king's final decision had come. At 15:45 he sent a representative to the German lines. He chose General Derousseaux, second in command at general staff. The latter set out at 17:00 to find out the conditions for the cessation of hostilities between the German army and the Belgian army. So this was a mission strictly limited to the conditions for a cease-fire.

—

General Van Overstraeten, who had wanted the king to wait until dawn on Tuesday, May 28, to take this step, also changed his mind as the news arriving at GHQ became increasingly more alarming and distressing.

In addition to the 800,000 inhabitants in the zone between the line of fire and the French border were the 700,000 or so refugees who were in a state of great distress. Following the bombing raids, the area had been almost without running water, electricity or gas. All food supplies had been exhausted and there were already some outbreaks of typhus. Even the smallest roads were so congested that it was impossible for a motor vehicle to advance at more than walking pace. The dead and the wounded—a large number had died, despite the care they received from volunteers, through the lack of medicines and basic necessities—were piled up in the hospitals, visited untiringly by Queen Elisabeth, who felt completely powerless to help them.

At 16:00, the king's decision was communicated to General Champon and Colonel Davy, head of the British military mission. It is unthinkable that General Champon had not been informed by General Koeltz about the conference at Cassel with no Belgians in attendance: nevertheless, he protested immediately, arguing that "the three armies in the north formed a unit, whose dissociation had never been contemplated until now." He was astonished that the Allies had not been forewarned, yet he had every opportunity to know, from the messages the king had asked him to pass on, that the collapse of the Belgian army was only a question of hours, prolonged to the afternoon of May 27 by its heroism. Had he not personally intervened that morning with Lord Gort to mount a counterattack requested by Belgian GHQ, knowing well that if it was not done, the enemy would open up a breach on the Lys front that could not be sealed? Had he not, with General Koeltz, just heard the most precise account of the situation from General Michiels? Had he not seen for himself the indescribable chaos on the roads, which made the question of retreat impossible?

Yet General Champon insisted that there could be no question of Belgium negotiating with the enemy without prior consultation with the Allies, and should this be approved, then the French and British should control those negotiations. General Michiels replied that there could be no negotiations given the army's situation; the only issue at stake was surrender. "Your protest will be conveyed to the king," continued the chief of general staff. "Our representative has only been sent on an information mission. No decision has been made."

A message from General Champon, chief of the French military mission attached to the Belgian army, was received at Vincennes GHQ at 18:10 on Monday, May 27, 1940:

"We have learned from a reliable source (a communication from Belgian general staff to General Champon) the following: the king of Belgium has sent a negotiator to German high command to ask about conditions for a cessation of hostilities between the Belgian army and the German army. The king is proposing a cease-fire at midnight tonight."

---

This dramatic message contained both a contradiction and an assumption that was quite erroneous.

General Michiels had told General Champon that the representative sent to the enemy by the king had only gone on an "information mission" (which General Champon interpreted as a "negotiator" sent to ask the "conditions for a cessation of hostilities"), showing he did not know the meaning of the words he was using. General Derousseaux could not become a "negotiator" until after he had given the king an account of his first mission and obtained a mandate from the king, commander in chief of the army, to accept the enemy's conditions.

Besides that, it was untrue that the king wanted a cease-fire at midnight May 27. On the contrary, the king intended to comply with the message he had received from his general staff on the afternoon of May 27, where it was suggested that a discussion with the enemy would benefit the Allies by giving them until the following morning, which could not have been obtained if the battle had continued without incurring heavy losses and the collapse of the Belgian army.

---

At 18:15, another message from General Champon reached Vincennes GHQ:

"General Champon wishes to point out that any discussion on this situation will be invalid and cannot take place except in the presence of qualified representatives from the three commands: French, British and Belgian. The three armies are part of a whole, and the Belgian army cannot act alone (General Champon's reply to the Belgian chief of general staff)."

General Derousseaux, authorized by the king to sign the Belgian surrender, would have to be present after he had told the king the enemy's conditions; I do not know whether the British government thought it should send a representative to General von Reichenau, but it would seem to me highly unlikely. It is a pity, just to complete the picture, that General Champon did not want a say in the "discussions" held before the head of the German VIth Army, who acted as Hitler's spokesman. Undoubtedly, he could have gained some important concessions from the Germans by acting as spokesman for a government that had gone adrift, while the entire French army was on the verge of collapse!

General Blanchard had more foresight and sent a message at 7:00 A.M. on Monday, May 27, to General Georges: "The situation is worsening by the hour especially on the Belgian front. The Belgians have just sent the 60th Division back to 'Admiral North.' "

———

Communications between Army Group I and Paris had been cut for several days, so that message was sent via the French embassy in London and did not reach Montry until after 18:00. If General Weygand had received it earlier, he would have understood that the object of the king's maneuver was to remove the 60th Division, which he commanded, from a position of danger. Weygand would have acknowledged this magnanimous gesture and deduced from it that the surrender of the Belgian army was only a few hours away. But, trusting the chief of the French military mission, he still thought, even two days before the surrender, that the situation was "rather good," and counted on

General Champon to "keep up their morale," which had been described by the latter as "excellent." When a man with his back to the wall is resolved to die rather than face dishonor, one does not say his morale is "excellent"; he is the epitomy of courage.

———

King Leopold tried to reach Lord Gort to inform him of his decision, but in vain: besides the fact that the telephone center in Lille had been destroyed, nobody at his GHQ knew where the chief of the British Expeditionary Force was. When they heard that a representative was going to the German lines, Colonel Davy, head of the British military mission, left GHQ. It was he who sent a message to London, received there at 17:54. Colonel Thierry states that the king was able to contact General Blanchard by telephone to inform him of his army's imminent surrender. At 18:00, Leopold issued the following order to his army: "As the front line has broken down in several places, the army will retreat at nightfall to the general area of Damme-Male-Hille-Koolskamp-Lisière, south of Roulers."

A glance at the map shows that Male was situated barely ten kilometers away from his GHQ

———

Because General Weygand had not been informed at the right time about the true state of the Belgian army, we can guess his reaction when he read General Champon's two messages.

In his book *Recalled to Service*, he wrote, "That day (Monday, May 27) ended with a new and disturbing event.

"At 18:00, during a conference at Vincennes, where I had summoned Generals Georges, Doumenc and Besson, there was a telegram from General Champon informing me that the Belgian army had given up the fight and we should expect a cease-fire from midnight. That news was like a bolt from the blue, as I had no warning, no intimation, to anticipate such a decision. General Koeltz, who had spent part of the afternoon with the chief of the

French military mission, had given me no indication of it. Belgian command had even requested the cooperation of one of our divisions in an area where it was having difficulties."

This extract from General Weygand's book shows how ill-informed he was. I have already pointed out that General Champon had some responsibility in this matter. But besides that, how is it possible that General Koeltz, who was in direct contact with the commander in chief, had never given him any indication that the Belgian army's surrender was inevitable, after General Michiels very detailed account that very day, Monday, May 27? It is tempting to believe that when Koeltz replied on April 17, 1951, "I understood, as did General Champon, that the Belgian army, which was being attacked from the front and threatened on the right flank, would have to retreat west," he wanted to absolve himself of that responsibility and, at the same time, that of the chief of the French military mission who was seriously compromised. The latter, it would appear, had kept to himself General Michiels's report of Sunday, May 26, that should have been passed to General Weygand. If he had simply telegraphed the last line, "we have almost reached the end of our resistance," to Vincennes, the commander in chief could not have failed to draw the obvious conclusion. But he had said clearly that there was "no warning, no intimation . . . no indication," to alert him of the extreme plight of the Belgian army. Whose fault was it? Certainly not King Leopold's, who had never ceased to stress the danger threatening the Allied armies in the north, and particularly his own army, ever since the Germans had broken through to the Ardennes. I can find no trace of those warnings in the messages sent by the French military mission to Vincennes.

I have already said that the commander in chief was ill-informed. Here is yet another example. He mentions in his book that "Belgian command had even requested the cooperation of one of our divisions in an area where it was having difficulties." If I am not mistaken, he dates that request to May 27, and must, therefore, have received the information from General Koeltz.

Far from asking for help, we know that the king sent the French 60th Division under his command to "Admiral North" (Abrial) in Belgian army trucks to spare it from violent attacks. General Champon must have known that; had he neglected to give that information to General Koeltz? Or had he said it in such a way that Koeltz had understood the opposite?

Distressed by General Champon's two messages, Weygand telegraphed Blanchard, asking him "to dissociate himself from the Belgian army and to make the necessary decision with British command to counter this act of surrender." For the reasons I have stated, this accusation was unfair: the Belgian army had not abandoned the Allies, it had succumbed after fighting heroically to the utmost of its ability, under attack from an opponent possessing vastly superior means. It was only experiencing the fate the French army would shortly suffer.

---

As soon as he had dictated the telegram, General Weygand left for Paris with Captain Roger Gasser, his aide-de-camp, to inform the prime minister. I had the privilege of hearing this account of the interview from Colonel Gasser himself:

"By 18:45 we were at 10 Rue Saint-Dominique in the premier's office. He knew nothing about what had happened.

"During our discussion on the new situation, Pierlot and General Denis arrived. Pierlot declared his loyalty to and cooperation, etc., with France. Paul Reynaud thanked him, adding, 'I must inform you of what I have just learned from General Weygand. The Belgian army is going to surrender.' Pierlot and his defense minister were dumbfounded; they knew nothing about it. Then the British ambassador and General Spears arrived. Marshal Pétain was already present. As Pierlot and Denis were leaving, General Weygand said to me, 'If they were not sincere, they are certainly a fine pair of actors!' At 22:00 there was a cabinet meeting at the Elysée Palace."

---

Well, yes indeed! Pierlot and Denis were in fact "a fine pair of actors." To see this we need only read Pierlot's undated account of the interview he, Spaak, Denis and Van der Poorten had with the king in the reception room at Wynendaele Château early on Saturday morning, May 25. I quoted the entire text, and I wish to take up the last part once more:

"The audience was drawing to a close. The king stood up. Before leaving, the prime minister asked one more question. Referring to something the king had said a few moments ago, whose meaning was not quite clear to the ministers, Pierlot asked what the king meant when he announced he would prolong the resistance as long as possible, and while there was some hope of it being useful.

" 'Does the king consider that, barring some unforeseeable event that might change the situation, the Belgian army's surrender might still be avoided, or is it certain?'

"His reply was, 'It is not certain; it is inevitable.'

" 'For how long could it be delayed?' asked the prime minister. Reply: 'Twenty-four hours at the most.' "

—

There is also Major Defraiteur's testimony which I have quoted. But to go back to the account written by Pierlot himself, how did he have the nerve, when he visited Paul Reynaud at Rue Saint-Dominique on the evening of May 27, to feign amazement at the news of the surrender, which the king had told him was *inevitable* and would take place within *twenty-four hours*? Besides, if the two ministers had not been certain that surrender was inevitable, why did they feel the need—having left the king in the meantime—to present their credentials to the French prime minister, assuring them of their *loyalty* and *cooperation*? They should have been amazed the Belgian army was only just about to surrender, sixty hours after they had hurriedly left Wynendaele Château, showing a tenacity that went beyond the king's own expectations.

If the scene described to me by my friend, Colonel Gasser, had not taken place at such a tragic time, I would be tempted to say that he and General Weygand had been watching a black comedy. For while Pierlot and Denis feigned amazement, Reynaud responded with righteous indignation when, as we know from Colonel Thierry, he had already been informed, before General Weygand's visit, that General Blanchard considered the Belgian army's capitulation unavoidable and imminent.

Indeed, to echo his commander's words, Captain Roger Gasser saw some "fine actors" that evening of Monday, May 27. In Pierlot's speech the next morning, broadcast over French radio (after which he tried to have King Leopold struck off the Legion of Honor before instigating the infamous dispatch, published under cover of the Havas Agency), he capped the previous day's charade with a most detestable action.

—————

While waiting for General Derousseaux's return, everyone at Belgian GHQ was busy collecting the standards of the units on the front which was rapidly caving in, to save them from the enemy. After Derousseaux had crossed the Belgian lines at Egemkapel, near Koolskamp—still held by the cannons of the 5th Artillery Regiment—he met up with the Germans and was driven to Count de Lannoy's château at Anvaing, where General von Reichenau, commander of the German VIth Army, had set up headquarters. When he returned to the Belgian lines at Laakbos, defended by recruits from the 1st Training Center, "a volley of bullets hit the car, smashing the windows and slicing through the thumb of the standard-bearer," said Chevalier de Fabribeckers. When General Derousseaux made his report to the king he described Hitler's brutal, five-word response to General von Reichenau: "*Der Führer fordert bedingungslose Waffenstreckung.*" This meant that the Belgian army was requested, in very condemning words, to make a total surrender without the right to any conditions. That certainly put paid to General Champon's desire to take part in the "discussion," a point which did not concern his counterpart at the British military mission attached to Belgian GHQ, who was preparing to leave for England. Quite undaunted, General Champon sent a message to Vincennes GHQ, received at 01:35 on Tuesday, May 28:

"General Champon has just been advised, at 0120, by the chief of Belgian general staff that the following message has been sent: 'Lay down arms. Cease-fire at 0400 on May 28.' General Champon maintains his view stated to Belgian GHQ at the time of his first message at 1810 that representatives from France and Britain should be present during the discussion on the terms for the Belgian army."

—

The courageous Belgian William Grisar—whom we shall meet again on May 28—wished to corroborate on his oath as an officer Admiral Keyes' account to him of his last meeting with the king at the end of that tragic day, Monday, May 27, 1940:

"The admiral had talked to Churchill by telephone during the day and returned from La Panne, where he had made the call to London, reaching the provincial government office in Bruges late in the evening, due to congestion on the roads. The king insisted that the admiral rest after his long journey. They began to talk, and the king gave his opinion that the French would end all resistance within two weeks. Then he asked, 'What about England?' Lord Keyes replied, 'We shall continue the struggle whatever happens.'

" 'I am sure of that,' said the king. 'You will get the upper hand, but not before going through a hell of a time!'

"Queen Elisabeth came in. She put her hands on the king's shoulders and added: 'Yes, it will be hell, but England will not perish!'

"Admiral Keyes begged the king to leave Belgium with him, keeping his promise to Churchill to try one last time to persuade the king. The king drew him to the window and pointed to the crowds of refugees hurrying in all directions, saying, 'It would be easy for me to leave but, even if I wanted to, I could not after having seen such a sight. Before you leave, however, I would like you to take a personal message to King George.'

"In his haste—Admiral Keyes was about to miss his appointment off the Nieuport coast where a destroyer was waiting—the king had to begin his letter again. The admiral copied the second page by hand, then the king signed it and they made their farewells.

"When the admiral reached Nieuport and boarded a little fishing boat, there was no trace of the destroyer. Sitting in the prow, he sent a morse-signal "K.E.Y.E.S." for several minutes. At about 2:00 A.M., the message was picked up by a fast patrol-boat. On May 28 at 11:00 A.M., Admiral Keyes reported to Churchill at Downing Street in London."

# "SUBMISSION IS NOT ACCEPTANCE"

Although Hitler's "*Der Führer fordert bedingungslose Waffenstreckung,*" was rude and imperious, it was only directed at the army and carried no political implications. This consideration induced the king to accept, and he replied, "We shall lay down our arms. Cease-fire at 0400 on May 28," thus giving the Allies the benefit of the maximum possible delay and conforming to the message from general staff. The king tried to inform Lord Gort and General Champon immediately, but only the latter could be contacted. There was so much confusion that some Belgian troops, who could not be reached in time, continued the desperate fight until 8:00 A.M., although four hours previously General von Reichenau had ordered his army to cross the lines immediately. He had no inkling that his powerful VIth Army, overjoyed at this victory, would suffer an even more humiliating defeat at Stalingrad in January 1943 than the one they inflicted on the Belgian troops, who had only succumbed because of the huge disparity in fighting strength. General von Bock noted in his log, "The twenty-two Belgian divisions defended their country with tenacity and courage, using many blocks and fortifications. They were disorganized by incessant attacks from Army Group B and were forced to surrender." This was no mean compliment coming from Fedor von Bock, World War I veteran and a personal friend of the crown prince. Hitler had given him the command of the German troops who entered Austria during the "Anschluss," and von Bock had then commanded the Northern Army Group during the Polish campaign before invading Holland at the head of Army Group B, which was to overrun the last resistance line on the Somme eight days later, to enter Paris on June 14.

———

"Blocks and fortifications." Among the latter was the fortified position at Tancrémont, which had been forgotten by GHQ as it was situated so far from the front line, near Pepinster, south of Herve, between Liège and Verviers. On the night of May 27 to 28, it was like the other side of the world. The position was known as "HSW," and during the evening of May 27, while General Derousseaux was on his way to the German lines, a radio message from "HSW" reached Saint-André GHQ, sounding like a ray of sunshine in the darkness of defeat: "Greetings to the campaign army and its chief. Still holding out, but alone. Long live Belgium!" There was no signature, but it must have come from Captain Devos, who was in charge of defense of the fortification.

Had Devos heard of the example set by his neighbor, Commanding Captain Charlier, who was in charge of the Boncelles fort just south of Liège? That day Charlier had only seventy men left out of four hundred, as the reserve reinforcements had unfortunately left. Nevertheless, he succeeded in doing some damage to the Wehrmacht's 251st Division with four howitzers fired from his old fort that dated back to 1888. The enemy replied with 150 mm. shells, which crushed three of the four gun-turrets on May 15. Charlier replaced his terrified men who had abandoned the fourth gun with volunteers, and began firing again. The next day he was repaid with a Stuka bombing attack that shook the fort to its very foundations. Charlier let the fainthearted leave as the reinforcements were about to surrender, and retained only thirty or so men who like him were determined not to be captured. Enraged at this stubbornness, the enemy placed mines, and at 12:30 P.M., a tremendous explosion destroyed the fort, killing Charlier and his adjutant Hurlet, burning or severely wounding most of the defenders. In the Royal Museum of Army and

Military History in Brussels, there is a moving triptych painted by the talented James Thiriar, who dedicated this work to the epic of Boncelles. The central picture depicts the coffin containing the remains of Captain Charlier, protected by six of his men. The coffin is preceded by German soldiers in full dress, saluted by the German colonel in command of the 88th Infantry Regiment who, like his soliders, wished to pay final homage to their indomitable foe.

Unlike Boncelles, the Tancremont fortification had been recently constructed, but only had two 7.5 cm. cannons. The men there did not have dealings with the enemy until May 22. Asked to surrender, Captain Devos said to the officer with a white flag who had come to accept his surrender, "This fort will be defended to the very last. Do not come back here again."

By supercharging his radio transmitter—which had a range of only 25 kilometers—he managed to contact the Namur forts, but only for forty-eight hours as they fell on Friday, May 24. Three days later, his radio-operator succeeded in contacting GHQ, which picked up the message I quoted earlier. The same operator received the general order to cease fire on May 28.

Refusing to believe that the Belgian army had been forced to surrender, Devos sought confirmation, but there was no reply from GHQ. Then he fired at some Germans, without helmets and unarmed, who were nearing the fort. On the morning of May 29, another representative arrived, who confirmed the cease-fire along the entire front, thus explaining GHQ's silence. Leaving the fort, Devos was brought to the German General Sprang, who gave his word that all fighting had ceased. Devos asked for two conditions to his surrender: the fort would continue fighting until 11:00 and would not surrender until 15:15. That would give him time to destroy documents, arms and ammunition. It was understood that the men would receive battle-honors and that he and his officers would retain their swords. These conditions were accepted, and in this way Tancrémont fort prolonged the Belgian resistance by thirty-five hours and fifteen minutes.

At 7:40 A.M. on Tuesday, May 28, another message from General Champon reached Vincennes GHQ:

"General Champon has just seen General Blanchard. The latter received no telegram. He was informed of the situation by a liaison officer who came to see General Champon. General Blanchard is looking for Lord Gort to try and take some joint action. We have not been able to contact Lord Gort since 0015, and General Blanchard does not know what the British want to do."

We know from Colonel Thierry that the day before, General Blanchard had been told by King Leopold himself on the telephone that the Belgian army's capitulation was imminent. It may be true, as General Champon says, that the chief of Army Group I had "received no telegram" (one wonders how Belgian GHQ could have managed to send one), but how come the chief of the French military mission, who had been informed the previous day that a representative had been sent to the German lines, waited until the arrival of General Blanchard's liaison officer to inform the latter of this news which was of such importance to the commander?

Vincennes GHQ also wondered, and replied immediately to General Champon:

1. Order to maintain contact with General Blanchard through radio-control car.

2. Order to stay and find out what happens to the Belgians while preparing for the embarkation of the mission.

Colonel Hautecoeur was already doing just that. Vincennes GHQ had been informed at 6:05 A.M. that he had telephoned La Panne while General Champon was away at General Blanchard's command post. Since the operation seemed impossible at Dunkirk, the colonel requested that a boat be sent to Nieuport or Ostend, or to a "point on the coast yet to be determined." Having been notified of this, General Fagalde informed him at 7:50 that only Nieuport was possible, and then "only for a very short time." Five minutes later, General Blanchard told GHQ he was still trying to locate Lord Gort. He finally succeeded at 10:20, but General Swayne from Lord Gort's staff replied he could not pass on his call to the chief of the British Expeditionary Force. "He is resting, and must not be disturbed."

At 10:55, GHQ registered the following message:

"The conditions of the Belgian armistice are now known. General Blanchard no longer needs the French mission attached to the Belgian army. The navy is giving powerful support at Dunkirk, protected by warships and other ships. General Doumenc has asked General Georges to tell General Champon that his mission is over and he should leave for France at the earliest opportunity, via England if necessary, and be at the disposal of high command."

But General Champon's troubles were not yet over. The details of his crusade continued to swamp GHQ until almost midnight, when they finally petered out.

1105. General Champon states he cannot reach Dunkirk. Admiral "North" (Abrial) says Dunkirk is unusable. General Champon must be picked up at La Panne. The English had offered him fifteen places, but because the English are panicking, those places are now uncertain.

1315. Without warning, the British rearguard have abandoned the Deule River line (a severe blow).

1600. Champon's mission is nervous and worried. The boats have not arrived. British boats are taking British soliders on board, and armed naval officers are preventing the French mission from boarding.

Aerial bombardment everywhere. All telephone communications have been cut. No information on the situation. It is raining, but the weather is not bad enough to stop the enemy air force.

1640. General Champon has managed to contact the British

admiral (?). The latter said he is not in charge of the reembarkation. "He couldn't care less about the French!" (verbatim
report from Champon's mission, five witnesses). He only knows of
a radio signal from Admiral "North" that a French boat is going
to Nieuport to pick up the mission. But Nieuport is inaccessible.
Please do what is necessary at the admiralty: the boat must come
to La Panne."

To panic, according to the dictionary, means to be in a position
where it is impossible to move forward. I think that destiny, which
tends toward irony, chose to register this last message concerning
the chief of the French military mission, who at 1:35 that day
still claimed he should be "present during the discussion on the
conditions for the Belgian army." It was recorded at Vincennes
GHQ at 23:15 on Tuesday, May 28:

"GENERAL CHAMPON IS STILL ON THE BEACH AT LA PANNE
WITHOUT ANY NEWS OF HIS REEMBARKATION."

But now, we must return to serious matters.

—•—

Five minutes after the order to General Champon to maintain
contact with General Blanchard was sent, an order of the day
signed by General Georges went out at 7:45 from Vincennes
GHQ:

"The Belgian army has defected and will abandon the Allied
ranks at 4:00 A.M. on May 28. The final bell has tolled. The fate
of the country now lies in the hands of the French troops. Their
mission is clear: hold fast and prevent the Germans from taking
the road to France. May each of you, in the glorious tradition of
our country, have the determination to give our defense the
aggression and resoluteness that will render our nation indomitable. Officers and soldiers, you shall be as great as your forefathers.
Take courage!"

That order of the day, followed by the words, "approved by

Weygand," made a serious accusation against the Belgian army that in those circumstances came very close to a charge of treason and echoed Paul Reynaud's speech made over the radio at 8:30 that morning. Coming from a politician in dire straits, such an accusation is only of relative value; but when spoken by the chief of the Northeastern Army with Weygand's approval, it is quite categorical. I hope I have been able to convince my readers how completely unjust it was, and I have no doubt that if General Weygand had been better informed, he would not have said it, nor would General Georges, whose honesty was well known.

That order of the day had already been replied to in the opening lines of King Leopold's order addressed to his officers, NCO's and soldiers: "Despite your being thrown into war of untold violence, you have fought courageously in the defense of our national territory. Now, exhausted by this continuous struggle against an enemy superior in numbers and resources, we are forced to surrender. History shall testify that our army did its duty. Our honor has been upheld."

General Weygand, a perfectly honest man, made public reparation ten years later for this injustice, committed through an inexcusable lack of information. If the liaison mission attached to Belgian GHQ was guilty of indolence on Sunday, May 26, and General Koeltz's silence in front of his commander in chief on his return from Belgian GHQ is incomprehensible, the deplorable communications between Vincennes GHQ and General Blanchard largely accounted for the bad shock General Weygand received on Monday, May 27, at 18:10. Admiral Keyes, whose word cannot be doubted, stated—as recorded in the Appendix on his libel suit against the *Daily Mirror* Newspapers in London—"At 5:00 P.M. May 27, King Leopold informed the British and French authorities that he intended at midnight to ask for an armistice so as to avoid further slaughter of his people. . . . Although wireless messages were repeatedly made, it was now known that they did not reach the commanders in chief." (We know from Colonel Thierry that this was not true of Blanchard.) We also know, as I pointed out, that General Blanchard's telegram sent on the morning of Monday, May 27, to General Georges, telling him of the rapidly deteriorating situation on the Belgian front did not reach General Georges until after General Weygand had received General Champon's first message at 18:10. It was in view of all this, that General Weygand wrote the following in 1950 in *Recalled to Service*:

"When I recall my impressions of May 1940, I cannot forget that the decision by Belgian command to withdraw from battle made me react very violently. I knew the Belgian army was in difficulties with the enemy's strong attacks. But that situation was not peculiar to Belgians alone, as the same went for the French and British armies during that critical time. However, I had absolutely no idea that the Belgian army would cease fighting on the night of May 27. The news did not reach me until after the request to lay down arms had already been made to the enemy. Faced with this *fait accompli*, which ruined my last chance, I reacted strongly. And yet during my long hours of imprisonment in Germany, I could not forget our comradeship at arms during World War I and King Albert's noble and courageous attitude in 1914. When I returned, I wanted, just as I had done with Lord Gort, to discover the motives behind Belgian command's decision. I examined the facts and read Lord Keyes's correspondence. On May 27, the Belgian army was in a perilous position. The army was too far away from the Yser to retreat there in reasonable time. Its right wing was in danger of being surrounded, and it could neither be assisted by the French nor the British, who had already begun to retreat to Dunkirk. Belgian command, no doubt, felt it had been abandoned by its Allies. That is how I view that decision, which, in time, history shall judge."

That is all very well, but it is not enough. When he wrote the above, General Weygand did not have all the documents that I have to refer to. If Belgian command considered it had been "abandoned by its Allies," there would surely have been some bitterness in its attitude to the Allies, but it was just the opposite: we saw how on May 26, the king had ordered the French 60th Division—for its own safety, and despite the difficulties the Belgian army was experiencing—to be transported behind the lines. The king and his general staff's primary concern was to protect the British Expeditionary Force, whose mission, like that of the French military mission attached to Belgian GHQ, was to be kept constantly informed on events and their implications. Just like their chief, the Belgian army—which had been thrown into a war not declared by Belgium—always remained loyal to French command (which since the opening of hostilities had planned to use Belgium as a gratuitous battlefield). The same went for Belgian attitude to the British Expeditionary Force when, evading the support asked of them, the leader of the Expeditionary Force was unable to forewarn the Belgians about the evacuation of the troops to England which had been planned since May 20. I believe *that* is what history will remember when the emotions surrounding this have finally died down. But it is never too early to establish the truth.

———

After the king heard General Derousseaux's account of his talk with von Reichenau, he decided: "We shall lay down our arms and cease-fire at 4:00 A.M. tomorrow morning, May 28."

At 00:20, the protocol for surrender was settled between General Derousseaux and the chief of the German VIth Army in the following way:

"The Belgian army will unconditionally lay down arms immediately, and from then on, shall be considered as prisoner of war. An armistice was initiated at 5:00 this morning at the request of Belgian command. German operations against the British and French troops shall continue.

"Belgian territory shall be occupied immediately, including all ports. No further destruction of the flood-gates or coastal fortifications in any form will be carried out.

"Additional protocol:

"In recognition of an honorable surrender, the officers of the Belgian army shall retain their arms. Laeken Château shall be put at the disposal of H.M. the King to live there with his family, court and servants."

It was obvious that Belgium could not object to the continuation of hostilities between the German forces and the French and British troops. When General Derousseaux insisted that the armistice—defined in the dictionary as a truce which may or may not lead to peace, which was to be France's case less than a month later—be set for 5:00 A.M. (German time), it was because the king wanted to gain the night of May 27 to 28 for the Allies, as expressed in the note from command the previous day. The formalities necessary to effect the armistice extended that respite until the end of Tuesday morning.

The following details for its application were added to the protocol:

"Between the commander in chief of the army, General von Reichenau, delegate for the Führer and commander in chief of the German army,

"And General Derousseaux, representative of the king of Belgium,

"The following has been agreed:

"1. The letters appointing the representative of the king of Belgium have been found to be correct and in order.

"2. The entire Belgian army will unconditionally lay down arms immediately and will be considered as prisoner of war.

"As a result, and at Belgian command's request, the armistice between the German and Belgian troops took effect at 5:00 A.M. (German time) and 4:00 A.M. (Belgian time) on May 28, 1940.

"This will not affect German operations against the French and British armies, which will continue to fight.

"To avoid any error, the Belgian troops will make themselves known by a white flag. They shall cease all movement immediately and wait by the roadsides for further instructions.

"3. Belgian general staff shall shortly hand over to German high command all the areas occupied by the Belgian army.

"In those areas and at other rendezvous points, the Belgian army shall lay down its arms undamaged; they shall keep them there and hand them over to the German troops. The Belgian army's departure shall be controlled by German high command.

"Belgian general staff has agreed to the German army's immediate occupation of the territory under Belgian sovereignty, including the coast. Its own troops shall ensure the flood-gates are kept in good order. These shall remain intact and closed until the arrival of the first German units. The coastal fortifications shall be handed over intact.

"To authenticate the above conditions of surrender, two copies of the protocol in German shall be signed and exchanged between the delegate of the Führer, supreme commander of the German army, and the representative of the king of Belgium."

—

If ever there was a bit of legal jargon, it was this appendix to the protocol. General Derousseaux—even if he had wished— could never have organized for the entire Belgian army to lay down its arms immediately. The order to retreat to a very indefinite line running from Damme to just south of the Roulers Canal, had little or no effect on the troops engaged in battle and did not reach the 14th Regiment until midnight. In fact everything depended on the morale of the soldiers. Some were disgusted at having had to retreat since May 10, without seeming to have fought at all; others, influenced by the propaganda leaflets dropped by the Luftwaffe, had given up the struggle, while there were still others who were so angered by those leaflets that they wanted to fight to the very end. A glance at the map will show that on Monday, May 27, Belgium's shores and territory were already almost completely under enemy occupation. The flooding that the enemy wished to avoid by demanding that the flood-gates be kept intact had already been effected for the benefit of the Allies, while the bridges on the Yser had been destroyed and the port of Zeebrugge blockaded on the king's orders.

———

It was already 5:20 A.M., Tuesday, May 28, when General Derousseaux had read and carefully checked the exact translation of the protocol. He then pointed out to General von Reichenau that several of Hitler's demands could no longer be satisfied. "It is certain," he said, "that some of our units have already destroyed their arms, and Belgian high command cannot be held responsible for the troops who are with the French or British on the Yser. Finally, I cannot guarantee that our fortifications on the coast will not be destroyed by the Allied forces occupying them. Moreover, as I said before, the king asked me to make sure that our troops surrender with full battle honors, but I can't find anything in this protocol or in its application that will spare the courageous Belgian army a humiliation that it does not deserve in the least."

Von Reichenau—who was acting directly on Hitler's orders— replied that he could not change any of the points already decided on, but that he would take measures to add an appendix on the last point raised by General Derousseaux to satisfy the king. "And what is to be the king's fate?" asked the latter. Embarrassed, von Reichenau replied that he had received no instructions on the matter. But the most valuable item had been gained in the process: time. For every second that passed was to the Allies' gain. Having dragged things out as long as possible, General Derousseaux finally added his signature to the documents presented him by the victor of the day. Von Reichenau might have found himself in a less enviable position if the general staff of the 2nd Corps of the British Expeditionary Force had had an officer who could read German on May 25. The complete battle orders of the Wehrmacht Army Group B, including the movements of the VIth Army, had been seized with Lieutenant Colonel Kinzel of General Brauchitsch's general staff. He had been captured by a British patrol. As no one in the 2nd Corps spoke any German, the precious documents were filed away and forgotten.

———

Their honor, primarily symbolized by their standards, was safe. I mentioned that on the evening of Monday, May 27, the Belgian regiments had been ordered, mainly because of the king's concern, to bring their standards to Saint-André-lez-Bruges GHQ, from which they were to be sent to England. Van Daele, an officer in charge of the operation, went to Ostend, but found the exits there blocked. So he turned to the Very Reverend Dom Nève de Mévergnies, abbot of the Benedictine Loppem Monastery just south of Saint-André, who was only too pleased to accept the precious charge. He entrusted them to Dom de Meeus, whose father, a commanding captain in the 1st Guide Regiment, had been killed leading his men in the last cavalry charge at Burkel on October 19, 1918, just before Belgium's liberation. He had already taken in thirty-six standards, when early on Tuesday, May 28, some German officers arrived at Saint-André GHQ demanding that the way be opened for General von Reichenau's VIth Army, according to the terms signed by General Derousseaux. Chevalier de Fabribeckers writes:

"It was too late to save all the flags at our GHQ, and thirteen were immediately burned; many others were disposed in the same way at army corps headquarters. That was the case for the 6th Corps's four flags, three from the 2nd Corps, two from the 4th and five from the regiments.

"Others preferred to hide them. Twelve flags were hidden by the military, five by civilians, nine in churches and three in France.

"Louis Leconte, curator of the Royal Museum of Army and Military History, hid many other flags in addition to the twenty-two already in his care. The king ordered General Van Overstraeten to take the standard of the 5th Artillery, and Colonel Herbiet—who had returned from captivity an invalid—gave him the flag of the 2nd Grenadiers, which had been hidden in a cave near the Albert Canal.

"Two flags were sent to England: that of the 2nd Air Squadron in December 1941, and the flag of the 1st Light Cavalry in April 1943.

"One went with the prisoners of war: that of the 1st Light Infantry. Commanding Captain Born took it to pieces and shared the bits among the officers of the regiment. One took care of the lion, the forager, the silk and the embroidery. The officers returned from Prenzlau camp in June 1945, after taking part in the last battles between General Henrici's army group from Vistula and those of Marshal Rokossovski's second front from white Russia. Madame Born had the honor of re-sewing the flag of her husband's regiment."

The youth of today, who think themselves "progressive" when they are only walking down the well-trodden paths of their elders, may smile at what seems like a childish fetish. But it is only at times of such national tragedy that this becomes a living reality. In 1943, in London, I saw a representative of the Central Committee of the French Communist Party sobbing openly at the showing of a color film taken in Paris just before the defeat, and one could see the French red, white and blue flag flying. Only with the fear that one's country may be lost for ever will one know the significance of a flag.

———

At the time when the Belgian army was laying down its arms after having fought to the utmost, William Grisar—the officer I quoted earlier in relation to Admiral Keyes—was bidding a last farewell to his men. He concluded with a phrase reminiscent of General de Gaulle's appeal from London on June 18. "But is this the last word? Has all hope been lost? Is this the final defeat? No!" Grisar said to his soldiers. "This is not the end. It is only one incident, and we shall meet again." This sentiment was shared by many of his comrades, who played a substantial role in the secret Resistance and the army, with which Belgium continued to oppose the enemy as it had done in World War I.

———

At 15:15 on Tuesday, May 28, 1940, General von Reichenau arrived at the provincial palace at Bruges to meet King Leopold, whom he had demanded to see. I received a firsthand account of the meeting which took place in the autumn of 1966.

The Belgian sector of my information network, *Confrérie Notre-Dame*, was directed by Charles Stockmans of Antwerp, who had fought against the Germans in the Great War. He and his other Resistance fighters were executed on November 20, 1942. If fate had ordained that I, too, should have died in this underground Resistance, his son-in-law Alexis Thys would have been condemned after Belgium's liberation for giving information to the enemy since he carried out a mission at my orders, an apparently dishonorable mission, to which his father-in-law was the only other witness. Like Charles Stockmans, Alexis Thys was a member (unknown to me) of the Belgian information network "Pipe" directed by our comrade Jean Vossen, former secretary general in the internal affairs ministry. When I was invited to the annual reunion of our Resistance movement in the autumn of 1966, sitting next to me was the honorable Colonel Hubert Rombauts, who twenty-six years previously had been secretary to Leopold's military set-up. In a speech at the end of the dinner, Colonel Rombauts said:

"One Tuesday, May 28, 1940, the day when the Belgian army surrendered in the morning, King Leopold was in Bruges at the West Flanders government office.

"His decision not to go to England or the Congo stemmed

from his fear of leaving his people defenseless against German reprisals. One should remember that from 1937, and after many negotiations, the Germans had tried to wrest the Congo from Belgium to satisfy the greed of the master of the Third Reich.

"On the afternoon of that tragic day, the German General von Reichenau, commander of the VIth Army, arrived at Bruges with his dazzling general staff—whose chief was General Paulus, who was to be defeated at Stalingrad—and a retinue of reporters from the German press (newspapers and radio). He had come at Hitler's orders to put himself at the king's disposal and to convey the Führer's greetings.

"The king was in the large drawing room on the second floor of the provincial palace and he had watched the arrival of General von Reichenau and his impressive retinue in the courtyard. The king called Major Van den Heuvel, director of the royal palaces, and asked him to inform the German general that he refused to take part in any showy spectacle.

"Major Van den Heuvel asked me to help him in this delicate mission. It was difficult to persuade the victor to comply with the king's wishes, but at last we succeeded. After he had dismissed his general staff and the phalanx of journalists and cameramen, General von Reichenau was received, alone, in the drawing room.

"His Majesty was standing rigidly in military fashion behind his desk at the far end of the room. After a brisk 'Heil Hitler!' General von Reichenau strode toward the king with outstretched hand. Then, sensing the king's cold impassivity, he stopped in midstride, although he had another ten meters or so to go. Then the king spoke, 'I have only one question to ask General von Reichenau. What is to become of my army?'

"The general remained silent for a moment, then stammered, 'I have received no instructions on the matter, Your Majesty. But you must realize that a defeated army is a prisoner . . .'

"The king was silent for a long time, then he replied calmly, 'In those circumstances, General von Reichenau should consider me his first prisoner.'

"The German went pale. Speechless, he could find nothing to say. One whole minute passed, then the king said firmly, 'I consider the meeting between General von Reichenau and myself to be over. Gentlemen, please show the general out.' "

———

Besides the humiliation suffered by the chief of the German VIth Army, the king's proud attitude was a slight on Hitler, who realized it. Furious at the failure of the little drama he had imagined, he ordered Leopold to be sent that day to a destination unknown even to his attendants. The following morning, a second procession left Bruges under heavy escort: Queen Elisabeth, the count of Flanders and a few people in their retinue were also sent to an unknown destination.

Did the master of the Third Reich expect to hold his royal prisoner in a fortress? I don't know. If he decided, against the king's will, to hold him at Laeken Château, I think it was to evade Belgian hostility and perhaps to lend credence to the misunderstanding caused by Paul Reynaud's accusations. No sooner had the palace gates shut behind the king, than huge bouquets of flowers were heaped against them: for like the army, the majority of Belgians realized that the king's refusal to abandon them meant that he wished to share their fate and protect them.

Somehow, news of the people's fervor reached the senators and members of the House of Representatives in Limoges. Gillon, president of the senate, said to his colleagues, "In Belgium, eighty percent of the population are against us and for the king."

———

On Tuesday, May 28, the king wrote two identical letters, one to the world's highest spiritual authority and the other to the leader of the most powerful nation in the world. I mean, of course, Pope Pius XII and President Roosevelt. The king said:

"Amidst the general confusion, caused by the swiftness of

events in which we are living, which have such far-reaching effects, I wish to state that Belgium and its army have fulfilled their duty. Belgium kept to its international agreements, firstly by scrupulously maintaining neutrality, and then by defending its national territory inch by inch.

"Attacked by tremendous forces, our army reached a powerful line of defense in good order, in contact with the Allied armies, to whom we had appealed for help. But military events outside our territory forced us to leave that battlefield and necessitated a series of retreats which pushed us back to the sea. Our army fought, regardless of cost, a four-day battle together with the Allied armies. We were finally surrounded in an extremely small piece of territory, heavily populated and already swollen by several hundreds of thousands of civilian refugees, who were without shelter, food or water, and who had traveled hither and thither to avoid aerial bombardment.

"Yesterday, our last means of resistance were crushed beneath a superiority of arms and air force. In that situation I wanted to avoid a battle which, today, would have led to our annihilation with no benefit to the Allies: no one has the right to sacrifice human lives needlessly.

"I wish to continue, whatever happens, to share the fate of my army and my nation. I rejected several requests to leave my soldiers, a move tantamount to desertion for the chief of the army. Moreover, by remaining in Belgium, I wish to support my people in the trials that lie ahead."

—

The king added another note to these two letters, which he passed to Frédéricq, his private secretary, and Colonel van Caubergh, his aide-de-camp, on June 2, to be handed to the Belgian ambassador in Berne. The message was to be circulated among all Belgian diplomatic missions abroad. Repeating the account given in the letters to the pope and President Roosevelt, the king added the following details:

"On the night of May 27, the army's front had been broken in several places. The army had used up all its reserves, and our last means of resistance were crushed beneath a superiority of arms and especially air force.

"After the military authorities had considered the possibility of holding out for another twenty-four hours, they reached a negative conclusion. It is certain that a further battle on the twenty-eighth would have crushed and routed the combat units immediately. In those circumstances, after taking all measures to give the Allied armies our active support until the last moment, command decided to avoid this useless debacle.

"The decision was not a sudden one. We had been concerned about this eventuality at Belgian GHQ ever since May 21, when the German armored divisions reached the coast via Abbeville. The king personally warned the Belgian government several times, as well as the British government and military authorities, that surrender might be inevitable. First the death of General Billotte, commander of the Northern Army Group, and then the breakdown of communications with France prevented us from contacting the French government directly. But the Belgian ministers, who left the king in such haste on the twenty-fifth, communicated their fears of a possible surrender to Paris and London."

———

I shall interrupt this note to correct it on one point. We can see from this that King Leopold had justifiedly assumed his ministers, who left him "in such haste" early on Saturday, May 25, would communicate "their fears of a possible surrender to Paris and London." But we know from Colonel Roger Gasser, present at their meeting on May 27 with Marshal Pétain, General Weygand and Paul Reynaud, that this was not the case. On the contrary, Pierlot and General Denis claimed to be "dumbfounded" by the French premier's "news."

———

The message to the Belgian diplomatic missions continued thus:

"The representative sent to the German lines on the night of May 27 was charged with a very specific and technical mission, inquiring about conditions for a cessation of hostilities. The Germans demanded an unconditional surrender, which we accepted on the twenty-eighth at 4:00 A.M. No negotiations took place. The French and British military missions attached to the Belgian GHQ were duly informed.

"The king had decided, whatever happened, to share the fate of his army and his nation. Requested several times by the Belgian and British governments to abandon his soldiers, he rejected it on the grounds that it amounted to desertion by the commander in chief of the army. Moreover, by remaining on national territory, he wished to support his people in the trials they would undergo. His honor and that of the army is safe. Belgium has done its duty."

———

I do not know how President Roosevelt replied to the king's letter, which was presented to him by his ambassador in Belgium, Mr. Joseph Davis. However, the latter made public this statement of his opinions on November 1, 1940:

"Whatever decision the king made, it could not but have conformed to the necessity of protecting Belgium and its people, which was compatible with his personal honor. History may say he committed an error of judgment. For my part, relying on facts I know to be true, I would oppose such a conclusion. But be that as it may, history will say that during these trials, King Leopold's personal honor and dignity are safe and unstained, even touched with greatness. In my opinion, it could not be otherwise."

Two former United States ambassadors to Belgium echoed that statement:

"The Belgian crown defended the cause of all that is noblest and highest among nations as in humanity," wrote William Phillips on November 17, 1940, with reference to World War I, "and King Albert became one of the leading figures in the world. It was during this tragic time and in this edifying atmosphere that his son, Leopold, spent the formative years of his childhood. He must have been aware of the powerful bond that united the sovereign to his people during those tragic years. So it is not surprising that he has inherited many of his parents' qualities: a highly developed sense of responsibility, the highest devotion to duty, a spirit of voluntary sacrifice and love for his people. These very real qualities make his person the symbol of independence in the eyes of his nation and of the whole world."

As for Mr. Hugh Gibbson, he did not mince his words when he wrote this on February 5, 1941:

"King Leopold has been accused of treacherously laying down arms, without having forewarned the Allies. This accusation is based entirely on a groundless statement made by Mr. Reynaud, which does not bear up to examination.

"During May 1940, I was in Paris. For several days all the diplomatic circles thought the situation was hopeless for the Belgian army, and its surrender imminent. We know now that the Allied governments had been informed in advance about the situation, and the reason for Mr. Reynaud's statement was that the French army had already collapsed, allowing the Germans to advance to the Channel, thus rendering the continuation of Belgian resistance impossible. The French people would inevitably ask for some explanation, which Mr. Reynaud would not be able to give. To avoid popular indignation, he had only one recourse, which was to find a scapegoat. He chose King Leopold, which was easy to do but hardly honorable, since the king was already a prisoner and could not defend himself.

"The king needs no testimonial to his morality. A man who has always led a loyal and courageous life does not suddenly become a coward and a traitor. He certainly had no illusions about the insults that would be thrown at him, but I am convinced that once the full facts are recognized, his action will be shown as not only loyal, but requiring courage of the highest order."

—

These are precisely my feelings. If on a modest scale my book has served to make to King Leopold of Belgium the respectful reparation due to him, I shall be very proud. In the autumn of 1940, the king thanked Pope Pius for the letter he received and concluded thus:

"I was always sure that in your foresight and your just bounty, Your Holiness would see, in my decision, the inspiration that comes from Christianity, and my concern for the good of the country in my charge, for which I would suffer a thousand deaths. For submission is not acceptance, silence is not approval; waiting is not giving up."

—

To submit without accepting; to remain silent without approving; to wait without giving up: these three attitudes adopted by the king to safeguard the people and the nation in his charge show a rare strength of spirit, for they prevent one from justifying oneself to the very people one is protecting and so expose one to criticism.

At his hermitage at Tamanrasset, Father Charles de Foucauld wrote to one of his friends—I think the letter was dated the very same day he was assassinated by Senussis plunderers: "Let us leave honor to whoever wants it, but danger, sorrow, should always be ours." What did he mean by honor, unless it is that petty vanity which so many men like to have? But there are other cases where honor, in the true sense of the word, makes such harsh demands on us that in order to serve it one must reject all appearances. Such self-sacrifice is so rare and so noble that it can only be understood by men of the highest spirit. It is to these men that I dedicate my book.

# MAPS
# APPENDICES

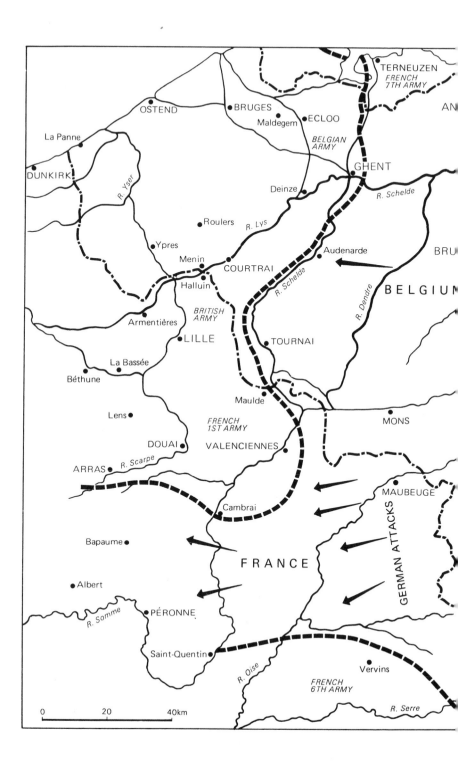

TERNEUZEN
*FRENCH 7TH ARMY*

OSTEND

BRUGES

ECLOO

Maldegem

AN

La Panne

*BELGIAN ARMY*

DUNKIRK

GHENT

*R. Yser*

Deinze

*R. Schelde*

Roulers

*R. Lys*

Ypres

Audenarde

BRU

Menin

COURTRAI

Halluin

*R. Schelde*

*R. Dendre*

BELGIUM

*BRITISH ARMY*

Armentières

LILLE

TOURNAI

La Bassée

Béthune

Maulde

Lens

*FRENCH 1ST ARMY*

MONS

DOUAI

VALENCIENNES

ARRAS

*R. Scarpe*

MAUBEUGE

Cambrai

Bapaume

FRANCE

GERMAN ATTACKS

Albert

*R. Somme*

PÉRONNE

Saint-Quentin

Vervins

*R. Oise*

*FRENCH 6TH ARMY*

0        20        40km

*R. Serre*

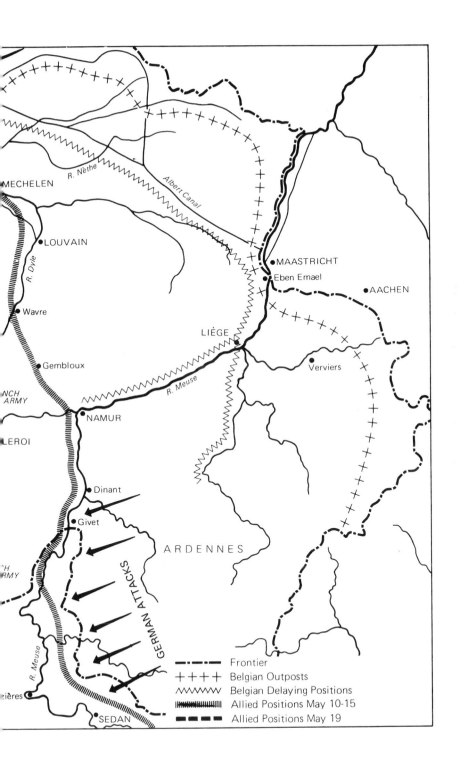

MECHELEN

R. Nèthe

Albert Canal

LOUVAIN

R. Dyle

Wavre

MAASTRICHT

Eben Emael

AACHEN

LIÈGE

Gembloux

Verviers

NCH
ARMY

R. Meuse

NAMUR

LEROI

Dinant

Givet

ARDENNES

'H
RMY

GERMAN ATTACKS

R. Meuse

ières

SEDAN

| | |
|---|---|
| —·—·— | Frontier |
| +  +  +  + | Belgian Outposts |
| ᶺᶺᶺᶺᶺᶺ | Belgian Delaying Positions |
| ▮▮▮▮▮▮▮ | Allied Positions May 10–15 |
| ▬ ▬ ▬ ▬ | Allied Positions May 19 |

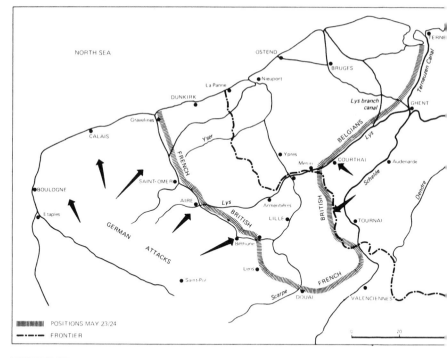

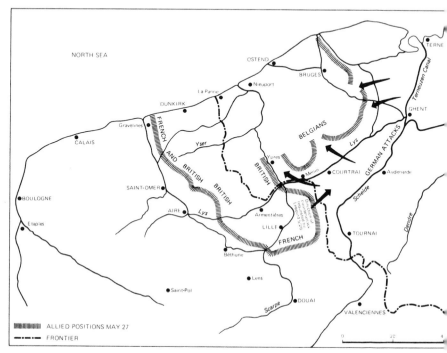

# APPENDIX I

## REPLY TO A FALSE ALLEGATION

The Havas dispatch broadcast over Radio-Paris on May 30, specifically stated the following:

"Furthermore, *before* assuming the command of the army in 1914, Albert I made a formal appearance in Parliament to show his intention of resisting the aggressor and of presiding over the Royal Council. Despite the ministers' request, Leopold III refused to go to the Palais de la Nation, and did not get in touch with his government. In vain did the Belgian ministers ask him to speak over the radio to denounce the invader. The king never said one word."

This is a good example, if ever there was one, of how the radio, like the press, will say anything.

---

Hitler's aggression against Belgium began at dawn on May 10, 1940, using aerial and mechanized attacks, means which the German Imperial Army did not possess in 1914. Although that attack had also been very brutal, King Albert had had a brief respite that was simply not available to his son. As commander in chief of his army, Leopold had to confront the enemy and had no time to waste on ineffectual statements to an assembly.

At six o'clock in the morning of that tragic day, May 10, 1940, King Leopold learned that the foward defenses at Liège were under heavy attack and Fort Eben Emael was in great danger of falling. His perfectly legitimate reaction was to join his soldiers immediately, but he first took the precaution of summoning to the royal palace in Brussels the prime minister, Pierlot, the minister of foreign affairs, Spaak, and the minister of defense, Denis. Surprisingly, Spaak gave a favorable account of that meeting on May 8, 1941, in *La Belgique Indépendante*, a pamphlet published in London thanks to subsidies paid by the "Belgian government in exile."

"We met in the large office where we had so often talked about peace, and our wish for it for our country, come what may."

I would like to stress here that "come what may" meant "despite all the pressures." I have no quarrel with this, though I am curious to know what Churchill had thought of it, since he had attacked King Leopold vehemently for enclosing himself in neutrality. Spaak continued:

"It was our first War Council. The king was firm and in control. There was no need to prolong the meeting. I was deeply moved and tears came to my eyes as we shook hands. When would we meet again?"

Despite Spaak's subsequent conduct, I am willing to believe these were not crocodiles tears. Before leaving for the front, the king asked Pierlot to present his apologies to the two Chambers for having been prevented "by the serious situation from going personally before Parliament." The prime minister assured him he would do what was necessary.

It is not surprising in this situation that Pierlot in Paris did not think it his duty to contradict a lie, which, according to the Havas Agency, comes "from Belgian political refugees in France who are in close contact with the Belgian government," even though Pierlot himself declared to the Chamber of Representatives on May 10, 1940:

"Before leaving to take command of the army, the king would have wished to speak to the representatives of the nation. The rapid course of events did not allow him to do so, for when a battle has begun, the commander must be with his army."

This was echoed by Van Cauwelaert, president of the Chamber:

"Obeying his duty with the same firmness and self-denial as his illustrious father, the king immediately went to command his troops. We have complete confidence in his decisiveness, and we know too well how chivalrously he shoulders such a heavy task not to give him our deepest admiration. He can count on our undying loyalty."

Gillon, president of the Senate, gave even greater praise:

"Our thoughts naturally turn to our soldiers. We are proud of them. They can count on the nation's total support in this tremendous struggle.

"The king is already at the head of his army. Worthy heir of the man who since 1914 has passed into history, he has vowed to share the dangers with his troops. The whole country will rally to his cause and willingly set aside any differences that may divide the nation. Belgium has only one soul: the king and his army are its perfect embodiment.''

———

One wonders how, during that terrible day of Friday, May 10, 1940, the king found time to speak to his nation over the air. However he did, in the declaration which opens with:

''People of Belgium! Despite the solemn pledges made to the world, the German Empire, for the second time in a quarter of a century, has attacked Belgium, which has always remained loyal and neutral.''

One wonders also how much more clearly he could have ''denounced the enemy.'' The same day he denounced Hitler's brutal aggression despite ''the repeated and formal promises to respect Belgium's neutrality,'' in his telegram to Pope Pius XII and in another to President Roosevelt.

That day, King Georges VI extended a friendly hand to Leopold, expressing Great Britain's hopes in the following way:

''The German troops are invading your country in flagrant violation of international law and the specific assurances of the German government. The aggression has been committed despite Belgium's strict neutrality since the beginning of this war.

''I wish to convey to Your Majesty my profound distaste at this crime and my deep admiration for the brave resistance now being staged by the Belgian army under Your Majesty's command.

''For the second time in a quarter of a century, Germany has launched an unprovoked attack against your country, and once again, in accordance with the obligations of my government and the French government, the Allied forces are hastening to your support. I have absolute faith that our combined armies shall triumph once again and that Belgium will maintain its freedom and independence. At this critical time, I extend to Your Majesty and your nation the sympathy and admiration for your country which is felt by my subjects throughout the world.''

I have not been able to find any trace of a telegram from Paris to King Leopold that Friday, May 10, 1940. It is true that King Georges

VI was, in the true sense of the word, a "gentleman." Besides the friendly courtesy of this message, which must certainly have been approved by the British government, one phrase should be noted: "once again, in accordance with the obligations of my government and the French government, the Allied forces are hastening to your support."

This clearly negates Paul Reynaud's allegation—which was deliberately outrageous—in his radio broadcast on May 28, 1940: "Eighteen days ago, the Belgian king, who up till then had seemed to believe Germany's word as much as the Allies', sent us an appeal for help." The appeal sent to France and Great Britain on May 10, 1940, was based on agreements subscribed to by the two nations with regard to Belgium. I shall return to this point in a statement Churchill made to the House of Commons on June 4, 1940. He made the mistake of adopting Paul Reynaud's opinions, no doubt for reasons of expediency, which bore no resemblance to the true facts.

# APPENDIX II

## "WE SHALL STAND BY THE ALLIES TO THE VERY END!"

In an interview with a reporter from the American United Press agency in Paris on Thursday, May 30, 1940, Spaak said:

"We are very determined to continue this war of liberation . . . We have enough soldiers to form twenty to twenty-five divisions, but we lack officers . . . . We have also taken the precaution of sending our machines and tools for arms manufacture to France. There, we shall be able to produce as many armaments as are necessary for our army."

The next day with equal fervor, he repeated this in his speech to the Belgian ministers at Limoges:

"Our position today can be summarized in two points. We shall stand by the Allies to the very end! If you harbor any doubts about the wisdom of this, remember, it is our last trump card, and for us there is only one chance, one hope of returning someday to our country, and that is to return in trimph side by side with the British and French. Until that day, our duty, our material interests and our honor are linked together. We must put all our assets at the disposal of the Allies: those young people who responded to our appeal will become tomorrow's army under General Denis, our economic and spiritual strength, our farmers and metal-workers. But that is only the first of our targets.

"The second, which will probably be as difficult to fulfill as the first, and which has been rendered more so by the king's capitulation, is to keep Belgium a nation. We must not only return in triumph at the side of the Allies: our goal is to rebuild our nation. And this is not a cry of despair from a minister in distress, but a heartfelt appeal. We can only achieve this by closing ranks in the face of tragedy, and the worse our misery, the greater must be the dignity we show abroad."

—

Such untruths! His allusions to the "twenty to twenty-five divisions" to the United Press reporter and to "those young people who responded to our appeal will become tomorrow's army under General Denis" at Limoges remind us of Denis's assertion during their last dramatic meeting with the king, that hundreds of thousands of Belgians capable of fighting were waiting patiently in France to enter the fray. It would seem that when Spaak said to the reporter "but we lack officers," he had recalled King Leopold's accurate observation. But no matter! According to him, the young men who had already responded in anticipation of Pierlot's broadcast on May 28 (it was not specified when or how) were to "become tomorrow's army under General Denis." Deluded like so many of his fellow politicians, he was beginning to believe in his own heady words, but this was only a temporary intoxication. (I remember that during a trip to Brussels from Paris in his company, I soon realized that he was his own best audience.) By a curious coincidence, on the very day that de Gaulle launched his appeal to the French from London, Spaak's enthusiasm for war disappeared. On that day, Tuesday, June 18, 1940, Marcel-Henri Jaspar, minister of public health in Pierlot's government, could only recall it was the anniversary of the Battle of Waterloo when he gave his impressions of the "ministers' council," held that day in Bordeaux, to the London *Evening Standard*. The article was printed in the edition of September 27, 1940:

The meeting was held on the second floor of an ordinary house where the Belgian colonial office had set up "a home." It was described by Jaspar as a "dirty, wretched hole," stinking of "the acrid smell of cheap cigars" smoked by the visitors, beneath a blotchy ceiling and with a decor to match.

"In the center of the room stood an off-white kitchen table with a few shaky chairs, the only furniture in this sordid house, whose very walls seemed to exude despair. A real thieves' den.

"As we moved from town to town, our meeting places seemed to get dingier, which reflected the fading hopes of the government. Each place seemed sadder, more miserable, more unreal . . . . On May 25, in Paris, when the Belgian government had sworn to continue the struggle, we had sat in most pleasant surroundings in the grandiose setting of the embassy. The next meeting was held at Poitiers where we were most disheartened by the dreadful confusion. In Bordeaux, the last destination, fate brought us to this hotel which could only breed disaster. . . ."

Getting up, Pierlot read the memorandum he had prepared throughout the previous night: "I have thought this problem over several times. We shall not leave for London. France has thrown in the towel. We, too, shall abandon the struggle.''

Pierlot sat down again after first suggesting they send the colonial minister to the United States to safeguard Belgium's interests in the Congo. Did he then remember King Leopold's insistence on getting formal assurances from France and Great Britain, both guarantors of Belgium's independence? Jaspar continues:

"It was all over. Surrender was complete and irreparable. These ministers were broken. In vain I reminded them of the decisions made by the ministers in Brussels on May 10, and again at Limoges on May 31. I repeated the words they themselves had spoken at Poitiers, reiterated by Mr. De Vleeschauwer, the colonial minister, but it was useless. The prime minister's proposal was adopted by an overwhelming majority, firmly seconded by Spaak, minister of foreign affairs.''

# APPENDIX III

## BELGIUM'S SURRENDER AS VIEWED FROM LONDON
### "Stop Admiral Keyes at All Costs . . ."

After meeting Admiral Keyes, who had left King Leopold less than three days earlier, Baron Cartier de Marchiennes, the Belgian ambassador to London, sent the following telegram dated May 30, 1940, to his foreign affairs minister. Spaak was preparing his exposé of the conditions that led King Leopold to decide on surrender, to be read to the assembly of ministers who had fled to France, at Limoges town hall:

"I saw the admiral, who defended the king's attitude at the cabinet meeting and who was instrumental in making the prime minister suspend judgment. The admiral and a liaison officer from GHQ have nothing but praise for the king, and are eager to justify his actions. According to them, we were in a desperate situation because the front had been extended too far despite our army's heroic resistance. Rumor of betrayal is false; the king stayed to share the fate of his army. I think we should look to the future and avoid any action harmful to the king. The measures already taken should only last during the hostilities. Beware of violent reaction from France. British opinion much more guarded."

———

The Belgian ambassador had every reason to fear violent reactions to Paul Reynaud's vicious diatribe of May 28, which had been exacerbated by the Havas dispatch. It had instantly provoked anti-Belgian feelings in France. Perhaps he had also heard of the curious telegram which Churchill received in the early afternoon of May 28, when Admiral Keyes was at Downing Street to make his report on his final meeting with the king. "After reading the telegram with obvious dismay, Churchill passed it to me," said Admiral Keyes to William Grisar, a major in the Belgian army. "It came from Frossard, the French minister of information, and said: 'Stop Admiral Keyes at all costs from defending King Leopold.'" That is why Churchill decided to make a statement that very day in the House of Commons: "We must not pass judgment until we know all the facts."

It is clear that the information was "controlled" in Paris. Surprised at the order he had received, Churchill replied in the following manner to the members of the House of Commons:

"The House will be aware that the King of the Belgians yesterday sent a plenipotentiary to the German Command asking for a suspension of arms on the Belgian front. The British and French Governments instructed their generals immediately to dissociate themselves from this procedure and to persevere in the operations in which they are now engaged. However, the German Command has agreed to the Belgian proposals and the Belgian Army ceased to resist the enemy's will at four o'clock this morning.

"I have no intention of suggesting to the House that we should attempt at this moment to pass judgment upon the action of the King of the Belgians in his capacity as Commander-in-Chief of the Belgian Army. This army has fought very bravely and has both suffered and inflicted heavy losses. The Belgian Government has dissociated itself from the action of the King, and, declaring itself to be the only legal Government of Belgium, has formally announced its resolve to continue the war at the side of the Allies."

There would be nothing to comment on in this statement—except to point out how much it contrasted with Paul Reynaud's statement against King Leopold the same day—were it not for that last phrase. Churchill was short-changing the agreements concerning Belgium that Great Britain had renewed in a joint declaration with France on April 24, 1937. I cannot stress often enough what is always overlooked by the detractors of this strict policy of neutrality based on "the determination, often and publicly stated to a) defend Belgium's frontiers with all its might from all agression or invasion, and to prevent Belgium from being used as a base for any foreign aggression, either as a passage or a springboard for land, sea or air operations, and b) to organize effectively the defense of Belgium." It was precisely because of this very explicit statement that France and Great Britain honored their agreements, and King Leopold did not make any "immediate request" on May 10: he was merely reminding the Allies of their promise.

"This Is Not the Time to Say Harsh Words against Your King"

The day before he sent the telegram to Spaak, Baron Cartier de Marchiennes accompanied Gutt, minister of finance in Pierlot's Cabinet, to see Lord Halifax, the British minister of foreign affairs. Gutt had been requested by Pierlot to make the following statement:

"On behalf of the Belgian government, I wish to confirm our wish to continue the struggle with France and England until the very end, to gain Belgium's independence. No doubt you heard our prime minister's speech to this effect on French radio yesterday. However, the government wanted one of its members to express this to you personally.

"Today must surely be the worst day ever for the Belgian ambassador and myself. It is cruel to have to make a choice between one's king and one's country, but when that day comes, one's country takes precedence.

"When I met you for the first time on Friday, May 24, I was already distressed by what I felt might come to pass. Perhaps you sensed my fears. We did all that was humanly possible to avoid that day, by fighting fiercely, but we were finally defeated. However, I wish to repeat that the Belgian government, which is and will remain the only legal Belgian government, is determined to fight to the very end, come what may. We shall form a new army to fight alongside yours. Belgium remains by the side of Great Britain and France. We ask Great Britain and France to remain by ours."

This is indeed a moving testimony of loyalty from a heartbroken man, and undoubtedly Lord Halifax listened carefully to what Gutt had to say. Lord Halifax, who was deeply religious—his father had worked hard with Cardinal Mercier in the "Mechelen Dialogue" toward the unity of the Christian churches—was a born conciliator, who had changed the course of history while he was viceroy in India without invoking any opposition from the extremists. He did his best to prevent war, and played an important role in the Munich Agreements, which were so criticized by those who, like France, did not stand to gain anything from them. In the meantime England had taken advantage of the respite offered to reinforce its fighter plane squadrons and its radar installations, which protected it from invasion in the summer of

1940. I do not know whether Lord Halifax had heard Paul Reynaud's speech, but I am sure he would have been shocked by it. This is what he replied to Gutt:

"I appreciate your statement and will convey it to the cabinet meeting to be held today. You know this is not the time—and I have no intention of doing so—to say harsh words against your king, for I am sure the motives which prompted him to make that decision were honorable. The other day you told me he was torn between his duty as king and his duty as head of state: I realize how tragic such a conflict must be, but having said that, we must face the situation. His decision is not only disastrous for Belgium, but, at least for the time being, a disaster for the Allies. We had always hoped our armies and the French armies could operate a retreat while fighting together with yours. Today we no longer have that hope, and we have to face arduous trials. But after all, a battle lost does not mean the war is lost. We must strengthen ourselves and concentrate on proving to Hitler that he cannot impose his will on us."

### WITH REFERENCE TO A QUOTATION

"A battle lost does not mean the war is lost." That sentiment was echoed in a headline boxed in the colors of the French flag which I saw posted on billboards in London during the last days of July 1940:

France has lost a battle!
But France has not lost the war!

Printed in italics, but not enclosed in quotation marks (it was attributed to Joan of Arc), those two lines were used as the opening words of an appeal by General de Gaulle which has often been confused with the speech he made on June 18, 1940, which gained him a place in history. If he had not had other things to think about, Lord Halifax could have claimed authorship of those lines.

### "THE KING OF BELGIUM HAD ASKED US FOR HELP . . ."

On June 4, Churchill once again spoke in the House of Commons about the Belgian surrender. Had Paul Reynaud pressured him to do so since May 28? Or perhaps the prime minister was irritated by an article printed six days earlier in the *Daily Mirror*, an illustrated London daily with a large circulation. It was a newspaper always hungry for sensation and had attacked King Leopold and, by inference, Admiral Keyes, liaison officer between the king and the British government. Perhaps Winston Churchill wanted to comfort his French colleague, who was in dire straits, by a gesture of solidarity. Whatever the reason, his statement on June 4 repeated the accusations made by Paul Reynaud against the king on May 28:

"The King of Belgium had asked us for help. If the Head of State and his Government had not set themselves apart from the Allies, who had rescued their country in the last war, if they had not sought refuge in neutrality, an experience already shown to be fatal, the British and French Armies could have saved not only Belgium, but probably Poland as well.

"At the last moment when Belgium was already invaded, King Leopold called upon us to come to his aid, and even at the last moment we came. He and his brave, efficient Army, nearly half a million strong, guarded our left flank and thus kept open our only line of retreat to the sea. Suddenly, without prior consultation, with the least possible notice, without the advice of his Ministers and upon his own personal act, he sent a plenipotentiary to the German Command, surrendered his Army and exposed our whole flank and means of retreat.

"Last week I asked Parliament to suspend judgment because all the facts were not known. Today I see no reason to prevent us from expressing our opinions on this lamentable episode. The Belgian Army's surrender has forced the British to cover their flank toward the sea over a distance of more than forty-five kilometers in a very short time, for fear of being cut off and sharing the fate to which King Leopold has condemned the finest army his country ever had. In carrying out this manoeuver, contact between the British and the two or three divisions of the 1st French Army was inevitably severed, as the latter were still very far from the coast, which seemed unreachable for a large number of Allied troops."

"The Belgian Surrender Was Not a Free Decision"

The least one can say about that speech is that it took considerable liberties with the true facts, including the reference to World War I: had it not been for the valor of the Belgian army, and in particular, the heroic resistance at the Liège forts, there would have been no French victory on the Marne. If it is true that without the Allies' assistance Belgium would have succumbed, it is none the less true that its admirable conduct, particularly in protecting Britain's communications with its troops in France, contributed greatly to the common cause. I have already shown that even at the price of deliberately forcing Belgium to revoke its neutrality, the Allies were incapable of giving Poland effective aid, while Belgium's neutrality was valuable to them in giving them time to establish their own defense systems. In all good faith, I do not think one can deny that all King Leopold's efforts helped toward the British Expeditionary Force's reembarkation and contributed to it by a sacrifice which commands respect. If ever there was a good witness, Admiral Roger Keyes said it clearly in a letter published in the *Daily Telegraph* in London:

"The brave resistance put up on the Lys against massive attacks over a period of four days—two days after the Belgian government had fled the country—allowed several thousand British soldiers to escape to Dunkirk. Had it not been for that, those soldiers would have been killed or taken prisoner. That is why we must thank King Leopold, whose encouragement to his army neutralized the effect of the thousands of propaganda leaflets dropped by the Germans to make the soliders believe that the war was over for them and that their leaders were preparing to leave by air."

Taking into account the extreme confusion existing in the relations between France and Great Britain, one wonders how the prime minister was able to "throw some light" onto the facts which Admiral Keyes had stated quite precisely one week earlier . . . It is to Churchill's credit that he corrected his June 4 statement in *La Libre Belgique*, which was published in London during the war. He stated that "The Belgian surrender was not a free decision. It was made *in extremis* through the irremediable force of events."

## The "Daily Mirror" Case

Admiral Keyes was not the type of man to allow the virulent attacks in the *Daily Mirror* to pass by without taking any reprisals. A libel suit was brought and heard in the High Court of Justice on June 13, 1941. The admiral was represented by Sir Patrick Hastings, K. C., and assisted by Mr. Holmes. Sir Patrick Hastings made a statement on his client's behalf, announcing the significant role played by Sir Roger Keyes in those decisive days:

"The Germans invaded Belgium on May 10 and a few hours later Sir Roger Keyes, at the request of the British Government, left England by aeroplane to join King Leopold as special liaison officer. He was with the King at the headquarters of his Army throughout the brief campaign in Belgium, and at the same time was in close touch with the headquarters of the British Army and with the Government. He remained with King Leopold until 10 P.M. on the night of May 27, the day on which King Leopold asked the Germans for an armistice. During that time he had unrivalled opportunities for observing events.

"On May 28 Mr. Churchill announced in the House of Commons that the surrender had taken place, and asked that judgment about the matter should be suspended until the facts were known. Sir Roger Keyes on the same day, in the lobby, echoed the same advice and trusted that judgment on King Leopold, a very gallant soldier, should be suspended until all the facts became known.

"That advice did not appeal to the persons responsible for the conduct of the *Daily Mirror*, and on May 30 that newspaper published an attack not only on the king of the Belgians but also on Sir Roger Keyes.

"How far justified Sir Roger Keyes had been in his advice to suspend judgment was now beginning to be understood. King Leopold, when his country was invaded, had placed himself and his Army under the French High Command, and the movements of His Army conformed with the orders of that Command.

"On May 20 the British Army and the French Northern Army were ordered to prepare to fight to the south-westward so as to regain contact with the main French Army, and unless the Belgian Army could conform to this movement it was clear that it would involve a breach of contact between the British and Belgian Armies.

"Sir Roger informed the King of the order, and he was asked by the

King to inform the British Government and Lord Gort that the Belgian Army had neither tanks nor aircraft, and existed solely for defence. The King did not feel that he had any right to expect the British Government to jeopardize, perhaps, the very existence of the British Army in order to keep contact with the Belgian Army, but he wished to make it quite clear that, if there were a separation between the two Armies, the capitulation of the Belgian Army would be inevitable.

"At the request of the French High Command the Belgian Army was withdrawn on May 23 from the strongly prepared position on the Scheldt to a much weaker and longer line on the Lys to allow the British Army to retire behind the defensive frontier line, which it had occupied throughout the winter, in order to prepare for the offensive which it was about to undertake to the southward.

"On the evening of May 26 a break through the Belgian line by the Germans seemed to be inevitable, and the King moved the remaining French 60th Division in Belgian vehicles to a prepared position across the Yser, which by now was flooded over a wide area and had its bridges mined.

"Fighting on the Belgian front had been continuous for four days, and the Belgian Army, by May 27, was running short of food and ammunition and was being attacked by at least eight German divisions, including armoured units, and by wave after wave of dive-bombers. On the morning of May 27 the King asked Sir Roger Keyes to inform the British authorities that he would be obliged to surrender before a *débâcle* took place. A similar message was given to the French. By the afternoon of that day the German Army had driven a wedge between the Belgian and British Armies. Every road, village, and town in the small part of Belgium left in Belgian hands was thronged with hundreds of thousands of refugees, and men, women, and children were being mercilessly bombed and machine-gunned by low-flying aircraft. In those circumstances, at 5 P.M. on May 27, King Leopold informed the British and French authorities that he intended at midnight of that day to ask for an armistice so as to avoid further slaughter of his people. That message, like the earlier one on the same day, was promptly received in London and Paris, but all communications with the British Army were then cut, and though wireless messages were repeatedly sent, it is now known that they did not reach the Commanders-in-Chief."

## "This Libel Action Has Been Extremely Useful"

From October 9, 1940, the *Daily Mirror*'s solicitors had been advising their client to drop the case. In a letter sent the same day, they acknowledged that the incriminating article was based on facts thought to be correct at the time, but which they now admitted were false. At the hearing on June 13, 1941, they proffered their deepest apologies to Sir Roger Keyes, and then went even further. In the report of that hearing in *The Times* the next day, the following article was printed:

"The judgment on this case requires something more, for as a result of the facts attributed to Sir Roger Keyes a serious injustice has been committed toward the King of Belgium who, with Sir Roger Keyes, has acted throughout in accordance with the highest traditions of honour and justice. Consequently, the defense takes this opportunity to proffer King Leopold, who was not present to defend himself, their most sincere and respectful apologies for the injustice done in good faith. They hope the king will hear of this apology and accept it in the same spirit as it is offered."

The hearing on June 13, 1941, was presided over by Justice Tucker. In his summing up the magistrate made an excellent comment: "Contrary to some people's opinion, it seems to me that this libel action has been extremely useful. I think the statement we have just heard will, all in all, be gratefully accepted."

## "A Taste of His Own Medicine"

Those words had a most unpleasant ring for the Belgian politicians who had sought to justify their behavior and associated themselves with Paul Reynaud's venomous allegations (and probably had something to do with the drafting of the infamous Havas dispatch of May 30, 1940). Their attitude was severely criticized by Sir Roger Keyes in the telegram he sent Churchill on May 25, stressing that the safety of the British Expeditionary Force depended entirely on the Belgian troops' resistance in the German offensive. He further specified that that resistance could only be successful if King Leopold remained at the head of his army. When Spaak heard of this telegram he was most upset. He bottled up his grievance for a long time and on July 20,

1945, at the tribunal of the House of Representatives, protested against the foreign interference in Belgian affairs. How unwise of him!

Admiral Keyes's reply was in character for a man who always gave an eye for an eye. That same day he sent a letter to King Leopold's truculent opponent. Moreover, since he felt that Spaak was unlikely to proclaim it from the rooftops, he sent a similar text to the Belgian daily *La Libre Belgique*, which published his article in the July 31 edition. Only these lines need be remembered, in which the man, whom General de Gaulle liked to call "the abominable man of Belgium" after the Himalayan monster,was administered a good dose of his own medicine by a master's hand:

"Spaak and his colleagues' continuous efforts between May 14 to 24 to persuade the king to abandon his army, caused me grave anxiety. In fact the small British army retreating on its northeast flank depended on the ability of the Belgian army to hold its ground.

"The Flemish and Walloon soldiers were torn between conflicting interests and did not feel eager to continue to fight for a lost cause, but they fought bravely, inspired by their commander King Leopold, just as their fathers had rallied to the side of Albert I in the Great War. In 1914, he, too, had been urged by his prime minister to abandon his army that was almost surrounded at Antwerp, but he refused.

"The Belgian army's determination throughout the 1940 retreat and its brave resistance on the Lys, until the morning of May 28—two days after the British troops had begun the retreat to the beaches—which had contained and stopped the powerful German army supported by its air force, is due to King Leopold, and we should thank him for it. Thanks to his refusal to board a plane with Spaak and his colleagues, thousands of British soldiers were able to escape to Dunkirk, and thus avoided death or capture."

# APPENDIX IV

## THE MINISTER AND THE CARDINAL

Of the four ministers who remained in Belgium until early Saturday morning, May 25, 1940, the most discreet—and probably the most efficient in the exhausting task of rescuing the refugees—was Van der Poorten, minister of internal affairs. Pierlot had heard Van der Poorten's statement to the king on the problem of food supplies. On September 25, 1940, Van der Poorten wrote to his compatriot Goffaux a letter greatly different in tone from the one Spaak had sent the king. This is not surprising since Van der Poorten's chivalrous nature made him express Pierlot, Spaak and Denis's feelings in a rather generous light:

"I think I should confirm the various conversations we have had, and particularly that of today. As I told you, I believe it is wise, desirable and useful to presume that nothing has changed regarding the men in power in Belgium at the moment.

"While His Majesty the king is a prisoner and continues to be one, he holds the future of our country in his hands until the peace settlement. Our sovereign, who is almost beatified by the public, is the focus of all the hopes and potentials of collaboration once war is over. The 'fateful misunderstanding' mentioned by the cardinal would never have taken place if the four ministers the king summoned to Bruges had foreseen the king's actions after their departure. Besides, the fatal lack of communication between the king and his government between May 25 and 28 only partly explains the final tragedy. As I said, not one of the ministers summoned to Bruges ever doubted the humanitarian motives that guided the king. On the contrary, they have always defended their king against outrageous attacks, which by inference reveals certain attitudes of the Belgian government.

"I hope that one day I shall be able to justify myself to the king about all this, and also about my administrative activities in Bruges from May 18 to 25 and in my duties as minister of refugees from the end of June (after my colleague Jaspar's departure). That is why I hope that no political action takes place now, so that the cruel rift between the ministers and their king may be bridged more easily. I sincerely hope for a reconciliation and I shall do all I can toward one.

"The king is the strongest unifying force in our nation, he holds the most power, and the monarchy represents our nation's continuity! We should all bow to this power, this link. Also, I am strongly convinced that the king believes his ministers had acted in good faith and they were following their souls and consciences. Therefore, in order to achieve this reconciliation, the ministers who are now in France must refrain from any political activity or any written or spoken demonstration of their feelings with regard to the armed conflict, in which they were powerless to intervene on the day the armistice prevented France from direct participation in the hostilities. From then on, they should only be concerned with the well-being and swift repatriation of our compatriots.

"In their exile in France they should tactfully refrain from taking governmental action until aid and rescue for the refugees and their own repatriation has been organized. In principle, they resigned from August 28, and this will become fact as soon as His Majesty the king accepts their resignation. In the meantime, all administrative work is conscientiously carried out by the board of secretaries-general in Belgium.

"I repeat that in my humble opinion nothing can be changed—until the situation warrants it—in this state of affairs. Only the king can decide the opportune moment, and then we must all follow his directives with the aim of the greatest good for the nation and the monarchy. I wish to make my feelings clear and ask you to use this letter in the way you consider best."

———

This letter is a great credit to its author, who may or may not still be alive. If he is, I ask his permission to make two comments which I feel are obvious.

1. When he refers to the "fateful misunderstanding" written by Cardinal van Roey, Archbishop of Mechelen, in his pastoral letter (which I shall quote shortly), Van der Poorten says "it would never have taken place if the four ministers the king summoned to Bruges had foreseen the king's actions after their departure." In Pierlot's report, written after their last audience with the king at Wynendaele Château on Saturday, May 25, there was no doubt at all: the king had expressly

stated his wish to remain with his army, and this meant he would become a prisoner of war, which formed the basis of Spaak's criticism against the king.

2. If communication between the king and his four ministers had broken down after the Wynendaele Château audience, whose fault was that? Leopold had given his ministers complete freedom of choice. Undoubtedly, he would have preferred them to remain at his side for obvious reasons, one of which will be given in Appendix V on the Belgian Constitution.

—

On Sunday, June 2, 1940, while the king was giving the order to send the note I quoted to all Belgian diplomatic missions abroad, a letter to his parish written by Cardinal van Roey, archbishop of Mechelen, primate of Belgium, was read in all the churches of the kingdom. Dated May 31, it said the following:

"The tragedy we are suffering has reached serious proportions because the painful accusations made by France against His Majesty King Leopold III has unforturately reached the ears of the Belgian people. To clear up the lamentable misunderstanding, we thought we should go direct to the source and see His Majesty in person. The king was most kind in granting us an audience, and has permitted us to make public the following statements."

These statements corroborate those the king made in his letters to His Holiness Pope Pius XII and President Roosevelt and the note he sent to Belgian diplomatic missions abroad. The prelate continued:

"These vile accusations of criminal behavior are quite false. At the last moment the king could have taken a plane to seek refuge abroad—as certain people were urging him to do. But he preferred to share the fate of his soldiers and the suffering of his people, which we consider more chivalrous and more honorable. The facts stated by the king and easily corroborated by other witnesses, should clear up the fateful misunderstanding that has caused thoughtless words and regrettable attitudes. For us who know that we share the same feelings as almost the entire Belgian population, we shall continue to respect, trust and believe in our king."

# APPENDIX V

## THE KING'S DECISION AND THE BELGIAN CONSTITUTION

Pierlot's speech of May 28, 1940, broadcast by French radio, condemned the king for violating the Belgian Constitution. According to him, the king had broken "the ties that bind him to his people," by refusing to flee abroad with his ministers on Saturday May 25, and by using his own authority to sign the armistice on May 28, and by placing himself under the control of the invader through his wish to share the fate of his army and be counted a prisoner.

As expected, the Havas dispatch of May 30 added fuel to the fire. On the authority of an "important Belgian politician," it denounced "one more deception before the final crime" because—it said—while the ministers were in conference during the night of May 26 (after their final audience with the king) "the king asked them for a blank signature which could be used to countersign the appointment of another minister." The Havas dispatch stressed that "according to the Belgian Constitution, the signature of only one member of government was needed to allow the king to overrule the entire Pierlot Cabinet." This was the basis of the accusation of "one more deception before the final crime."

Who was this "important Belgian politician," so well informed on the ministers' conference on the night of May 26, and on the mechanism of the Belgian Constitution? Only Frossard, who was briefly minister of information at the time the Havas dispatch was broadcast, could have told us, but he disappeared soon after the war. As a man who only acted when there was something to be gained, I would settle for Spaak.

——

The departure of the four ministers who had taken part in the early morning meeting at Wynendaele Château, made it impossible for King Leopold to continue to rule, while he retained his role as chief of the army with one reservation: without the signature of General Denis, minister of defense, he was powerless to confer rank in a necessary reshuffle of command, nor could he dismiss an officer who was incapable or unworthy, nor try a traitor, as the military courts had disappeared with the minister. Similarly, he was unable to take any new administrative measure to relieve the plight of the hundreds of thousands of refugees, who were increasing by the hour. Therefore, he urgently needed a new minister of defense and a new minister of internal affairs. Without them, did he still have the right to authorize a cease-fire?

When he found himself alone, the king's first precaution was to consult Hayoit de Termicourt, the attorney general. His reply to the king's query about a cease-fire was that if it was signed under certain conditions, surrender could not be constitutionally valid unless countersigned by a minister. However, the situation was desperate, as the king plainly told his ministers and General Blanchard, who visited him the previous evening. If the situation were to continue without a cease-fire, the army as well as the large number of civilians, which had increased due to the inflow of refugees, would be threatened with extermination.

Hearing that Henri de Man, director of Queen Elisabeth's charity work for the army, was at GHQ, the king asked the advice of this militant trade unionist, who had been a minister in Van Zeeland's coalition government before the war. "There is only one way," he replied, "and that is to ask one of the ministers now in France or England for a blank signature to nominate a minister who is needed here." Immediately, Count de Grunne, grand master of Queen Elisabeth's Royal Household, called London, which was something of a feat, and told the Belgian ambassador to Great Britain of de Man's suggestion, confirming his message with the following telegram: "The king wishes Frédéricq to get a minister's approval (Gutt if he is in London) for a signature which can be used to dismiss the present ministers and appoint a new one. Once verbal agreement has been reached, appropriate action should be taken at the embassy."

Frédéricq, the king's private secretary, had been entrusted with accompanying the royal children to France, for it was essential to protect the family. The ministers' reply was sent by the ambassador:

"All the ministers have approved their colleagues' attitude. Reply is unanimously negative."

That clearly showed two things: the entire Belgian government felt the king should have followed the example of Pierlot, Spaak, Van der Poorten, as well as General Denis, minister of defense (who was abandoning the army now engaged in combat, to try to levy a phantom army in France). The government deduced from the king's request, and his respect for the Constitution, that he intented to negotiate with Germany. Hitler soon put paid to that by asking for an unconditional surrender and a strictly military cease-fire that only required the signature of General Derousseaux, whom the king had nominated as his representative.

It is understandable that Spaak, in his harangue at Limoges on May 31, did not comment on the accusations of "deception" and "crime," but it is regrettable that in his interview published on June 1, 1940, in *Paris-Soir*, Pierlot did not correct that low charge, proven groundless by subsequent events.

———

From a legal point of view, it is interesting to reproduce the conclusions drawn up the day after the surrender by three eminent Belgian personalities: Joseph Pholien, former minister of justice, Albert Devèze, former president of the Belgian Bar and cabinet minister, and Hayoit de Termicourt, attorney general. They carefully examined the accusation that the king had "engaged in negotiations with the enemy" without the approval of his ministers, in the light of the Constitution. Here are their findings:

I. CIRCUMSTANCES LEADING UP TO THE ARMY LAYING DOWN ITS ARMS

"The decision to lay down arms is only justified if all possibility of effective resistance has been exhausted. Only the chief of the army can have all the facts that allow us to understand the decision he made during the night of May 27 to 28.

"Some of the essential facts are already well known, and most of them can be confirmed by the functions of the undersigned in the campaign army.

"1. Due to circumstances completely beyond the control of the Belgian army, the enemy managed to reach and hold a position on the Calais coast and thus enclosed the entire Belgian army and the Allied forces in a pocket that diminished in size daily, until on the day of the surrender, when it was only thirty kilometers in Belgium. Besides, the situation had prompted Allied command to withdraw its troops from ours, so that we were left to defend ourselves.

"2. In the Belgian zone of that pocket, supplies of arms and provisions were daily becoming more difficult. Several hundreds of thousands of refugees from occupied Belgium and the Franco-Belgian border were wandering on the roads in panic. They had no shelter, no food, no drinkable water, and were fleeing from bombing raids and congesting all the main roads, hampering troop movements and creating a harrowing spectacle. Some cases of typhoid fever had already been reported.

"3. All the while the enemy air force was systematically bombing the troops and the built-up areas. Entire streets were in flames, and there was never any reaction from the Allied air force.

"While a brutal enemy offensive was beginning, and losses of men and supplies had grown to the point where some were just skeleton units, the men's morale was very low. They saw how powerless they were in the constant air attacks, which the Allied air force never attempted to prevent, and with the enemy's armaments, lethal machines against which their own arms could not protect them. That explains why in the final hours some units surrendered to the enemy without orders, and why several officers regrettably failed in their duty.

"So it was obvious to all that there was only one choice left between the hideous slaughter of the soldiers and civilians—which could only have prolonged the battle in Belgium for a pitiably short time—and the decision taken by the chief of the army.

## II. THE KING'S PRESENCE AMONG HIS TROOPS

"We believe that the king, chief of the army, had the inalienable right to remain with his soldiers.

"The enemy had falsely claimed in the propaganda leaflets dropped from planes that the king had left. If the king had not been able to deny this immediately, the army's resistance would have collapsed in an instant. By sharing the fate of his army, the king assured them the best possible treatment whatever happened, from a military standpoint and from one of morale. Finally, it was the king's presence that ensured that order and discipline were maintained after surrender.

"It is worth noting that this problem never occurred for His Majesty King Albert because the troops he commanded were never surrounded. Therefore, there can be no comparison. King Leopold cannot be held responsible for the fact that our last possible line of resistance on the Yser was directly threatened by the enemy in two places, and that as opposed to 1914, it was no longer possible to communicate with the Allies' territory.

"The king preferred to carry out his military task to the advantages he would have enjoyed by leaving the country, thus showing his courage and personal disinterest.

### III. The Legal Ramifications of the Order to Lay down Arms

"Contrary to what was alleged, the king did not treat with the enemy: he did not sign or negotiate any agreement with Germany. Only the strictly military order to lay down arms was given.

"The order was issued on behalf of the king by the chief of general staff, invested by the king and the government. All orders to the army during this war, as the previous war, were given in a similar manner. Prior warning of that order had to be given to the enemy and the cease-fire announced.

"No prior conditions were agreed to by the king and the enemy; after arms were laid down it was the enemy who said that because of the bravery of the Belgian soldiers, they considered the surrender an honorable one, and authorized the officers to retain their arms.

"Although a treaty or an agreement must be personally signed by the minister responsible, this does not apply to a military action. Undoubtedly, if the head of the army is in contact with his ministers, he does not take any important decision, even a military one, without conferring with at least one of his ministers. But when all the ministers have abandoned national territory and communication with them is made impossible, then the chief of general staff has the power of decision, with the king's approval, over everything of a military nature. So that kind of order does not constitute a violation of the Constitution, even for those who do not recognize the king's power to decide alone, as commander in chief of his army, everything of a military nature.

IV. As Prisoner of War, the King, Head of the Army, Is Temporarily Unable to Rule

"The king is actually a prisoner of war. That is the logical conclusion to the laying down of arms without a treaty or an armistice agreement. The king had neither demanded nor accepted any waiving of that rule. As prisoner of war the king is temporarily unable to rule.

"Article 82 of the Constitution lays down the procedure to be followed in such a case: it is up to the government to determine whether, in the present circumstances, they can reunite the Chambers when the representatives of the nation, either abroad or in occupied Belgium, do not have a voice.

V. Conclusions

"The above points of fact and law lead us to the following conclusions:

"1. The tragic mistake of accusing the king of negotiating with the enemy and thus violating his oath must be corrected at once. The king concluded no pact, treaty or agreement with the enemy. He acted only in his capacity as head of the army and in accordance with the chief of general staff, after having ascertained that in the circumstances, any continuation of the struggle by the army in Belgium would lead to disastrous consequences, without any appreciable military benefit. The king could have left this last piece of free territory. But on May 25, in a moving message to his army, he tried to encourage his troops by the announcement that whatever happened, he would share their fate. This admirable self-sacrifice helped to sustain their courage and prolong the resistance. Everyone, officers and solidiers alike, concerned over the mistaken interpretation of the facts abroad, have shown their loyalty to their sovereign. The same goes for the civilians, who have expressed similar sentiments.

"2. We cannot conceal the fact that the situation has opened up an ever widening gulf between the Belgians in the country and those abroad. The enemy will use it to foment their policy of a divided Belgium, a policy which is impeded by the king's presence, an impediment we sincerely hope will remain.

"3. We believe, in all good faith, that in the interests of the country and above any personal considerations, truth must be established, the Belgians reunited and the king's prestige totally restored.

"4. As for the administration of the country, the May 10, 1940, law permits much delegation. Over and above that, as the king is a prisoner of war, the procedure according to Article 82 of the Constitution should be applied.

"In any case we have indicated above the procedure to be followed when all the members of Parliament have left. But, whatever the outcome, we wish to repeat that it is most important that the king's moral authority and the viability of public authority in Belgium should remain unblemished."

—

I would like to comment on five points in this text which will serve as a fitting end to this book.

1. If the false allegation that the king had fled had not been disproved by the king's physical presence among his troops, "the army's resistance would have collapsed in an instant." This is enough to answer Pierlot and Spaak's exhortations to the king to leave the country. He could not have dealt a more devastating blow to the Allies, to whom the ministers claimed loyalty.

2. When Pierlot and Spaak fled early on Saturday, May 25, to the coast, they relinquished their powers with regard to a cease-fire to General Michiels, chief of general staff, who was the first, together with General Nuyten, to recommend such a step on the afternoon of Monday, May 27. The arguments subsequently used by Pierlot and Spaak could have no basis of truth unless one of them had remained behind to oppose the measure.

3. At the meeting of senators and members of the House of Representatives at Limoges, Pierlot and Spaak claimed they were defending the Constitution, but they deliberately discounted their colleagues who had remained in Belgium by ignoring their opinion.

4. The situation created by their attack on the king could only have served to divide Belgium, a move that was to the enemy's advantage.

5. The eminent jurists, whose conclusions I have just quoted, said unequivocally that the enemy would find the king's presence their most powerful obstacle (and later events proved them correct). In order to

contain the occupying power's methods as far as possible, it was not necessary for the king to rule; his prisoner of war status forbade him from entering into any agreement with the enemy: his moral authority alone (which was attacked in speeches at Paris, Poitiers and Limoges) was sufficient to spare his people what Holland had to suffer at the mercy of a *gauleiter*. Hitler would have imposed such a person on Belgium, too, if the king had given in to his ministers and forsaken his duty.

Pholien, Devèze and Hayoit de Termicourt, as Belgian citizens, were able to sum up legally what I as a Frenchman have tried to show as best I could. I have used facts and texts which I sincerely hope have served to demonstrate to my fellow countrymen the seamy side of a tragedy in which a doomed politician forced France into an invidious role.